The End of Revolution

The End of Revolution

A Changing World in the Age of Live Television

Frida Ghitis

Algora Publishing
New York

Algora Publishing, New York
© 2001 by Algora Publishing
All rights reserved. Published 2001.
Printed in the United States of America
ISBN: 1-892941-66-X
Editors@algora.com

Library of Congress Cataloging-in-Publication Data 2001-005298

Ghitis, Frida.
  The end of revolution: a changing world in the age of live
Television— / by Frida Ghitis.
     p. cm.
  ISBN 1-892941-66-X (alk. paper)
  1. Ghitis, Frida. 2. Television journalists—United
States—Biography. I. Title.
  PN4874.G359 A3 2001
  070'.92—dc21

                    2001005298

Cover photos
Top: Tuzla, Bosnia, December 1995. Waiting with UN peacekeepers for US
    forces to arrive.
Bottom: Tibet, July 2000. Pilgrims at Jokhang Temple.
Back: Armenia, Colombia, Febuary 1999. Discussing earthquake in the Andes
    with CNN headquarters via satellite telephone.

New York
www.algora.com

Table of Contents

Live, The End of An Era

What better time for live television news — the world was changing in unexpected and dramatic ways and at dazzling speed. In the past
two years history had taken a sharp turn, demolishing the constructs of
historians and politicians. Now, the Soviet Union was about to be
signed out of existence.

The repercussions of the transformation unfolding on Moscow's
side of the Iron Curtain would be monumental. Lives would be
changed, from Gorky Street to the Amazon jungle, and the entire planet
would have to redefine itself. The nations of the world would have to
decide who they were and what they stood for. A new era was unfolding, one with a world in search of a new identity.

The end of the USSR came not by atomic explosion or bloody battles, but by a series of legislative changes, leading up to the moment
when the leaders of the Union's republics would get together in Alma
Ata (the capital of Kazakhstan, in Soviet Central Asia) and sign an
agreement dissolving the USSR outright. This act was to give birth to
the new CIS, the Commonwealth of Independent States.

All the while, professional sages were making terrifying prognos-
tications about the future of the former communist world. Secretary of

State James Baker III prepared the ground for tough times to come, telling an audience at Princeton University, "The dangers of protracted anarchy and chaos are obvious. Great empires rarely go quietly into extinction." Rampant poverty, nationalist passions, nuclear weapons and short tempers — warned the pundits — were combining into a potentially catastrophic cocktail. At the same time, there was a sense of exhilaration. The Cold War was now officially coming to an end. If properly handled, the future held extraordinary promise. It was a time of high adrenaline.

Like most news organizations, we at CNN had our plane tickets in hand for the milestone meeting in Alma Ata (later to be known as Almaty). Like everyone else's, our bookings were on Aeroflot, until recently the biggest airline in the world and the only one serving the Soviet Union.

Then an airline employee, chatting with a friend who worked at the CNN bureau in Moscow, revealed a little secret: keeping pace with the rest of the USSR, Aeroflot was running out of just about everything. In a few days — before the Kazakhstan meeting — Aeroflot would be completely grounded for lack of fuel.

Out came the trusted Rolodex of the news bureau's office manager. We set out to call every private pilot in the region, and everyone with access to a decent airplane.

As it was, Aeroflot's monopoly was quickly becoming a thing of the past. The Soviet Republics and the autonomous regions, rushing headlong into independence, had simply taken possession of any Aeroflot planes on the ground in their territory. More than 30 slices of Aeroflot had been carved out. Still, nobody would guarantee us a trip to Alma Ata for one of the most significant historical events since the advent of television. Even those who claimed to have enough fuel for a flight to Kazakhstan could not be sure about the return trip.

The Soviet Union and Russia, incidentally, have some of the largest oil reserves in the world. But that seemed as useful for our purposes as a wealth of diamonds buried deep under the taiga.

We widened our search to the outside world, where capitalism would surely produce results in exchange for cash. A company in

Finland proved willing to charter a plane, for a hefty sum wired in advance to a Frankfurt bank account. We had our aircraft.

And so, on Saturday, December 21, 1991, we saw the end of seven decades of a communist experiment that had given direction to much of what transpired in the 20th century. With the USSR out of the picture, the threat (and the promise, to some) of world revolution also died.

Academics, revolutionaries, politicians and common people would debate what the Marxist movement had wrought, for years to come. It clearly had failed to deliver on its promise of a worker's paradise, even while it had brought some measure of equality. The Stalinist approach to revolution had left an indelible mark in the souls of a people who had learned not to trust anyone. The new Republics would be characterized by cynicism — a self-defeating quality for the nascent democracies of the old Soviet Union, in sharp contrast to the idealism of other new democracies coming to life throughout the old Eastern Bloc.

Millions had perished in the name of revolution in political purges and in man-made famines. Millions had also received a superior education and had seen — until the system began to collapse — many of their basic needs adequately met.

Now, with the winners setting out, as they generally do, to write the official version of history, any achievements would quickly fade from memory, making room under the bright spotlights of recent history for the endless catalog of failings of the communist experiment. Alas, after enduring seventy years of privations for the sake of a better future, the Russian people's suffering — and that of their neighbors — was far from over.

What would replace the old order became the subject of even more protracted debate. We were ushering in a new era. The old familiar Cold War was over, replaced by a work in progress: an era to be named at a later date.

In Alma Ata, eleven of the original fifteen Soviet republics signed the agreement. The turbulent republic of Georgia, with its fierce nationalism already bubbling over, did not sign. The three Baltic States, Latvia, Lithuania and Estonia, had already left the Union and had no interest in stronger links to Moscow.

For Mikhail Gorbachev, the Soviet leader who had pulled the thread that unraveled the empire (thus becoming a celebrated icon in the West), it was the end of the road. Like a factory worker unceremoniously laid off in the capitalist world, he was informed that his job had been eliminated. The leaders of the eleven new nations sent him a message explaining that like the Soviet Union, his position had ceased to exist, and they thanked him for his contribution.

The Kazakhstan meeting produced a loose confederation of nations trying to forge ahead in their new identities. Their agreement recognized each republic's existing borders and its independence, and called for economic cooperation and a unified nuclear command.

The hero of the new democratic Russia, Boris Yeltsin, had flown to Kazakhstan directly from Rome, where he had been talking with business leaders and meeting with Pope John Paul II (a man many credited with sparking the anti-communist chain of events that was now culminating). For Russian journalists covering the trip to Rome, the experience was a painful eye-opener. Moscow-based Western journalists, also covering the trip, had to lend money to their Russian counterparts — their salaries, paid in what now were practically worthless rubles, came to about $20 a month, barely covering one meal in the outside world. Joining the world economy was going to prove painful, indeed.

Not long after the Alma Ata meeting ended, I received a frantic call from Helsinki. It was the airplane's owner, demanding to know why our agreed itinerary, from Moscow to Alma Ata and back, had changed. Why, he shouted, were his plane and his crew in the middle of a war zone?

The same team that had covered the Kazakhstan meeting, with Christiane Amanpour reporting and Siobhan Darrow as producer, had persuaded the pilot to fly into Tbilisi, the capital of the Republic of Georgia. Fighting had broken out there in what some believed was a sign of things to come in the former Soviet Union. The opposition in Georgia had attacked the parliament building, where President Zviad Gamsakhurdia vowed never to surrender.

These were boom times for analysts and pundits, whose sound bites filled the airwaves with warnings of doom and worse. A Rand Corporation analyst, Arnold Horelick, invoked the bloodshed in a disintegrating Yugoslavia to prophesy his vision for the region, "Multiply what you've seen in Croatia ten times." Croatia was in the midst of what would become just one of a series of devastating Balkan wars — celebrating the end of communism by destroying Yugoslavia.

Friction between Ukraine and Russia, Horelick explained, could spark a conflict with both sides armed with nuclear weapons. There was danger between Russia and Kazakhstan, a Muslim-majority country with a huge Russian minority, also armed with nuclear weapons. The 12 new independent Republics were ripe with potential for violent outbreaks to settles disputes over borders, natural resources, and ethnic nationalism.

The foreboding that permeated the pundits' words was in sharp contrast with the triumphant optimism that had reigned earlier the same year, when an aborted coup by old-guard Soviets tried to end Gorbachev's six-year tenure at the helm of a steadily weakening Soviet Union.

Instead of a return towards Soviet socialism, the coup plotters — one of whom committed suicide at the end of the ordeal — managed to propel an energetic and charismatic reformer, Boris Yeltsin, to the front lines of history, while setting off the Soviet Union's relentless march to disintegration.

Boris Yeltsin's dramatic speech from the top of a tank in August 1991 has been burnished in history's memory. He urged his countrymen to resist a return to communism, declaring himself the "Guardian of Democracy."

Before long, even children were climbing on top of tanks. The military retreated and the coup plotters were forced to accept defeat. Yeltsin had made it clear that he would defend the move towards democracy, barricading himself in the parliament building. Only a few years later, as Russia's ruling president, it would be Yeltsin who would call out the tanks and attack that same building.

Following the failed coup of 1991, the mood was utter euphoria.

Jubilant crowds raised the white, blue and red Russian flag. The statue of Felix Dzerzhinsky, founder of the KGB, was thrown off its pedestal. All over the crumbling empire, likenesses of Lenin were taken down and smashed to pieces.

Even Yeltsin warned his people to resist the tempting excesses of overflowing joy. But the West was exultant, too, in the early days leading to the final collapse of the "Evil Empire," as Ronald Reagan had branded the USSR. Corporate moguls promised to invest untold billions. U.S. Ambassador Robert Strauss, named by President Bush in the middle of the coup, offered grandfatherly advice to adventurous investors, telling one interviewer that if he were young and had $10,000 to lose, he'd try his hand in Russia. The promise of prosperity was palpable, but the bakeries were running out of bread.

During the glory days of serious live television — the glory days of CNN — I had the immeasurable privilege of traveling the world with some of the CNN teams that brought the spellbinding news to all corners of the globe. The massive political earthquakes that took place in the late 1980s and early 1990s set in motion a number of forces that have continued to reshape the world ever since. More than a decade later, the world has moved forward enough to allow some perspective on what these changes have wrought.

With the Cold War over, the stakes, at first glance, seem much less consequential. The old mantras of idealistic revolutionaries, dreaming of transforming the world to fit their utopian plans have been replaced by a drive to extract economic gain by nations and individuals. And yet, the new era is still a work in progress. The most powerful nations are trying to find their place in the world. Young people, with a revolutionary flame still flickering inside, are trying to take on the seemingly unstoppable wave of globalization, trying not so much to turn it back, but rather to keep it from sweeping the weakest away.

As I, too, move on from almost two decades at CNN, I offer my own account of some of the moments that propelled the world in a new direction, and of some of the major forces unleashed along the way. I hope to bring back my recollection — along with a few articles I wrote at the time — of how those forces came to dominate this new era, and of some of the events that stand like markers, showing how we arrived here, and where this road might lead.

Dominos

The August 1991 "Putsch" itself was the culmination of a process Gorbachev had set in motion almost two years earlier throughout the Eastern Bloc, when he allowed what used to be Soviet satellites to spin out of Moscow's orbit, throwing communists and would-be revolutionaries around the world into stunned disarray, and unleashing waves of euphoria among democracy activists, free-marketers, and legions of communism's foes.

In places like El Salvador, in Central America, leftist rebels with Moscow's support had spent more than a decade fighting the Washington-backed government, trying to reach their hilltop on behalf of World Revolution. Only a few weeks after the USSR ceased to exist, this twelve-year-old war also came to an end. While rank-and-file guerrillas were in shock at the collapse of their ideological beacon, their leaders later revealed that the years of Gorbachev's rule in Moscow had shined a clear, discouraging light on their future.

One high-ranking official of El Salvador's Communist Party, a member of the anti-government rebel coalition known as the Farabundo Marti Liberation Front, said the final days of the Soviet Union were not exactly a surprise. It was, he said, "not like a bucket of cold water, but of water which has already warmed."

Rebel leaders who had trained in the USSR and who were counting on significant financial support from Moscow (if they reached power) had been told by Gorbachev that support would not be forthcoming.

FMLN commanders kept a close watch on events in Eastern Europe. A few weeks after the Berlin Wall fell, an internal FMLN document praised the "social forces that demand more freedom and democracy," a telling, albeit secret, show of support for anti-communists forces, expressed by avowed Marxists.

Before long, the FMLN had become a political party in a Latin American democracy. Events in Moscow, Kazakhstan and Eastern Europe had had a direct impact on the signing of a peace treaty in El Salvador. Marxist guerrillas everywhere were mesmerized by the spectacle riveted to the chain reaction of falling communist regimes in the Eastern Bloc. Plainly, their world revolution was dying.

If there is a birthplace for the death of revolution, it is Gdansk, Poland — the Lenin Shipyards, to be more precise. That's where, in the summer of 1980, the workers, led by the young electrician Lech Walesa, went on strike demanding rights never granted in an Eastern Bloc country, including the right to strike and to form a union outside the control of the Communist Party. The workers, energized by their charismatic leader and by an enormous wave of popular support, gained concessions from the government. *Solidarity* was born, and quickly grew into a powerful engine for change. Pope John Paul II, originally from Poland, had stirred emotions with his inspiring visit in 1978. He now gave the movement public support and international legitimacy. Solidarity caught the eye of the world as its membership quickly grew to 10 million — one in every four Poles.

Amid all the expectations, observers from Warsaw to Washington worried that Moscow might put an end to the Polish unorthodoxies, much as it had done over the years when it had sent tanks to crush previous democratic revolts in Eastern European nations. With the unspoken threat of intervention from an enraged Moscow, Walesa toned down the group's demands; but others in the movement demanded more change. What they got was martial law under the new government of General Wojciech Jaruzelski. Jaruzelski ordered an end to the Union's activities, imprisoning thousands of activists, closing universities and cracking down on all dissent. He would later say he had acted to prevent a Soviet invasion. The General dissolved the workers' union, but the movement persevered.

In 1985, a new Soviet leader took power in Moscow. Mikhail Gorbachev had inherited an economy in a tailspin. Like a termite-infested building, the Soviet economy had maintained a shell of stability, even as it was crumbling within. Soviet communism had proven that it is virtually impossible to control every aspect of an economy through central planning, and that it is fatally inefficient to operate without real incentives for workers. It was a system where raw material often cost more than the finished products — a "value subtracted" method that was leading the nation farther and farther behind the rest of the world, even as it furiously spent its dwindling treasury in an effort to keep up with the U.S. in the arms race. Gorbachev knew the times called for major changes. It was time to try something unprecedented in Soviet history. His reforms made two unlikely words from the Russian language well known around the world.

Glasnost and *Perestroika*, the policies designed to rejuvenate the Soviet Union through Openness and Restructuring, also signaled to Eastern Europe that Moscow was less likely to intervene. In Poland, Solidarity was still illegal, but it was powerful and visible. The country's economy was in a desperate state. With fears that chaos would break out, Jaruzelski began talks with the opposition.

History would record 1989 as one of the century's pivotal years. In February, the Soviet Union at last decided to end its disastrous campaign in Afghanistan. Eastern Europe watched closely, hoping the troop withdrawal meant Moscow had decided it would no longer hold its empire together by force.

In Poland, the government decided to open talks with Solidarity and with the Catholic Church. In April, communist authorities agreed to call for elections and allow Solidarity to run for some of the available seats. At the same time, Soviet forces, a despised symbol since the crushing of the 1956 uprising, begin withdrawing from Hungary.

The whole world was watching, and waiting for Moscow's reaction. Even in China, young pro-democracy activists were becoming inspired by the palpable changes in Europe's communist countries.

The Chinese efforts at democracy were brought to a world audience thanks in part to the enormous media presence in Beijing for coverage of Gorbachev's visit to China. Communist authorities demolished the uprising, in the ignominious tradition of Prague in 1968 and Budapest in 1956. Around the world, Tiananmen Square became synonymous with the brutality of Chinese authorities and the heroism of pro-democracy students.

But in Europe the experiences of Soviet intervention in Prague and Budapest decades earlier were not repeated. The Polish opposition routed the communists at the polls. In Moscow, Gorbachev advised the communists to accept their defeat. By crafting alliances with smaller parties, Solidarity managed to place a non-communist in power for the first time in more than 40 years. The new Prime Minister, Tadeusz Mazowiecki, vowed to dismantle communism and bring Poland to the free market economy. Poland's neighbors were inspired.

In Hungary, the transition also came gradually. Janos Kadar, the man who had headed the country since the Soviets crushed the 1956 uprising, was removed from the Politburo in 1988. The new leader, Karoly Grosz, began making overtures to the West. In February of 1989, as Soviet involvement in Afghanistan was coming to an end, Hungary's Communist Party Central Committee drafted a new constitution permitting a multi-party system.

Perhaps the crucial point in the country's return to democracy came when the hero of the 1956 uprising, Imre Nagy, was reburied, bringing hundreds of thousands of Hungarians to what became an anti-communist demonstration. Nagy had been prime minister in 1956. In 1989, with reformist winds blowing, the Central Committee declared that Nagy's execution for his role in the 1956 uprising had been illegal. At the same time, the government and the opposition officially agreed to start designing the system for a transition to a multiparty system.

When Hungary opened its border with Austria, the Iron Curtain was raised and Eastern Europeans, particularly East Germans, started flooding across to the lands of freedom and plenty. Hungary was well on its way to democracy and East Germany would soon be reunited with the West.

One by one, the peoples of Eastern Europe and Central Europe (as the Western-most ones among them now insist on being called) cut the cords that had tied them to Moscow and proclaimed that they were ready for freedom and prosperity. They believed both prizes were assured.

In early November 1989, the icon of the Cold War, the Berlin

Wall, came crashing down. Thousands of elated Germans rushed across the dividing line between East and West. With a pickaxe in one hand and a champagne bottle in the other, they set about destroying the most concrete reality of the once unbreachable divide between East and West.

Only weeks before, East German leader Eric Honnecker had joined in a kiss with Mikhail Gorbachev to celebrate the 40th anniversary of his country. In a most un-Soviet way, Gorbachev had warned Honnecker, "History does not forgive those who refuse to move with the times." With the forces of history moving inexorably forward, Honnecker's deputies quickly deposed him in a desperate bid to save themselves.

After Berlin came Prague. The Czech people, betrayed by the West in its appeasement of Hitler and later crushed by the Soviets in 1968, now broke the shackles with a dignity undiminished by their joy. Under the leadership of the playwright-politician Vaclav Havel, they took to the streets, overthrowing a previously unmovable communist regime in what came to be known as the Velvet Revolution.

Less dignified was the exit of Nicolae Ceausescu. The Romanian leader was summarily executed on Christmas Day by his opponents after he tried to put down the protests in Bucharest and Timisoara.

The Soviet leader, Mikhail Gorbachev, refused to subdue the uprisings, allowing the era to be ushered out by the common people. The next year he was awarded the Nobel Peace Prize. The world was infatuated with the "magnetism" of Gorbachev. His own people, watching their once mighty nation losing a grip on its own future, were quickly losing all respect for him.

The famed Domino Theory, wherein Washington warned the West that one country after another would fall to communism if the U. S. failed to act, had proven true — but in reverse. Communism in the Eastern Bloc had fallen like a neatly arranged design of dominos, with the designer — the USSR — falling last.

The press prepared for the shockwaves from the falling pieces to reach across the ocean and topple Cuba's communist leader. But the wait proved too long and the plans for a quick crossing of the Florida straits to Havana had to be postponed indefinitely. President Bush declared the failed 1991 coup in Moscow "the death knell for the communist movement around the world," adding (with his Bushite brand of eloquence), "There's only a handful of people that stick out like a sore thumb. I think of one down there in Cuba right now that must be sweating."

Cuba, in fact, struggled, but Castro's regime outlived Yeltsin and Bush and many of the experts who confidently heralded its demise.

A Bright and Prosperous Future?

Revolutionaries around the world found themselves in crisis. Lifetimes of devotion to Marxist-Leninist revolution suddenly seemed futile. Clever communist politicians in many countries quickly changed their stripes, quietly merging into the new mainstream. A few years later, the governments in many former communist countries were in the hands of the same men who had once been communist leaders, now governing under a different banner but deftly assured of influence and privilege.

The Free Market became the new creed. Even countries whose governments officially continued to espouse socialism opened their arms to the forces of the market, attempting the difficult balancing act of opening up the economy while keeping a tight grip on all political aspects of society.

Gorbachev's experience showed communist leaders who were searching for a way to reform their troubled economies that political reforms could veer dangerously out of control and take on a life of their own. They therefore stuck to economic reform only, improving the material standard of living for millions without loosening their control on other aspects of their countries' lives.

Communist leaders in China, for example, had managed to suppress the pro-democracy hopes of Tiananmen Square protesters and remain in power. Now their country, along with the rest of the world, had plunged into the Capitalist currents of trade and competition.

Many of the experts confidently predicted that China would soon join Eastern Europe, adding its name to the growing list of ex-communist countries. When the Soviet Union collapsed, the Chinese communist leader Deng Xiaoping had just turned 87. Scholars proclaimed the collapse of the regime after Deng's passing. Ross Terrill, of Harvard University's East Asian Research Center, wrote, "Mao's dictatorial excesses in the end brought heavy blows to the Communist Party's prestige, and Deng's dictatorial excesses may, after his death, bring an end to Communist Party rule itself."

When Deng finally died at the age of 92, his designated successor took the reins of the country, honoring the man who surprised communist China with the news that "to get rich is glorious." The Communist Party remained in power, controlling a society where Adam Smith might have felt more at home than Karl Marx. Deng had sown the seeds of economic growth, allowing for a new class of wealthy Chinese and their inevitable Capitalist counterparts: an underclass of the poor.

The optimists in the West, looking beyond the dangers of strife in the ruins of the Soviet Empire, saw the promise of wealth for the newly freed Russians. Now that the Cold War hemorrhage of military spending could be staunched, Moscow and its former satellites could get on with the business of doing business. Russia, they explained, is a nation of enormous natural resources, monumental oil reserves, and a highly educated population. Russia, they said, will become an economic power. Some predicted the Russian economy would soon surpass that of China.

But cynical Russians weren't exactly squinting at the sunny prospect. After the failed coup in the 1991, army Col. Nikolai Petrushenko said, "We will now see how the Soviet people like capitalism. My guess is that Russian capitalism won't turn out any better than Russian communism."

Ten years later, the colonel's forecast proved accurate. With the economy crumbling, the life expectancy of Russian men plunged below that of Paraguay's. A few people made monumental fortunes but most Russians struggled to make a living as the country made what at times seemed a hopeless effort to join the world economy. For decades, the workers and the State had survived under an unspoken rule, commonly described as the workers pretending to work while the State pretended to pay them. Obsolete factories with ancient technology simply could not compete in the globalized world market that quickly permeated every aspect of the economy around the planet.

Globalization Conquered in the Blink of an Eye

With the battle between Moscow and Washington over, small nations couldn't simply count on the largesse of the two superpowers to prop up their economies. During the Cold War, many regimes had become adept at persuading the big powers to offer enormous financial assistance in exchange for political and ideological allegiance in their region of the world. Corrupt dictators with practically no popular support could stay in power by convincing Washington that they were the only ones capable of keeping the communists out, or by telling Moscow that they wanted to keep the Americans out. Now Washington wasn't worried about keeping the communists out, and Moscow had no money to give and no ideology to defend.

In order to survive, the nations of the world had to lure investors to their markets. Now that market efficiency and productivity were the driving goals for virtually every nation, many believed a new age of worldwide prosperity was just around the corner.

Just days after the official demise of the USSR, President George Bush, facing an economic slump at home, set out on a tour of Asia designed to push down trade barriers, open markets, and practically implore American voters to give him some credit for the defeat of communism. In the new world, the ability to hold back the Russians, which had been a crucial factor in U.S. elections, had become a non-issue. All that mattered now, as a young governor from Arkansas knew, was the economy.

In his Christmas address to the nation Bush vowed to use his upcoming trip "to fight for open markets and more opportunities for American workers, because exports abroad mean more jobs right here at home." And he told Americans mired in recession that he was "committed to attacking our economic problems at home with the same determination we brought to winning the Cold War."

That same day I was still in Moscow, where we were juggling a number of problems, befitting what was one of the most newsworthy Decembers since the advent of live television. After weeks of begging for interviews from Yeltsin or Gorbachev, after boxes of chocolate and bottles of whiskey had been strategically placed in the hands of their aides, both men agreed to live interviews. . . on the same day! The interviews were conducted by CNN bureau chief Steve Hurst and his wife, Claire Shipman. We managed to organize a motorcade so that we could do the two interviews, live, at different locations, within minutes of each other.

While we were organizing this, we faced the more daunting logistical challenge of finding a Santa Claus hat for the president of CNN, Tom Johnson, who was in Moscow at the time. He informed me that he wanted to throw a little Christmas party and wear the hat. "Shouldn't be a problem," he confidently told me.

As if that weren't enough, the team in Tbilisi, Georgia, had obtained an exclusive interview with President Ghamzakhurdia, under siege in his bunker. That night, after the party and the interviews, we would have to figure out a way to get a videotape out of the battle zone in the Republic of Georgia.

Of all these challenges, finding a Santa hat, of course, was the most difficult. Store shelves were empty in Moscow. Even if they hadn't been, the Russians didn't really celebrate Christmas, and to the extent that they did, they celebrated it in January.

I sat down with one of the many energetic young Russians who were working with us as translators and general assistants. We put together a list of locations where Santa Claus might make an appearance at this time of year in Moscow. He went to every restaurant and shop catering to foreigners in the diplomatic corps, the press or the nascent business community. He came back empty-handed. The next list we made included the seamstresses for the Moscow Circus, the Bolshoi Ballet and other groups requiring exotic costumes. The seamstresses said they'd be happy to do it, but there was no fabric to be found in Moscow.

Then I caught Eileen O'Connor studying the local English-language newspaper. On the cover was a story indicating that a Norwegian charity would be distributing Christmas presents to children in the orphanage. The story included a picture from last year's visit. A fully-attired Santa Claus was doing the honors. In the end, we bought the hat from the Norwegian Mr. Claus.

The party, of course, was a bust, in spite of Johnson's lovely hat and matching white beard. Everyone was much too busy preparing for the two interviews. Both went off without a hitch, and everyone came back to the office at the end of a very long day.

That's when the phone rang. It was a crackling call over a satellite phone, telling us the interview with the Georgian leader in his bunker was ready. All we had to do now was get the tape back to Moscow so we could show it to the world.

After hours of discussing the options, a long-time producer at the bureau dug into a stack of business cards and phoned an acquaintance from the Soviet Air Force. He said he would do it for US$10,000. He would fly in (presumably in a Soviet Air Force plane), pick up the tape, and fly back with it. It wouldn't take long. We offered him half the amount, and he agreed to go. But first, he would come to get the money.

It was well after midnight when we heard an alarming banging on the door. When I opened it, I was almost knocked over by a powerful blast of vodka breath from a small man in a large fur hat, flanked by two gigantic bodyguards.

Tom Johnson himself wanted to conduct the negotiations. It was about 3:00 AM and everyone had been up since before dawn. The adrenaline-pumped Johnson called for a translator and resolutely told the man he would give him $5000 in U.S. dollars, and another $5,000 in Russian rubles, half now, half after delivery of the tape. Not a penny more. That was his last offer. It was also double the amount the pilot had agreed to before his encounter with the vodka bottle and the president of CNN. He said "Thank you, Mr. President." They shook hands, we gave him the money, and he solemnly announced that he'd be back in two or three hours with our precious tape.

Six hours later, there was no sign of our daredevil pilot. By noon the next day, the BBC had already aired its own interview with the Georgian leader. By then, Tom Johnson had left Moscow. Our interviews with Gorbachev and Yeltsin done, he had returned, triumphant, to Atlanta.

At about two o'clock that afternoon, another man showed up at the door with a tape and a letter, saying we owed him $50. Our folks in Georgia had found him attempting to leave for Moscow, and had given

18

him a copy of the interview. If he succeeded in reaching Moscow, they told him, we would give him money for the tape.

The drunken Air Force hero finally showed up at about 8:00 PM that night, proudly brandishing the tape, again flanked by his two goons. By then, of course, the competition had already beaten us, and we had already aired our material from the copy we had received earlier.

He gave us the tape and demanded another $5,000. We had a long chat with him, trying in vain to explain concepts of journalism and a free press. He didn't quite grasp the notion of an "exclusive interview" and he didn't seem impressed with the fact that the competition had done it first or that someone else had brought the tape several hours before he did. When we pointed out that it had taken him almost twenty hours, not two or three, to get back from his appointed rounds, he pounded the table and stood up. "The president told me I would get another $5,000."

I was having this friendly social encounter in the company of Alessio Vinci who, along with his then-girlfriend Siobhan Darrow, was about to relocate to Moscow. We excused ourselves to have a little conference out of earshot. We didn't want the guy to hear the fear in our voices! Alessio and I decided that for the sake of his longevity as a future resident of Moscow, we would pay the man every penny "promised" to him by "The President." We paid the money, received the tape, and put it in the trash. The New Russian Capitalism was making its way into the old Soviet Union.

From Moscow I traveled directly to Singapore, to prepare for the arrival of President Bush. I was there in time for the dullest New Year's Eve I ever thought possible. The streets of that extraordinarily prosperous city-state with the surrealistically authoritarian regime were lightly populated with couples strolling, playing their radios at an unobtrusively low volume. (Chewing gum, incidentally, was about to be declared an illegal substance in Singapore.) Five minutes after the stroke of midnight, everyone went home. Party time was over.

A couple of days later, I went down from to the hotel room that was our office in Singapore to the bustling hotel lobby. Suddenly, there was hush in the giant hall. As if they had practiced for just this moment, all the people in the lobby suddenly stood and applauded spontaneously. President Bush had walked in — the leader of the capitalist world, in the flesh.

At the start of his Asian tour, Bush, with his inimitable rhetorical deftness, had told the people of Asia that the U.S. would not disengage after the Cold War. "WE WILL stay involved," he declared, "right up till the end of eternity." Asia, home to 60% of mankind, was widely believed to be the region holding the greatest economic promise.

Nobody knew just how involved the United States would be. In the years to come, American corporations would expand, along with other multinationals; technology and commerce would sway the politics of the new era. Asia would boom, but the boom would not last forever. The nations of the world would discover that the same open door that allowed billions in foreign investment to pump their economies would also allow the billions to gush out, leaving them in an economic drought.

Bush, along with his entourage of high-powered business executives, continued his tour in Japan, where he was supposed to impart his commanding presence in the service of his country and the free market. Instead, the president caught a stomach flu and vomited on the Japanese Prime Minister's lap, before collapsing.

CNN came within seconds of being even more embarrassed than the President, when someone called into the Atlanta newsroom, claiming to be the president's doctor, to report that President Bush had died. On the sister network, *Headline News*, the anchor went on the air saying, "This just in to Headline News. . . " A producer stopped him within a heartbeat of utter journalistic shame.

Despite Bush's less than illustrious performance in Asia, the world had no choice. The global economy proved unstoppable. The world grew smaller and smaller as commercialism and globalization became the new religion.

The cult of the market came together with the gospel of democracy. But neither absolute prosperity nor total freedom and peace became the order of the day. Developing countries and former Eastern Bloc nations had to compete with each other for financial assistance from the World Bank and the International Monetary Fund. Financial help came with strings attached — strings designed to help pull the economies into the all-conquering globalized marketplace.

The economic growth in Asian countries was spectacular for many years. Some predicted that the debt-ridden U.S. economy would lose its preeminence to countries like Japan, or to the newly re-unified colossus of Germany. The future looked unclear, but an air of optimism permeated boardrooms around the world.

With trepidation, poor countries began removing trade barriers only to find that, on the economic playing field, it was strictly hardball. They had trouble obtaining loans at affordable rates, and they now had to compete for credit against the old Eastern Bloc. They also discovered that some of the same powerful nations that had persuaded them to drop their own barriers were still blocking access to major markets. In return for money from international institutions, they were required to cut government spending; so they began eliminating subsidies that had helped the poor to survive, and they fired thousands of workers to trim government payrolls. Some mused that it was all much more difficult than the old days, when all you had to do was convince Washington that your country needed money because you could hear communist footsteps nearby.

In Eastern Europe, the euphoria of the end of the decade gave way to the cold reality of laissez-faire capitalism. Some people were getting rich, but millions were growing poor.

Poland took the strongest medicine, but it also seemed to show the most improvement — although the economic reality one decade after the end of communism looked nothing like the glorious expectations of the heady days of the younger, thinner Lech Walesa. Poland's economy in 1999 was 17% larger than in 1989, one of only two Eastern European countries whose economy had not shrunk to below pre-1989 levels. In Romania most people said they wouldn't have been able to survive without growing their own food. In Ukraine, 42% reported going hungry "frequently." The benefits of capitalism came more abundantly to nations bordering on the West, like Poland, and enjoying large populations of generous compatriots abroad. Still, even for Poland, the growth wasn't uniform. Those living in the countryside continued to struggle. Unemployment and poverty, something most people only read about under communism, became commonplace.

A decade after communism, only Hungary and Poland seemed to be doing well. Much of the rest of the old communist world seemed to have joined the Third World. The questions to which so many had thought communism was the answer were still unanswered.

A United Nations report said the 20th century was ending with "a crisis of development," as the gap between rich and poor continued to widen. For the poorest of the poor, the end of communism only brought more misery. Much of Africa seemed to dissolve into chaos. The regimes that were no longer useful in the Cold War calculus collapsed, leaving in their place war, strife, and confusion. When the new century began, more than half a dozen African countries faced internal insurgencies, while another half dozen were mired in a war in the Congo. The majority of people in Sub-Saharan Africa barely managed to subsist on less than one dollar per day. Perhaps worst of all, the continent was caught in the grip of an epidemic more devastating than anything seen since the Middle Ages. In some countries, as many as one in every four people were infected with AIDS, and there was no money to pay for drugs as the local economies stagnated, in debt to the West. The rest of the world seemed to write Africa off as an unsolvable quandary.

Despite dire predictions for America in the early years of the post-Cold War era, the U.S. economy eventually managed to benefit mightily from the changes. The winds of free trade allowed American companies to sail easily across new commercial frontiers. The expansion into new global markets came in tandem with a booming technological advance, ushering in an era of unparalleled growth that some believed would never end.

In poorer countries, a few made millions, while small middle classes began to emerge. But the vast majority continued to struggle. The nations of Asia had proven just how well the markets could function. Prosperity indeed was reaching many levels of society, even in countries where so-called "Crony Capitalism" made the market less than free. Friends of the powerful carried an enormous advantage, benefiting enormously from favoritism and other forms of corruption. Still, average incomes were rising steadily for millions, and middle classes were emerging where none had existed.

Then, suddenly, at the height of the rush to worldwide integration, a new, ominous game of dominoes came to be played on the game board of the international economy, with the pieces falling one after the other, principally in Asia.

Thailand, Korea, Indonesia, Malaysia — practically all the Asian economies collapsed. Then the pieces fell in Brazil, Ecuador, Russia . . . The global economy, it turned out, had the power to destroy what it had wrought. The same investors who had pumped enormous sums into economies, without regard for national borders, had just as quickly siphoned out the money, causing currencies to collapse, businesses to close and children to go hungry. Standards of living plummeted, almost overnight.

When the West came to "help" (desperate to salvage its investments), it offered rescue packages with more strings attached, and international organizations again required governments to cut spending, fire employees and reduce subsidies.

Capitalism was still the accepted world religion, but its miracles didn't always work.

What to Believe

Just as leftist guerrillas were stunned by the end of communism, leftist intellectuals around the world had felt the ground tremble beneath their feet when the Berlin Wall collapsed. For decades, the notion that socialism had the power to end poverty and greatly diminish human suffering had kept the bustling cafés in Paris' Left Bank thick with smoke as pensive poets and novelists deplored the evils of capitalism behind their filterless cigarettes. Moscow was the beacon. One day, they believed, a new social justice would reign.

Much of the early idealism managed to survive for years among the left-leaning elites, just as it had in the jungles where revolutionaries fought. Evidence of oppression under communism was written off as Western propaganda.

Communism had become a secular religion, offering spiritual sustenance even for devout atheists. The news from the East was tantamount to the dreaded headline, "God is Dead." The most disheartening aspect of the crushing news was not just that communism had proven incapable of delivering prosperity or happiness, it was that communism simply was not being replaced. The new order would resemble the old. The problems that communism was supposed to solve, in its cherished, unattained Utopia, would now go unsolved — and unchallenged. Concerned idealists worried that an uncaring society would become the uncontested norm. Homelessness and poverty would go unquestioned as a necessary evil in society.

Capitalism, the triumphant force at the end of the 20th century, was a system devoid of morality, they argued. Even the Pope warned that Capitalism has no morality and must be regulated.

As the relentless march of globalization proceeded over the ashes of the old world, intellectuals found a new focus for their efforts. Globalization, unfettered and unquestioned, would become their target. Despondent liberal activists suddenly found their energy. They rallied against the forces of globalization, not necessarily aiming to stop it altogether but rather seeking to restrain it and humanize it. Just as the people of Eastern Europe had once sought Socialism with a human face, the new rebels now demanded Capitalism with a heart. They made their case with street protests, newspaper articles and vandalism, and even though sharply rejected, their arguments had already started to make headway even before the fall of the Berlin Wall.

Capitalist countries in varying degrees had already adopted many socialist ideas. Western Europe had solidly built the foundations of a welfare state. Many rich countries offered their people free education, protection from unemployment, and health benefits. Virtually all countries offered the poorest of the poor some form of support. Pure Adam Smith, laissez-faire Capitalism was nobody's idea of a perfect system.

Although wealth was indeed concentrated in a few hands, the number of affluent people in many countries was growing. Thriving stock markets meant millions of people were partial owners of the great engines of Capitalism. Still, when Marx called for workers' ownership of the means of production, it wasn't stock options he had in mind.

Even in countries where prosperity came gushing after the Cold War, sharp inequalities continued to prevail. On a global level, inequality also became much greater. The growing distance between rich and poor became a big enough threat that some scholars and politicians warned the next wave would be away from democracy, toward authoritarianism. In poverty, they said, lay the seeds of the destructive scourge of nationalism, which would prove that the hoped-for peace on earth, after communism, would not become a reality.

One Big, Happy Global Family

Perhaps it should have been taken as an omen that peace was not about to wash over the earth when we found that the first major international event after the collapse of the Berlin Wall was the start of the Gulf War. When Iraq invaded Kuwait in August 1990, the U.S. found that it could intervene without fear of triggering World War III. But the Gulf War was seen as a sign of positive changes to come.

An impressive coalition of 34 countries united to enforce what appeared to be shaping as a new international set of rules — rules no country would be allowed to break. The United States led what only months earlier would have been an unthinkable coalition of nations. Former communist adversaries of the U.S. like Czechoslovakia and Hungary joined with Arab countries like Syria, Saudi Arabia and Bahrain. Under the banner of the U.N., the coalition provided cover for what was largely an action carried out by the United States and its NATO allies.

When the war was over, the U.S. found it had new friends in the Middle East. Again, with the Cold War confrontation out of the way, the region was no longer a proxy for East-West enmity. The Russians said it would stop supporting the Arabs and the U.S. said it wanted to become what it called "an honest broker," helping to at last settle the Arab-Israeli conflict.

But it turned out ethnic conflicts had a life of their own, outside the parameters of global politics. The conflict in the Middle East came closer than ever to being resolved, but it did not end.

Conflicts in other parts of the world went on, as well.

The worst fighting in Europe since World War II came in Yugoslavia, which quickly disintegrated into ethnic carnage after the death of the country's unifier, Marshall Josip Broz "Tito." Without Tito, and without the powerful motivator for unity that was the expansionist Soviet Empire, the dormant forces of nationalism were awakened from their enforced slumber — in a very bad mood. A vicious hatred came to the fore in a crumbling Yugoslavia, where soon there was no shame in admitting the worst kind of prejudice against one's neighbor. And a refashioned democratic nationalism was erupting in Western Europe, with racist, right-wing candidates making gains in popular elections.

In Asia, what was supposed to be the rapidly spreading fires of democracy instead turned into a raging inferno of ethnic hatred in places like Indonesia, whose sprawling collection of far-flung islands had been held in place by the dictatorship of Suharto for more than three decades. Despite his autocratic and corrupt rule, Suharto, a proven anti-communist with strong support from the West, had helped bring prosperity to many in Indonesia. His family and other cronies, certainly, became immensely rich, but the standard of living of the average Indonesian improved dramatically, too.

But when the forces of globalization turned away from Asia in the economic stampede of 1998, Suharto's grip on power quickly slipped. The power to bring prosperity carried with it the power to take it away; when investors took it away, a devastating economic crisis hit Asia in 1998. Suharto was forced to follow the harsh measures imposed by the IMF in exchange for a financial bailout. The restive population's pain under the economic crisis was intensified by the mandates of the international organizations. Suharto's regime collapsed. At last, democracy had arrived in Indonesia.

But just as Tito's death had left a vacuum in Yugoslavia, and just as Tito had managed to keep his disparate nation together, Suharto had been the architect of Indonesia's unity. In his absence, that unity began to fall apart. The dawn of democracy was quickly clouded by the gathering storm of ethnic violence. Before long, the archipelago-nation lost its cohesion. Old separatist, nationalist and religious conflicts exploded again. Vicious fighting erupted in East Timor, Aceh, Irian Jaya and Kalimantan.

In Africa, country after country collapsed into warfare, with the rest of the world generally taking little if any action after an early traumatizing experience in Somalia. The heart of the continent became mired in a five-nation war in the Congo — a country looted by long-time ruler Mobuto Sese Seko, another anti-communist propped up by Western support. The continent saw fighting in countries from Ethiopia to Sierra Leone, Sudan, and Rwanda.

While the powerful in the West talked globalization, the forces of ethnic nationalism and religious intolerance wreaked havoc with millions of lives. Instead of worrying about the advances of communism, the West now worried about the advances of desperate people fleeing warfare and poverty. Refugees, not nuclear blasts, became one of the most feared side effects of war.

For the rich and the powerful there was now a new moral and strategic dilemma: when to intervene in other people's wars.

The Russians Aren't Coming

The entire machinery of foreign policy decision-making had been built for the Cold War. Containment of Soviet expansionism had been the overriding objective of practically every action taken by the U.S. beyond its shores since the end of World War II. The new decisions proved excruciatingly difficult to make.

In the new scheme, the U.S. had to start from the very beginning. It would have to wrestle with its conscience to decide what it would stand for and what it would fight for. Would economic progress and prosperity, democracy, human rights, or some other lofty goal be worth dying for and killing for? A new "national interest" would have to be articulated.

The pragmatists now had to contend with the so-called "CNN Effect," as millions of television viewers were able to watch suffering in real time on their televisions. The horror of millions of viewers at the sight of famine, massacres, or worse, brought a new kind of pressure on political leaders. In the age of instant mass communications, sometimes it would prove impossible to say that involvement was not in the national interest.

Articulating a new guiding principle for intervention proved enormously, maybe impossibly difficult. The process evolved — or at least changed — from administration to administration after the Cold War.

In the fledgling days of the "new era," with George Bush in Washington and Mikhail Gorbachev still in Moscow, the formation of the Gulf War coalition seemed to indicate there might be an international standard of accepted behavior which, when violated, would be enforced by the international community, with the stamp of approval of the United Nations. Then, when starvation in Somalia reached the world's living rooms, intervention in the internal affairs of another nation became an option even when the national interest could not be defined as anything more pragmatic than saving millions from dying. That, by itself, had never been considered reason enough for action in the past. But when its intervention in Somalia turned into disaster for the U.S., the rules began to change again.

Defending democratic principles emerged as a *raison de guerre* when an election was overturned by a military coup in Haiti. The exodus of refugees to U.S. shores seemed to underline the need for democracy — a system that presumably would help keep the refugees away.

Yugoslavia presented the most daunting dilemma. In the end, it was its geographical location — in Europe — that brought the West to intervene. Not only was the threat of a spreading conflict an encouragement to action but, again, the refugees were arriving too close to the homes of NATO allies.

By the time George W. Bush arrived in Washington, a decade after his father had led the conflict in the Gulf War, the attitude had changed again. His Secretary of State, Gen. Colin Powell, who, as the country's top soldier in the previous two administrations had opposed intervention in Bosnia, stepped into the new Bush government as Secretary of State. During his confirmation hearings he declared that America couldn't respond to "every 911 call that's out there."

What had become clear by then was that if anyone did have the power to jump at 911 calls, it was the United States. America's overwhelming pre-eminence in the military sphere had become plain over the course of the decade.

The King of the World

The European Union had transformed itself, gradually becoming a single entity and an important power; but militarily, it could do little without Washington leading the way.

In the economic arena, the U.S. had defied predictions from earlier in the decade that it would become a lesser power, losing ground to economies like Japan's and Germany's. The 1990s had, in the end, been the American Decade. Millions were drawn to America's shores, lured by the promise of freedom and prosperity. Beyond the U.S., American culture had sprouted roots and was growing strong. U.S. popular culture was becoming the world's culture, and American values held great appeal.

Indeed, to much of the rest of the world, America's influence had become a sore subject. Even as they tried to imitate many aspects of America's success, particularly its economic system, criticism and resentment grew.

The resentment was fostered by the less-than-humble attitude of many in Washington and the rest of the United States who proudly proclaimed the U.S. "the Indispensable Nation." In reality, few disputed the truth of that statement, at least when it came to dealing with international crises, but America was proving to be far less than perfect, particularly in the eyes of Europeans who pointed to troubling aspects of American society.

The United States showed itself to be a profoundly uncaring society, where the pursuit of wealth came at the expense of everything else. The country's two-tiered health care system, for example, where the poor and the elderly receive chronically inferior care and where many had to choose between buying food or buying medication, offered proof of this callousness. The ever-present homeless people, hardly even a subject of discussion anymore in America, reinforced this view. But perhaps nothing outraged the rest of the industrialized world as much as America's infatuation with guns and with the death penalty.

The deadlocked national elections of the year 2000 gave much of the world a welcome chance to laugh at the country they felt had done a little too much lecturing and preaching while promoting its own ways.

At the turn of the millennium, America had become the focus of envy and scorn. Throughout the world, the U.S. was widely imitated, its culture imported wholesale, its currency and its language adopted en masse. But criticizing the U.S. became a way of defining oneself outside U.S. borders. By attacking aspects of America, and of the global economy the U.S. promoted, it was possible to express a political position about the system that now permeated the globe.

In the new millennium, just as the U.S. and Europe were redefining themselves, and just as small countries and ethnic groups tried to set their own direction, the world as a whole was engaged in defining its goals.

After one decade, it seemed the early euphoria of the end of the Cold War had produced an overly optimistic picture of the possibilities for a new world, at least for the short run. But the era was young, unnamed, and still in the process of being created.

The Rebels and the Cause

If you grew up in the United States, you may have missed out on one of the great debates of the twentieth century. The debate was not just an intellectual, philosophical exercise. It spilled far beyond that, into everyday life and into history. It sparked wars and built alliances; it guided governments and fueled uprisings. It was about revolution. It focused on one of the most important questions a society must answer: which road leads to a better future? What is the way to the greater good?

In the twentieth century, the choices seemed defined by the issue of whether communism, capitalism or some combination of the two offered the best answer to the problems of a nation.

At the end of the millennium, the world made up its mind. Communism, as an ideology, was defeated.

But not all revolutionaries put away their rifles with the news of the collapse of the Berlin Wall. The death of revolution came suddenly to some places, gradually to others. Some revolutionaries went on fighting. After all, revolution making was the only occupation they'd ever known. It was their job. In countries where they had achieved victory, such as Cuba, they held on — much to the chagrin of their detractors.

Where they were now defeated, some resisted change, as in Russia — hoping against hope for one more chance to make the old system work.

But in the United States, the Great Debate that had framed political discussions in much of the world had never gone far. The question had been answered almost before it was asked. As the Soviet Union became the embodiment of communism around the planet, the line was drawn, separating the world into two camps led by the two superpowers, with the U.S. and the USSR staring each other down. The Soviets crushed the debate in what became the Eastern Bloc, and the U.S. just as adamantly, if less overtly, stifled the debate: the Soviets were the enemy. The Soviets were repressive and despotic. There was hardly any point in discussing the merits of another system.

The U.S. was virtually defined by its position on the issue. It was a matter of Us versus Them. They, the communists, were the enemy, and they were wrong. But virtually everywhere else, it seemed that no more important decision existed. Granted, many people's positions were determined without a great deal of insight or introspection. Often, if you were wealthy, you abhorred communism. If you were poor, you yearned for radical change.

In a country like Colombia, where I grew up, it was nothing out of the ordinary to have lunch interrupted by a knock on the door from poor children begging for leftovers. It was a powerful and deeply disturbing image, the little smudge-faced children carrying plastic bags filled with an awful-looking miasma — a mixture of scraps, an assortment of what rich people had been too full to eat. The same children pressed their noses against restaurant windows until waiters shooed them away, protecting the dining experience of the well-off.

Poverty was rampant. There was no question; something needed to be done. But what? The argument was passionate.

The prevailing view among those in positions of power was that a free market was the best course to alleviate poverty, although some degree of government intervention would be necessary. It was the basic Adam Smith argument that businesses seeking to make a profit would create jobs, eventually benefiting society as a whole; but corruption plagued the system, leaving Mr. Smith's magic hand of capitalism too weak to reach most of the poor.

You couldn't set foot in a university without a visual onslaught of political graffiti. "Down with Yankee Imperialism," "Down with the Oligarchy," "Long Live the Proletariat," "Viva la Revolucion!" For a child growing up in that environment, the questions were endless. (For the child's parents, they were even more interminable!)

In many cases, the young minds of the undecided, just starting their university education, were being swayed by the rhetoric of professional "students" trained in Moscow and Havana, student-agitators who remained in the university year after year and somehow never completed a degree. Ideologically, most academics in the public universities seemed to reside firmly in the camp of the radical left (at least the louder ones did; those who disagreed were much quieter). They called for an overhaul of the economy and of society. They frequently and vociferously sided with workers in labor disputes, bringing classes to a standstill, and they often supported the aims of guerrilla groups fighting in the countryside.

Some of the most devoted university recruits ended up taking arms and joining the guerrillas. They often cut off contact with their families to live in muddy, insect-plagued, rain-soaked jungles, fighting government soldiers who lived in conditions just as dismal, without the benefit of idealism to help them survive.

Those were the days of the Cold War. The whole world was a battleground. Both sides, Washington and Moscow, invested in this debate, trying every strategy to score points like lawyers in a rich man's trial. The truth seemed secondary. Only winning mattered. It was hard to believe the world hadn't always been this way, and it looked as if it would never change.

But change came. And it came practically without warning, catching history by surprise.

It started far away from Latin America — far from most of the Third World countries whose revolutions and insurrections had been funded, financially and ideologically, by the two superpowers. But the waves of change reverberated to every corner of the world.

First came Mikhail Gorbachev and his unexpected willingness to open up and restructure the Soviet system. Then the Berlin Wall fell, and before long, the Soviet Union decided it would cease to exist altogether. Just like that — as far as anyone could tell, from outside. But what about revolution?

Many of the professional students who were in Moscow, training to return to their universities, suddenly found themselves at the most peculiar of loose ends.

Working in Moscow on CNN's coverage of those remarkable days, I visited the Patrice Lumumba University, just at the time the Soviet Union collapsed. Students from Third World countries seemed to be walking around in a daze. Many of them had come to Moscow to learn about communism, to learn how to replicate the Soviet model in their countries. Now the plan for their lives had suddenly evaporated.

The plight of leftist students, however, was almost trivial compared to that of armed revolutionaries whose side had surrendered in mid-battle. In the Amazon jungle, for instance, Marxist guerrillas didn't follow the news moment by moment; but the news arrived like an overwhelming enemy ambush — a defeat of the worst kind. And the extent of the carnage was almost incomprehensible. The source of their inspiration, Moscow, was conceding ideological defeat. What to do now?

One of the most dramatic final acts in the quest for world revolution came in South America, in 1996.

The government of Alberto Fujimori, in Peru, had effectively destroyed one of the bloodiest guerrilla movements in the hemisphere. The lyrically named "Shining Path" had sown terror among those they purported to defend. They killed the poor and the rich alike in their efforts to create the chaos that would allow them to usher in their brand of communism.

Fujimori had faced them head on, and won. When his forces captured the leader of the Shining Path, a man by the name of Abimael Guzman, known by his *nom de guerre*, Presidente Gonzalo, the prisoner was put on display wearing the black-and-white striped costume of the prisoner. It was a scene out of a comic book: the man paced about in a tiger cage, wearing his cartoonish outfit, railing against his captors. The humiliation was complete. And the message was clear: terrorism was coming to an end in Peru.

But Shining Path was not alone in its revolutionary struggle. The MRTA, or Revolutionary Movement Tupac Amaru — named after an

Inca leader who had refused to surrender to the Spaniards long after the Inca empire was completely defeated — had been seriously weakened, its leader captured; but it had not been destroyed. Like other Third World guerrilla groups, it stubbornly held on in the face of massive losses, and simply refused to give up. Much like the MRTA, the FARC (the Spanish acronym for Armed Revolutionary Forces of Colombia) also continued its fight into the twenty-first century — the longest guerrilla war in the hemisphere — scoring some successes fueled by the financial power of protection money from drug traffickers.

Drug money had played a major role in Peru as well. That country, along with Bolivia, had supplied the raw materials for cocaine production to Colombian drug cartels, but Fujimori's crusade obliterated much of the coca-growing business in Peru. The business simply relocated to Colombia.

With their ideology defeated and their adversary stronger than ever, the remaining members of MRTA, the *emerretistas*, as they were known in Peru, faced the decision of their lives.

They decided to gamble everything in a last act of terrorism. On December 17, 1996, a group of MRTA operatives stormed the residency of the Japanese Ambassador to Peru. They blasted into the luxury mansion in Lima's exclusive San Isidro neighborhood, interrupting what was supposed to be a quaint gathering under the stars by the city's political and diplomatic upper crust. The annual gathering celebrated the birthday of Japan's emperor, and it brought together a Who's Who of Lima's most influential residents. This glittering celebration turned into a terrifying hostage ordeal. Ambassador Morihisa Aoki pleaded with his captors to let his guests go home, but some 500 guests were taken hostage — among them, the entire senior staff of the country's foreign ministry, including the foreign minister himself, and the head of the supreme court, President Fujimori's brother, and a significant portion of the country's diplomatic corps. The guerrillas, led by Nestor Cerpa, gradually allowed hundreds of hostages to leave the residence, finally keeping 72 men in captivity. Eventually, talks with President Fujimori's government got off the ground.

For Fujimori, the challenge was manifold. Under normal circumstances, the president would have charged ahead without hesitation, retaking the house by force. But these hostages were technically on Japanese territory, not Peruvian. And with ambassadors from several countries among those captured, the crisis had international dimensions that sharply narrowed Fujimori's room to maneuver. The Japanese Prime Minister, for one, repeatedly and publicly urged Peruvian authorities to exercise caution. Still, from the beginning, Fujimori made it clear that meeting the principal demand of the MRTA — releasing their comrades from Peruvian prisons — was out of the question. They were, after all, convicted terrorists.

The Tupac Amaru rebels were at pains to distinguish themselves from the better-known Shining Path. The group had always been smaller, and their ultimate goals differed. The Shining Path followed a Maoist ideology while the MRTA aspired to a Cuban model. Shining Path had been the more ruthless organization, but MRTA also had blood on its hands. It had gone from staging high-publicity, low-bloodshed acts to more daring actions that had left many people dead, turning away some of their supporters. MRTA had once been described as "Revolutionary Chic." No more. They had compiled a dossier of killings, bombings and kidnappings that allowed Fujimori to navigate the uncertain waters of this hostage crisis with the conviction that these rebels must be defeated.

The four-month ordeal proved a challenge to the press as well. When the residence was overtaken, a group of Peruvian journalists took positions in an apartment overlooking the compound. It was a prime spot from which one could clearly see the tent under which, on the night of the attack, the buffet was served on the expansive lawn. Local law enforcement authorities soon closed access to the buildings immediately adjacent to the Ambassador's home. No more journalists would be allowed to enter. The Peruvian journalists held their positions, remaining in the apartments for weeks. The police made it clear that if they left, they would not be allowed back. Bags of food and supplies were hoisted to their perch, using a makeshift pulley from the nearby street, where the rest of the media stood waiting for something to happen.

The competition was intense among Japanese journalists as well. On one occasion, a Japanese television reporter managed to slip into the compound, only to be arrested and later deported by Peruvian authorities.

It wasn't the first attempt at a face-to-face encounter with the protagonists of the drama. Earlier, a large group of journalists had managed to obtain an interview with Nestor Cerpa inside the house, an incident that embarrassed and angered Peruvian security forces. That was two weeks after the siege began, and the security cordon had allowed journalists to come close to the house. That was about to change.

A group of cameramen was standing in front of the house when one of the Japanese photographers boldly walked up to the door and asked a guerrilla to let him in. The doors opened, and about a dozen members of the media rushed inside. They were greeted by Nestor Cerpa, the leader, wearing a red bandana over his face and hand grenades around his belt. Cerpa spoke of the group's demands. There were strong hints that the rebels already knew that things weren't going well. Their demands were shrinking.

Immediately after the MRTA raid, they had maintained contact with the press, often calling to make statements, sometimes simply writing messages on posters and placing them on the windows of the residence. The first list of demands was made through the press in what they called "Communiqué No. 1." It included the release of hundreds of Tupac Amaru rebels being held in Peruvian jails; transportation of the captors and hostages to a jungle location where the hostages would be freed; an economic program to help Peru's poor; and payment of something they called a "War Tax," of an unspecified amount.

Struggling to maintain his bravado before the press, only a couple of weeks into the siege, Cerpa no longer talked about releasing the prisoners; instead he demanded that the conditions in which they were held should improve. Peruvian prisons and, for that matter, the entire legal system that had convicted the inmates, had for years been sharply criticized by human rights organizations.

From the day of Fujimori's unexpected rise to power in 1990, Peruvians had viewed him with a mix of admiration and mistrust. It was a sentiment echoed in the international community, as people watched him walk a thin line between democracy and dictatorship, frequently stepping over and landing squarely on the side of unabashed authoritarianism. Even as he stabilized the country's economy and brought an end to the wave of terrorist violence from left-wing guerrillas, Fujimori trampled over the most basic tenets of democracy. He closed down the country's Congress for a time. He oversaw the creation of a new constitution allowing presidents to run for reelection just once. Then he promptly decided to run for a third term. But it was his treatment of political prisoners that brought him the harshest criticism.

In the name of his war against the communist insurgency, he instituted the so-called faceless tribunals where suspected guerrillas were tried by judges in ski masks to protect them from retaliation. Human rights groups said the process was a travesty of justice. That controversial judicial system had sent to prison some of the people the MRTA now vowed to free through their takeover of the Japanese ambassador's residence.

The MRTA's list of prisoners to be released started with Victor Polay, the official leader of MRTA. Then there was a young American woman whose name was well known throughout Peru. Lori Berenson's story read like a Hollywood adventure movie.

Berenson grew up in a middle-class suburb of New York. As a student, she developed a passion for the downtrodden. She traveled to Central America during the years when that region was mired in Cold War-era civil wars. Berenson became a devoted follower of left-wing views. She moved to Nicaragua, trying to learn about the causes of poverty and the roots of the war. By the end of 1994, she moved to Peru. Accredited by a couple of leftist publications, she announced that she would work as a journalist to document conditions in the country; but it all came to a catastrophic end in the course of one year. In November 1995, the 26-year-old Jewish girl was arrested by Peruvian security forces, accused of being a high-ranking operative of MRTA and of plotting an attack on the country's congress. She was taken before a faceless tribunal and given no opportunity to testify, cross-examine witnesses or present a well-prepared defense.

Berenson's life sentence was all but ensured when she made a statement in a televised pre-sentencing hearing, saying, "If it is a crime to worry about the subhuman conditions in which the majority of the population lives, then I will accept my punishment." Then she defended MRTA, saying they were not terrorists but revolutionaries.

Berenson was taken to the Yanamayo Prison high in the Andes, a place whose conditions are the subject of constant criticism by international groups. For years, political and diplomatic pressure did little to sway President Fujimori. In the human rights community, few proclaimed her innocence but all agreed that she had been denied the most basic elements of due process. And Berenson, they said, was not alone. Peru held some 4,000 political prisoners accused of supporting rebel groups. The tribunals handling the cases convicted 97% of defendants. Still, after an era of violence that left some 30,000 people dead, many Peruvians shrugged off the excesses of the system; those who remembered well the bloodshed in the heyday of violence by the Shining Path and the MRTA believed terrorists should be in jail.

Berenson was unexpectedly granted a new trial in September 2000. Fujimori had just won reelection to a third term. The entire process that resulted in his reelection had brought thousands of Peruvians to demonstrate in the streets, and had drawn sharp criticism from the international community, accusing him of again trampling on democracy. Perhaps trying to smooth their way back into the good graces of other governments, Peru revoked Berenson's life sentence and ordered a new civil trial. The civil trial resulted in another conviction, with a sentence of 20 years in prison. For Fujimori, a dramatic reversal of fortune was in store.

Not long after his fraudulent election to a third term, a damning videotape of his powerful security chief, Vladimiro Montesinos, became public. In it, he was seen clearly bribing a lawmaker. Before long, Montesinos' extensive library of incriminating videos unleashed a scandal of gargantuan proportions. It became clear that Montesinos had orchestrated Fujimori's re-election, and that the administration had been plagued by endemic corruption at the highest levels.

Fujimori initially made a big show of going after Montesinos, who had disappeared. With the scandal growing out of his control, the president traveled to Asia on official business. Amid rampant speculation about his future, he sent a fax from Japan resigning the presidency. Fujimori, a child of Japanese immigrants, held dual citizenship.

During the hostage crisis at the ambassador's residence, CNN's reporting was watched carefully in Lima, where the hostage-taking had caused almost unanimous outrage. Journalists often referred to the MRTA as rebels or guerrillas, and many Peruvians were angry, demanding they be called terrorists — a term for which they clearly qualified. Occasionally, our words were twisted by zealous Peruvians who accused us of calling the kidnappers "freedom fighters," a term we never used.

Initially, it seemed the siege might end quickly. Once it became apparent that the situation would continue for some time, we started looking for new ways to enhance our coverage. The MRTA had once dominated a portion of the country. Sources told us there were other so-called *emerretistas* still in the Amazon jungle, preparing to follow up on a possible success of the Lima operation. One of the original demands of the hostage-takers had been transportation to the jungle, where the last hostages were to be freed. It seemed logical to expect that some of their comrades had remained there. We set out to look for MRTA members in the Huallaga Valley, a region that once had achieved notoriety as the world's foremost coca growing area.

We allowed ourselves just a few days in the jungle, since the situation in Lima could change at any moment. One of our contacts in the Huallaga town of Tarapoto was a seasoned journalist who had lived there his whole life. He recalled the days when the MRTA completely controlled the area, from levying taxes to imparting their version of justice for major and minor crimes. He had promised contact with active members of the group; but shortly after we arrived, it became clear that the Peruvian intelligence service would make it all but impossible to reach our goals anytime soon.

With the hostage crisis consuming the attention of the country, Peru's security forces were in a full state of alert. Our small expedition had not escaped their notice. On the first night, we were summoned to the hotel lobby. Two men wearing mirrored sunglasses, despite the late hour, politely said they had come to help us. They said they would protect us. We thanked them, telling them we were not really looking for protection. Then the men pulled out a piece of paper with the names of each member of our group, including passport information and a number of other items of personal information.

It was obvious who they were and what they were doing. After that first evening, the same men (or others with the same signature glasses — the international tough-guy uniform) managed to show up near us at almost every turn. On the phone, calls that started out with a tolerably good connection would suddenly fill with static after a loud click. They wanted us, and anyone else with any interest, to know we were under surveillance.

The people who had spoken to us earlier became visibly reticent and our journalist friend said no active guerrilla would surface under those circumstances. We settled for a "retired" MRTA commander.

Sistero Garcia had once ruled with an iron hand and a loaded rifle. He was the man we were going to meet. He had accepted a government amnesty program and was now in business for himself. The ex-rebel leader was now a chicken farmer.

Garcia was in Tarapoto, on the way back from a shopping trip to town, and ready to return to his farm. We could save him the difficult bus trip, and the harsh climb from the main road, if we would give him a ride in our four-wheel drive. Between our camera crew, Mr. Garcia, and a friend he insisted should come along, we were packed shoulder to shoulder in the car. We tied his supplies, including several crates of eggs, to the roof of the vehicle.

The hot jungle air was dense and humid and the muddy road was rough, with giant craters, rocks and fallen trees. We drove out of town and bounced along to the Huallaga River, where a "ferry" made up of logs tied together with a rope transported us to the other side, where the road deteriorated steadily. A couple of times we got stuck deep in the mud, but somehow managed to pull out. The worse part of the trip, however, came after one last bounce brought the contents of Mr. Garcia's purchases slithering from the roof into the car, covering us with a coat of raw eggs.

It kept raining eggs, but we couldn't close the windows. Not only because of the debilitating heat but the stench, which grew worse by the moment as the eggs hardened on the car floor, the windows, seats, and — of course — on us, the avid jungle travelers.

And so, covered with scrambled eggs, we arrived at Garcia's farm.

We clambered off the crusty four-wheel drive and the old rebel started to show us around his domain. The man whose gun had sown fear in this region picked up a tiny yellow chick and gently stroked her pale feathers. Then he told us his amazing story, and his views of the happenings in Lima. The article that follows recounts his tale.

Retiring from Revolution
January 1997

(Tarapoto, Peru) The Peruvian jungle seems a galaxy away from the stage of the hostage drama that refuses to end just 400 miles away, in Peru's capital of Lima. It seems completely unconnected from the world of East-West politics, the Kremlin, the Berlin Wall, and the places where the course of history suddenly took a sharp turn less than a decade ago.

In tiny villages nestled deep inside the rain forest, Peru's poor struggle to make a living in a country that they say appears to have forgotten them, in a world that remembers them only when the war on drugs takes center stage. But the people of the jungle towns here keep a wary and keenly interested eye on developments in the crisis where 72 hostages remain in captivity more than 2 months after left-wing rebels blew their way into a cocktail party at the residence of Japan's ambassador to Peru.

Some of these mild-mannered farmers know that what is happening in Lima is just one more aftershock of the world changes that transformed their own lives. And in Lima, the people have hardly forgotten what this troubled land in the Upper Huallaga river valley spawned. It is here that the revolutionary movement of the Tupac Amaru managed to cleave for itself a big slice of the country. It is here that Peru became one of the world's top growers of coca, the leaf where all cocaine begins. It is here, also, where many who once fought with fervor for social change have now returned to join the mainstream of Peru's rural society.

Sistero Garcia was once the top commander of the Tupac Amaru's northeastern front in Peru. He reported directly to Nestor Cerpa, the leader of the group now holding the hostages in Lima. In his heyday, Garcia practically governed this breathtaking land of thick air and lush vegetation. Here he fought the government in a war that he believed would eventually lead to a communist government and a better life for the wretchedly poor people of Peru. Revolution was Garcia's life, and national borders only a minor concern. He was one of the founders of the "America Battalion," joining with other Marxist guerrilla groups in Latin America to bring a tide of revolution that would change the world. But the world changed him first. Betrayal came as quickly and powerfully as a jungle storm. It had been brewing out of sight, on the other side of the horizon, and when it started it washed away his beliefs and made him question everything he had worked for. When the Berlin Wall crumbled, when Moscow gave up on communism, Garcia says he felt like someone had ripped away his floor and his roof. The ideological Motherland had no ideology. Those who had succeeded in getting to power now said the idea was a failure. Ever pragmatic, and in the throes of a profound personal crisis, Garcia quietly admitted a new truth: "If a country as advanced as (East) Germany cannot make it work in 50 years, it would take us in Peru 200 years, and we still would not get anywhere." And that would be, IF they could ever make the shift from fighting to governing.

Still, Garcia remained a rebel in a movement that continued to control a large region, where men and women where fighting with some success against a determined government. He tried to establish a debate within the Tupac Amaru. He proposed the group establish talks with the new government of President Alberto Fujimori. He wanted the rebels to enter the political arena and press for social change within the admittedly flawed democratic institutions of Peru. But he found little support. Instead, he saw the erosion of ideological conviction among his comrades. The Huallaga Valley was becoming critical to the cocaine trade, providing most of the coca plants in the world. Armed rebels established a symbiotic relationship with the drug runners, protecting them in exchange for hefty sums of cash. The war against communism and narco-traffic became one and the same. The rebels began extorting money from the civilians who had once welcomed their promises of a better life.

Garcia decided to leave.

After sending a letter of resignation to his commanders, he went into hiding in the jungle that had been his home. The rebels tried to hunt him down, but they too were starting to lose their drive. The Fujimori government, meanwhile, was gaining the upper hand in the war against the Tupac Amaru, as well as the much-feared Maoist rebel group, Shining Path. Garcia went into exile in Venezuela to ponder his future. Experiencing what many other Marxist fighters around the globe felt, Garcia tried to chart a new course for his life. The Tupac Amaru too, were starting to change their views, even as they were losing their war.

Fujimori surprised Garcia when he offered an amnesty program for so-called "repentant" rebels. Garcia accepted the amnesty and returned home to the Huallaga Valley. He returned to discover a life of struggling to make ends meet, a much more tranquil struggle than the one for world revolution. He now travels through the muddy roads of the Andes, rather than the machete-cut paths in the brush of the jungle. His voyages now take him to markets in the larger towns in the area, searching for chickens and feed for his new business, rather than for government soldiers to kill in the name of revolution.

Garcia believes his former comrades holed up at the Japanese ambassador's residence in Lima, are playing their last hand in the game of revolution. They want to exit with honor. They want to move on with their lives, and perhaps join the side they could not beat. He still believes Peru must change. He still hopes that one day this land will join the rest of the world, giving its people a share of the prosperity that lured people in Berlin and Moscow to say their system was not the answer. He says he still hopes there is a better way for his country.

Garcia's story appeared to have something of a happy ending. Despite the defeat of his cause, he had managed to do well in the world he'd spent decades trying to destroy. But not all retired rebels did as well. We also visited another man, who told us his name was Tarzan. He and his wife lived in a tiny one-room hut with their little daughter. They had met in the jungle, fighting against "the system." Their life together had started while they were both guerrillas, even though they were not supposed to form that kind of attachments. They too had accepted Fujimori's amnesty, officially becoming part of those known as "the repentant ones." When we asked if they really were repentant, if they truly regretted their previous lives, they just smiled.

Now Tarzan had no job. His daughter had a nasty cough. He said she'd had it for some time, and he was terribly worried about it, but he couldn't afford to see a doctor.

The conditions that made revolution appeal to him were still there, all around him. But far away, the world had changed.

When we returned to Lima, the press had been discovered by the fortune hunters. A local newspaper had published an article saying we were paying five thousand dollars a month for the house that had become our base of operations. It was a terrific location, and we had found it by knocking on every door in the neighborhood as soon as we arrived in Lima, just hours after the start of the crisis. The man who answered the door showed as around, and when we asked if we could rent the place, he said we were welcome to stay. He was running a business and was using only a small part of the house. He didn't want to charge us, but we insisted on paying.

Our monthly rent was a small fraction of what the papers were quoting, but by then the truth carried little weight in the swirl of gossip that followed the international media. As we soon discovered, the man who had invited us to use his house was not the owner. He was renting it, and when his landlady read the newspaper story, she came storming in with attorneys in tow. She demanded we pay her retroactively for the time we had been there, in spite of the fact that we had already paid her tenant. The tenant, who had been nothing but hospitable, begged us to deal with him and not the enraged landlady. After fruitless negotiations, we packed up our satellite dish and moved.

Whenever there's a major protracted story, it seems inevitable that a point like this is reached. The process is usually the same. After we reach an agreement and have been paying for a while, rumors about our expenditures begin, quoting fantastic sums. Invariably, a newspaper prints the rumors as indisputable fact. Then the landlord demands we pay what the newspaper says. At the same time, landlords for other news organizations read the story and go to their tenants, complaining they've been short-changed. And a spiral of hyperinflation spreads to every aspect of the operation. It happened in Bosnia, too, where our landlord did everything possible to gouge us, from harassing us to kidnapping our equipment. One might have expected him to keep a lower profile given that, as we discovered, he was a convicted murderer serving a prison sentence. He kept appearing mysteriously, demanding more money. Apparently the prison door wasn't well locked.

Back in Lima, at the hostage compound, security vehicles started blaring deafeningly loud music. It seemed like a tactic out of U.S. military psy-ops. It was used in Panama, against General Manuel Noriega, but in this case, military psychology wasn't the main rationale at work. The music was intended to cover the noise and vibrations from the tunnel being excavated below. President Fujimori was in the subterranean phase of his climb to international hero status.

The talks between the government and the rebels seemed to be going nowhere; both sides seemed intransigent, and suspicions as well as tempers were beginning to flare. Throughout the ordeal, the Red Cross had been coming and going from the compound, organizing deliveries of food, medical care, letters and other items to the captives. As part of those deliveries, authorities managed to smuggle communications equipment to a few of the hostages, inside a thermos and a guitar.

Fujimori's plan was as daring, dangerous and spectacular as the initial hostage-taking operation had been. Five tunnels were dug, leading to the compound. The raid came when most of the guerrillas were distracted by a soccer game.

Latin America's longest hostage siege ended on April 22, 1997. After communicating with one of the wired hostages, Peruvian commandos blasted their way into the building. Every one of the fourteen MRTA members was killed, as were two commandos. All but one of the hostages were brought out alive. For the hostages, it was release from an eternity of terror and boredom. For President Fujimori, it was the beginning of an international apotheosis. For the MRTA, it was all but the end.

A Peruvian newspaper reported that two MRTA rebels — teenage girls — had raised their hands and shouted, "We surrender. We surrender," but everyone was killed. Published reports said that after the hostages had gotten out, the commandos went back through the house and shot each one of the 14 guerrillas in the forehead. Any hint of criticism was drowned in the accolades. Japanese Prime Minister Hashimoto congratulated Fujimori on the "admirable" rescue operation (adding that it would have been nice to have been advised of it beforehand, since it did take place, technically, on Japanese territory).

Ambassador Aoki was sharply criticized in Japan, and accused of permitting the security lapse that allowed the crisis to happen. He resigned from the diplomatic service.

The MRTA is said to maintain a handful of members in the jungle. It has a website and a spokesman — a blind man living in Hamburg, Germany. But their strength seems to have been pulverized, along with the Japanese ambassador's residence, now demolished. Elsewhere in the world, a few other revolutionaries held on with more success.

The Reluctant Domino

The collapse of communism in Eastern Europe had caught much of the world by surprise, but the pundits were not about to be left behind again. Everybody, it seemed, predicted confidently that Fidel Castro's days in power were numbered. In Miami's Little Havana, Cuban-Americans could hardly contain their joy and anticipation. The state's governor, Bob Martinez, named a Free Cuba Commission to look at how Castro's imminent demise would affect Florida, and he named the legendary leader of Miami's Cuban community, Jorge Mas Canosa, to head it. The powerful Cuban American National Foundation, chaired by the exiled millionaire, drafted a new constitution for Cuba and invited U.S. businesses to join in establishing a "blue print for a market economy in a post-Castro Cuba."

Some in Miami said they were having trouble sleeping ever since the fall of the Berlin Wall. It wasn't just the effects of the powerful Cuban coffee of Miami's Calle Ocho. The moment they had dreamed of for forty years was almost at hand. There were reports of Cuban boat owners gassing up their motorboats, virtually revving up for the short trip to the island. Bumper stickers promised "Next Christmas in Havana."

Many rushed to their lawyers for advice on how to reclaim the lost property they were about to regain.

President Bush congratulated the American people for successfully standing up to the enemy; and he declared the death of the communist movement around the world (while acknowledging there was still a smattering of communists here and there). A senior State Department official proclaimed "the contagion of democracy" would soon spread to Cuba. Washington was prophesying the reverse domino effect, and all eyes were on the last piece, 90 miles from Key West, that was about to tip over. It made sense.

We all prepared to cover the Fall of Fidel. It was bound to begin, at any moment. We were ready. We didn't know exactly how it would come, but we knew it would be a tremendous story. Journalism, the first draft of history, had been busy writing draft after draft. The world had changed more than anyone expected in the last several months; now, it seemed nothing could surprise us first-draft historians. Communism had lost the battle for the future; what nobody seemed prepared for was communist Cuba's refusal to move along with history.

It's a good thing we didn't buy any non-refundable tickets or charter any ex-Aeroflot jets to go and cover Castro's overthrow. The Cuban leadership buckled up and prepared the population for tough times ahead; they euphemistically called it "The Special Period."

When the 21st century arrived, the Special Period showed no signs of reaching its conclusion, but neither did the Cuban Revolution. In Miami, the celebration was postponed.

Over the years, as Fidel Castro's revolution took a sharp left turn into socialism and away from any prospects of democracy, Havana's ties with Moscow had strengthened. By the 1980s, the Cuban economy was dangerously dependent on trade with the Soviet Union and its satellites in Eastern Europe. The island received billions of dollars every year from Moscow; as much as 80% of its trade was with the USSR. The Soviets bought Cuban sugar at premium prices and sent just about everything to their Caribbean friends. More than 200 thousand barrels of oil each day were supplied by Moscow, as was virtually all the machinery and spare parts needed to keep the Cuban economy moving.

The Kremlin was making sure that the one nation in the hemisphere where Marxist revolutionaries had managed to stay in power was able to give its people a decent standard of living. Cuba was the inspiration for thousands of revolutionaries fighting in Latin American jungles — the island where everyone knew how to read and write and everyone had access to adequate health care. Fidel Castro and Che Guevara had become the romantic embodiment of a struggle for justice.

Now the dying Soviet Union was stepping aside. The virtually invincible protector was saying that it could barely hang on. U.S. Secretary of State James Baker, visiting Moscow, promised a weakened Soviet leader Michael Gorbachev and the newly-powerful Russian President Boris Yeltsin that the U.S. would do its utmost to provide food aid during the winter months — but insisted that all forms of aid to Cuba most stop.

With economic assistance from Moscow becoming a thing of the past, the hard reality of life without subsidies stung the Cuban people. After some 30 years of Washington's embargo, the island was dealt the worst hand — an empty one, by its former friends in Moscow. It was time for a new economy.

Amid widespread predictions of Castro's impending demise, Havana worked hard to attract foreign investment and set out on a crusade to live still more frugally and develop new sources of hard currency. From a workers' paradise, the island would transform itself into a haven for hedonists, and a land of opportunity for capitalists from all over the world — except the United States.

Throughout the island, bicycles filled the streets and oxcarts replaced tractors. Economists scrambled for new ways to support the economy and the people scrambled for new ways to support their families.

Two years later, in early 1993, the exiles in Miami had not given up. A report from Mas Canosa's Cuban American National Foundation announced that the Cuban economy had shrunk by almost two-thirds, and confidently predicted that Castro wouldn't last beyond July.

Without a doubt, the situation was desperate. Electricity outages of more than 10 hours a day were imposed. Officials asked the people to search their homes for pencils and notebooks they could donate to schools, and reports of rampant malnutrition surfaced. Fidel Castro announced that the vital sugar harvest had been a disaster, and again declared, "The next years will be years of sacrifice."

The lives of the Cuban people had been and continued to be inextricably tangled in the politics of Washington and Moscow. They could hardly separate their personal lives and the fortunes of the Island's economy. A Cuban woman told me that 1993 had been the worst year of her life. "My mother died, the sugar crop failed, and my husband left me."

Desperate Cubans, sunburned and dehydrated, began washing up on the beaches of Florida. A small group of pilots from Miami's Cuban community set out to spot rafters from the air in an effort to help them survive the dangerous voyage. "Brothers to the Rescue," formed in 1990, became known the world over in just a few years. By 1996, they would be at the heart of one of the most dangerous confrontations between Washington and Havana.

With economic pressure mounting, Castro did the unthinkable. In August of 1993 he decided to allow Cubans to deal in the enemy's poison — U.S. dollars — encouraging them to receive funds from abroad and from tourists. A month later he loosened the reins of the proletariat's dictatorship, allowing some form of private enterprise. One of the last passengers on the sinking revolution would keep from drowning by grabbing on to the raft of capitalism. The measures helped to relieve some pressure, but life was still terribly difficult in the Special Period, and the flood of Cubans across the Florida Straits continued.

The rafters' exodus climaxed in 1994, when Castro let tens of thousands take to the seas, sparking a crisis with the United States. Refugees were taken to camps at the American base in Guantanamo Bay, as U.S. authorities pleaded with Cuba to close its doors. After more than 30,000 rafters had left, a migration agreement was finally reached between the two countries, both governments agreeing to let some 20,000 Cubans emigrate to the U.S. every year.

As the rest of the world slowly responded to Cuba's developing tourism and foreign investment economy, criticism of U.S. policies mounted. The country that had once been the ideal staging ground for a Soviet attack on the United States, the place where the ultimate nuclear Armageddon had seemed at hand in the early 1960s, could hardly be considered a threat any longer.

But the lobbying efforts of Miami's Cuban exile community had managed an almost seamless transition from the Republican Reagan-Bush era to the New Democratic Clinton administration. As candidate Bill Clinton campaigned for a crucial victory in Florida, Mas Canosa persuaded him to support the Cuban Democracy Act of 1992. George Bush signed it into law. Bill Clinton went on record in favor of the legislation.

The law tightened the embargo's stranglehold on the Cuban economy, making it illegal for subsidiaries of U.S. companies to do business with Cuba, and requiring any ship that docked in Cuba to stay away from the U.S. for six months. It was a harsh blow to Castro's effort to revive his economy, but it gave him an effective shield against criticism from his people: any economic hardships could be blamed on the evil U.S. embargo — which they would later label as genocidal.

Clinton later softened his stance on Cuba, allowing for easier travel from the U.S., money transfers among relatives, cultural and religious exchanges, and other personal interactions between Cubans and Americans. Some say the new, friendlier policy worried Castro, who preferred to maintain a more adversarial relationship with Washington. Others say Cubans in Miami wanted to torpedo the changes. Whatever the reason, these eased conditions were now, in early 1996, abruptly tightened up again.

Brothers to the Rescue, the Miami group that had been helping to rescue rafters making the crossing, had grown much bolder in its anti-Castro actions. The small planes had started buzzing the Cuban capital, dropping political leaflets. Castro was enraged. He told the U.S. that if the flights did not stop, he would have to stop them himself. On February 24th, the Cuban military shot down two Cessnas; four men were killed. In the White House, the president met with the chairman of the Joint Chiefs of Staff and explored the possibility of a military retaliation against Cuba. A decision was made not to attack, but Castro was secretly warned that another move against the planes would meet with a military response.

International reaction was firmly on the side of Washington, but what came later quickly swayed the international community the other way. Only weeks after the incident, Congress passed the Helms-Burton bill, tightening the embargo. To the outrage of many countries, the law imposed penalties on foreign companies doing business with Havana. The president's shifting policy towards Cuba sharply regressed, as the November election came into view; Clinton signed the Helms-Burton Act in March of 1996, bringing a storm of diplomatic protests.

Clinton more than doubled his support among Florida's Cuban American voters compared to 1992.

The number of communist countries in the world was quickly dwindling, and most of those countries showed signs of loosening their Marxist orthodoxy in an effort to survive. From Eastern Europe to Asia, Africa and Latin America, the Cold War had come to an end. But in Cuba, the United States had retrenched and gone back to the Cold War battle lines half a decade after defeating the enemy. For years to come, U.S. policy towards a wilting revolution 90 miles away remained firmly rooted in the strategy dictated by a conflict now relegated to history. Cuban-inspired revolution had lost its strength, as had Fidel Castro's ability to export his brand of Marxism.

Cuba: Staying Alive After the Cold War
March 1996

(Havana) The Executive Lounge on the top floor of Havana's legendary Hotel Nacional is alive with the buzzing sounds of multiple conversations in many languages. An Italian businessman — cell phone in hand — talks business with a government official. A Colombian couple relaxes, waiting for confirmation of their reservation at a plush hotel in the resort of Varadero. The executive floor hostess counts the stack of U.S. dollars handed over by a businessman checking out of the hotel: every guest a symbol of American foreign policy that is producing little benefit.

Ever since Fidel Castro came to power in 1959, the United States, prodded by exiled Cubans living in Miami, has tried to strangle the communist regime in its backyard. But rather than toppling Fidel, American policy towards Cuba has brought suffering to the Cuban people and scorn to the U.S. from the international community. The latest act in the theatre of Cuban-American relations is no exception.

After Cuba shot down two civilian airplanes coming from Miami, the U.S. had the support of the international community. The planes were piloted by Cuban exiles who had been goading both governments with their flights in and out of Cuban airspace. The planes were flown by members of an anti-Castro organization called Brothers to the Rescue, a group specialized in rescuing Cubans fleeing their country on rafts and other precarious vessels. But the group had also violated Cuban airspace, dropping leaflets on Havana in defiance of Fidel's warnings. Whether the flights were right or wrong, the overwhelming international consensus was that Cuba went too far when it downed the planes. Then the U.S. government responded, signing into law the Helms-Burton Act that tightens the screws on an economic embargo that was supposed to bring down Fidel a long time ago. International public opinion changed sides.

There is something stubborn and relentless in the way the island hangs on for dear life. It's the one nation in this hemisphere that refuses to give in to the tide of democracy sweeping the world, the country with a regime whose imminent death is continuously postponed.

When the Soviet Union — along with all its communist puppets in Eastern Europe — collapsed at the turn of the decade, all eyes turned to Cuba. Clearly, the tiny nation could not survive without its patron. Cuban exiles in Miami got ready to buy summer homes on the beach, and U.S. businessmen rubbed their hands together, anticipating great profits through new investments in the Caribbean.

Now, 35 years after the U.S. tried to overthrow Fidel Castro at the Bay of Pigs, Castro remains solidly in power, causing headaches for the United States. Ironically, it is the United States that finds itself isolated on the world stage on the issue of Cuba, even after it had mustered world support and almost unanimous condemnation of Cuba following the plane incident.

The Helms-Burton Act seeks to take the embargo beyond the prohibition of U.S. firms doing business in Cuba. The U.S. embargo has consistently been repudiated by overwhelming votes at the United Nations. Now the U.S. seeks to punish other countries dealing with Castro. Already members of the European Community have said they may seek "retaliatory measures" against the United States for interfering in their relationship with Cuba.

Even Cuban dissidents on the island say the U.S. government's reaction to the downing of the planes played right into Castro's hands. With the Helms-Burton Act in place and the rhetoric from Washington carrying more venom, Castro can easily explain to the people of Cuba that their standard of living continues to suffer because of a U.S. embargo — not because Cuba has taken the route of socialism, which has failed virtually everywhere. In addition, Fidel can now point to the increased pressure from the U.S. when he cracks down harder on dissidents. The powerful enemy in the North is a strong unifying force in Cuba. It's an us-against-them mentality that strengthens the Castro regime, with Cubans proudly playing David to the American Goliath.

Many of Castro's opponents have left the island, but those who remain say Clinton's earlier policy towards Cuba, a relaxation of restrictions, was working well and was shaking Fidel's grip. According to some of Castro's critics, the people-to-people contacts that Clinton started allowing last year were bringing the type of information that showed people they would be better off in a different system.

Without a doubt, the U.S. embargo has had a severe impact on life in Cuba. When the Soviets supported Castro, the standard of living for the Cuban people remained satisfactory. Between the largesse of Moscow and the achievements of the revolution, the people had many reasons to love their leader. Fidel had taken a country mired in poverty, decadence and inequality, and turned it into a nation with a literacy rate higher than the U.S., at 100 %. Everyone had access to quality health care, and everyone was more or less living at the same level. Once the Soviet Union collapsed, Cuba had to fend for itself in the hostile world of a U.S. embargo.

To make matters worse, at the same time the Russians deserted communism and Cuba, the sugar harvest (Cuba's lifeline) was one of the worst in years. Without Russian oil, the Cuban people started driving bicycles to work and facing lengthy blackouts that crippled factories. With sharply reduced revenues from sugar exports, the daily diet of the average Cuban diminished to the point of producing nutritional deficiencies.

Then the Cuban government decided to open the doors to foreign investment, inviting the world to its beaches and to its oil fields.

Foreign investors started pouring in millions, and tourists started coming by the hundreds of thousands. American businessmen sat by in frustration as the prime pieces of land were grabbed by investors from Mexico, Spain, Germany and other countries. Some American investors tried to lay the groundwork for an anticipated change in U.S. policy. Already major U.S. firms had sent out teams to explore the financial landscape in Cuba. General Motors, Radisson Hotels, Sears Roebuck, and a host of other Fortune 500 companies sent advance squads to Cuba. In 1995, Cuban officials say they met with more than one thousand U.S. businessmen, and even signed letters of intent for a host of investments valued in the billions of dollars.

But investments from the U.S. will have to wait. Today's profits and tomorrow's prospects are being captured by other countries.

To be sure, the economy in Cuba is in serious trouble. The standard of living has declined sharply and most Cubans are living hand to mouth, many selling their belongings to get by. Castro has allowed the unthinkable — pockets of capitalism in his socialist economy — but he shows no intention of allowing his country to become a capitalist democratic nation.

The only desirable currency in Cuba today is the U.S. dollar, and stores offering a good assortment of products accept only U.S. dollars. Castro has also allowed some forms of private enterprise. Tourists can now dine in so-called *Paladares*, restaurants set up in private homes where meals are served by family members and prices are fixed in dollars. Paladares are not allowed to hire workers other than family members. This is supposed to avoid any potential exploitation. Private entrepreneurs are required to confront that capitalist evil, taxes. Many simply don't register so they can avoid paying the government. Private enterprise, with and without government approval, is starting to pop up everywhere in Cuba.

Clearly, Cuba is changing. The country is adapting to the new world reality in order to survive, and there is little doubt that change will continue. The question is, will Cuba undergo a true political transformation while Castro is still alive? Indeed, is a transformation possible without bloodshed? What seems assured is that when Cuba finally opens its doors to the world, the United States will stand far behind in the line to participate in the country's economic revival.

A War Un-won

With Marxism discredited in most of the world, market economies proliferated. By the end of the 1990s, according to the World Bank, there were more than twice as many democracies as autocracies — almost exactly the opposite of a decade earlier. However, poverty of the worst kind remains, and it remains in shameful numbers that have changed little since the end of the Cold War: in 1998 there were still about 1.2 billion people around the globe struggling to survive on less than one dollar a day.

The Mexican poet Octavio Paz noted, after the demise of the Soviet system, that communism had proved to be the wrong answer — but that didn't mean the questions had been wrong.

One More Battle

Of all the traffic jams in which I've been stranded, none could possibly compete with the one of October 1993, in Moscow. It's not just that I had to give up and get out of the car to walk the rest of the way to the office; it's that the road was full of tanks and armored personnel carriers. And, as it turned out, the tanks — part of the Russian military arsenal — would soon start firing on the Russian Parliament building. That's one way to solve a dispute with the legislature. It was starting to look like the road to democratic, free market Nirvana would be fraught with peril.

In Moscow, Boris Yeltsin was the symbol of change. Still a vibrant and energetic man, he was bringing his New Russia into the modern world. After his election in 1991, Yeltsin had taken on the Herculean task of transforming the gigantic, crumbling centrally planned economy of the Soviet Union into a working market economy; but his status as the hero who had stood on top of a tank two years earlier, staring down a communist coup, was not enough to clear the way for all his reforms. Would Moscow become the shining symbol of the new era, or the epicenter of a catastrophe?

Poverty was becoming visible in the streets, and wealth was now being openly flaunted by the early beneficiaries of the new system, bringing bitterness and resentment from millions whose standard of living had dropped continuously after the dissolution of the USSR. Under the Soviet system, the government had kept all prices tightly controlled. Its successor, the Commonwealth of Independent States, decided to turn prices loose on most of the products it still controlled, on January 2, 1992. Inflation had already ballooned by a staggering 200%. The Russian ruble was plummeting and in some places it was rejected as a form of payment. Most Russians could no longer survive on their earnings — and this was only months after the end of the Bad Old Days of communism. If these were the good days, people moaned, the bad ones were better.

Russia was plunging into the free enterprise system with a work force that was used to paying little attention to real productivity; with a society that barely knew the meaning of entrepreneurship; with major industries crumbling under the control of the central government and restricted international contact; and with inadequate laws and structures for making a market economy work. Nirvana was nowhere in sight.

My friend Boris said to me, one day, "We have freedom to say anything now, but what good is that when people are going hungry?" A couple of years earlier Boris, who was not nearly as old as he looked, had told me a story. When he was young, he said, he and his family had an orchard that had produced fruit for generations. Then someone told them that scientists had developed a new kind of apple, a more beautiful and better tasting one. They planted the new trees and took care of them for a few years, waiting for the tasty new apples to grow. The trees all began to die. "That's communism," he told me. In the beginning it looked good, full of promise. But it's not natural. It can't survive. Now Russians wanted out of the orchard business altogether — they were growing increasingly cynical about their leaders and the future.

By the summer of 1993, Yeltsin's economic reform plan seemed to be going nowhere in Parliament. The president and the legislature were mired in infighting while inflation raged at 20% per month. The economy slipped into a downward spiral. With popular discontent growing, hard-liners in parliament seized the moment, trying to score populist points. They stood up to the man who had led the country into the unknown and called for an easing of the capitalist pain for their constituents. Finally, Yeltsin had had enough.

After a summer of discontent, Yeltsin gave up on the old Soviet constitution and on the Parliament that was standing in his way. On September 21, the Russian president went on television and gave another show of his compelling forcefulness. He announced that he was dissolving Parliament and calling for new legislative elections in December. That decision was fuel on the opposition's fire.

The man who had once been a close ally of Yeltsin, Vice President Alexander Rutskoi, along with Parliamentary speaker Ruslan Khasbulatov led what would be one of the most serious challenges to Yeltsin's turbulent administration. They formed a new government inside the Parliament building, with Rutskoi as President. They hoped the people outside, tired of painful reforms, would join with them in their revolt and bring an end to Yeltsin's government. But most people were in no mood for another revolution.

Inside the Parliament building — the White House, as it was known — rebellious parliamentarians issued weapons to their supporters. After an attempt to take over a military facility left a couple of people dead, Yeltsin ordered his forces to take charge of the situation. As the mutineers in the building voted to impeach Yeltsin, hundreds of armed men surrounded the White House, creating a tense standoff — which Muscovites either ignored, or observed with detached curiosity. Instead of a massive popular uprising, the city of Moscow saw another normal day, by and large.

But a few thousand die-hard Yeltsin opponents looked on the revolt sympathetically. The alliance of Neo-Nazis, monarchists and communists included many who passionately wanted to bring back the old Soviet Union. Among the parliament's supporters were Gen. Vladislav Achilov, a former defense minister, and Gen. Albert Makashov, who would both play a major role during the most dramatic hours of the crisis.

Yeltsin said he would not end the standoff with bloodshed. His adversaries were making no headway, and it looked like their revolt would fizzle out soon enough. They had no telephones, little access to the media, and no significant support in the armed forces.

But two weeks into the crisis the situation suddenly changed and, for a time, it looked as though those who wanted the Soviet Union back were about to carry the day. Weekend demonstrations by the parliament's supporters unexpectedly got out of hand. On Saturday, demonstrators took to the streets, breaking through police lines. When Sunday came, the demonstrations quickly became violent, energized by news that several hundred troops from the Interior Ministry had joined the rebellion. Alexander Rutskoi mobilized his supporters, telling them to take over the television station, the Kremlin, and the Mayor's office. As the attacks began, the leaders of the rebellion were sure the vast popular uprising would begin.

Gen. Makashov led the charge for the main television facility, crashing a truck through the door, shouting, "This is the free territory of the USSR."

At the Kremlin, Yeltsin had had a tense time of it, initially finding it hard to convince his military men to take up arms in defense of the fledgling new system. Eventually, they agreed — grudgingly — to turn their weapons against their fellow Russians. It also became clear that the feared mass movement would not materialize. Russian tanks took to the streets and fired on the Russian Parliament. Hundreds of people died as the world looked on in disbelief.

Boris Yeltsin went on to stay in power until the last day of the 20th century, surviving another impeachment vote by parliament. When he resigned from office, his level of popular support had dropped so much that it was hard to believe he had once been the darling of a powerful nation, and the people's great hope for a better life.

(Moscow) The scene appeared surreal from the roof of the building that houses CNN's Moscow bureau. A huge line of tanks and armored personnel carriers roared down the street, pouring out of Kutuzovsky Prospect to surround the shining marble building known as the White House. Suddenly, the Russian tanks started firing on the parliament building, making the earth shake with every artillery blast directed at what was soon sarcastically known as the "Black House." On the roof, as we watched the astonishing scene, a young, newly affluent Muscovite shook his head, "This is not Moscow," he muttered, telling me as if to reassure himself, "Tomorrow we will wake up and it will all have been a dream."

How could this be happening? The hero of 1991, Boris Yeltsin, ordering Russian tanks to fire into the Russian White House, killing scores of Russians?

To understand what led to this, one would ideally go back in history for centuries. My direct experience takes me back only a couple of years, and in that time Moscow had been transformed. When I arrived on my current assignment, three weeks ago (only hours after Yeltsin's dissolution of the parliament), I found a very different city from the one I had seen at the time of the August coup against Gorbachev in 1991 and during the dissolution of the Soviet Union in December of the same year. Gone are the long lines in front of barely-stocked stores. Gone are the days when spending U.S. dollars was a dangerous activity. And gone are the egalitarian incomes that provided most people with an almost identical standard of living, low as it may have been. Gone, too, are the remnants of paranoia sown during the repressive years of communism and the lack of street crime that went with it.

Suddenly, Moscow's enormous thoroughfares are filled with shiny new BMWs — and they don't all belong to foreigners. Young Russian entrepreneurs have started making a killing in the fledgling free market. As they drive along in their luxury cars, the young capitalists are urged by dozens of billboards to buy cigarettes promising "the taste of America." They can listen to America's top 40 hits on the radio, complete with commercials in English. Like the imported cars wending their way through a sea of sputtering Russian Ladas, U.S. dollars are also zipping past the decrepit Russian ruble. Two years ago I was getting 30 rubles for a dollar, today one greenback will fetch more than one thousand worthless rubles.

From a place where most people were poor but equal, and therefore surviving with a semblance of dignity, Moscow has become a place where poverty is plainly visible, and shame comes on top of frustration and anger, due to the high contrast with the lucky few.

Two years ago a fairly common income, the equivalent of about $20 per month, was capable of sustaining a person in the strictly controlled prices of Russia's economy. In fact, it was barely a cash-based economy at all, with housing (modest, it is true), medical care, childcare and many other necessities provided as part of one's compensation from the work place. It is not easy to know what the average wage is here now: estimates vary from $15 to $100 per month, with inflation solidly established in the triple digits. And, while wage increases keep incomes on the rise, they consistently stay behind inflation, pushing the average Russian's standard of living lower and lower. In street markets, women try to supplement their income, standing shoulder to shoulder, holding up their pathetic wares: a pair of used gloves, one bottle of perfume, a puppy for sale. Russians survive by eating a lot of bread, potatoes and cabbage, and by relying on the ever-thinning safety net of the government, supplemented by ingenious barter schemes.

During my last visit here, I went to GUM, the famous department store next to Red Square, to find a simple clock for the office. As we walked into the glass-ceiling cavern, my translator told me with short-lived pride, "This is the biggest store in the world." Only moments later we both laughed. The store was absolutely empty. There was nothing to buy. That has changed; today, GUM is teeming with people and products from around the world. However, nothing is cheap and most people seem to be there just to look longingly at what they cannot afford. At least now there is a reason to have money; but it has become much more painful not to have it.

Around the corner from the CNN bureau is a shop called Sadko, one of the many hard currency stores where outrageous prices guarantee an ample supply of most Western goods. Every time I walk out of the store with bags full of supplies for our staff, I am followed by an elderly Russian woman, begging for help in the international language of desperation: hand cupped in front of her, head slightly tilted as she utters the words I understand all too well, despite my limited knowledge of Russian. For some reason she reminds me of my grandmother. For some reason I can't help wondering what she has seen through her long years in this land. Did she live through the Russian Revolution, the days of terror under Stalin, World War II and the Cold War? Did she feel she was participating in the noble enterprise of creating fairness in the world? Did she believe that in exchange for the sacrifices she made in her youth she would be protected in her old age?

Russians have seen their nation go from Super Power to Super Basket Case. It's been a bitter pill to swallow. Yeltsin's reforms have brought products to the stores, but the stores might as well be museums.

The Russian president has maintained all along that he needed more authority to carry out his reforms, since only drastic measures could turn this ship around. Members of the Soviet-era Parliament — the ones that saw their White House go up in flames —repeatedly blocked his moves, saying that the people should be sheltered from some of the harshness of the changes. In the end, Yeltsin simply moved to dissolve the body. Parliamentary leaders refused to accept the decision and the standoff began.

Yeltsin claims his plan of turning over state industries to private hands and lifting price controls, once completed, will bring rising standards of living. In the meantime, however, life is becoming more and more difficult. When I ask people whether times were better or worse than when Yeltsin came to power, they invariably acknowledge that for young people there are opportunities, and everyone appreciates the freedom to talk and think without fear (many of the political reforms that allowed the freedom to speak were introduced by Gorbachev. Yeltsin has concentrated on economic reforms). When I ask whether times are better or worse for the majority, the answers come without hesitation: "Much worse."

And yet, most people did not participate in the uprising led by the former Speaker of the Parliament Ruslan Khasbulatov and the former Vice President Alexander Rutskoi. Most Russians seem to shield themselves from political activism with a thick layer of cynicism. Perhaps it has to do with that long history of fighting for ideals and then simply being told the old truths are now lies.

When I arrived in Moscow, a round-the-clock demonstration was underway behind the White House; but it was relatively small. When Yeltsin's forces surrounded the White House with barbed wire, a few days into the crisis, most Muscovites were only affected by the complications in traffic caused by the closing of a few roads. Most people appeared to be interested in what was going on, but it wasn't until the tanks rolled in that their attention was really captured by the unfolding events.

The people who ended up taking to the streets on Sunday, October 3, were a motley collection, probably never numbering any more than one percent of the 9 million population of the city. They included communists and nationalists who were in despair at their country's apparent ruin, run-of-the-mill nihilists, and everyday Muscovites. But most of them seemed unconvinced; they didn't particularly care to defend Yeltsin, but they certainly did not want to die for Khasbulatov and Rutskoi. They were concerned more than anything with the danger of civil war. And despite their suffering under reforms, it's hard to find many who would actually prefer a return to communism.

Yeltsin survived the latest crisis because the military backed him. And the country escaped civil war because, like the military, most people did not wish to fight one another. But the divisions that led to the crisis still lie just below the surface, and as long as the extent of suffering throughout the country — not only in Moscow — continues, the events of October 1993 could yet turn out to be the early scenes of a nightmare.

From Russia to Latin America

Perhaps it seems odd that one of the last holdouts of communism is in Latin America. However, the region has always been a forum for debates over politics and economics, and the battles that brought communist ideology to the forefront of modern history.

When the followers of Karl Marx took the reins in Russia, intellectuals around the world watched closely. When Lenin's successors fought for control, leftists in Latin America had already taken sides. In the violent history of Russia, one crucial event actually took place in Mexico City — where Joseph Stalin terminated the life of one of his most respected adversaries. The death of Leon Trotsky was the death of a revolutionary who had a different view of how to use Karl Marx's ideas to answer the great questions of our time. If history had bookends, Leon Trotsky's demise would stand opposite the demise of the Berlin Wall. Perhaps it is fitting that a major communist figure, Fidel Castro, remains in place at the end of the era, holding out not far from where one of the movement's early leaders perished.

The story that follows is the unlikely tale of Leon Trotsky's final days, so soon after the beginning of the revolution that helped give birth to the Cold War.

World Revolution Stops Over in Mexico
March 1995

(Mexico City) Sometimes, the turbulence in the life of one country is reflected in another distant land, almost by an accident of history. In one of those strange intersections of nations' lives, the world of Mexico's *avant-garde* bohemian artists became the stage where — with great novelesque flare — one of the great political battles of the 20th century came to a bloody, tragic end.

In the 1930s, the great forces that shaped politics for an entire era were jockeying for position. Around the world, cataclysmic changes were taking place, from painful economic downturns and crushing political conflicts to new artistic genres. The world was in turmoil. The United States, for one, was mired in a deep and painful economic depression that was hardly a persuasive argument in favor of capitalism.

Communism, on the other hand, was getting tired of tolerating theoretical debate. Leon Trotsky, regarded by many historians as Lenin's Number Two in the Russian Revolution, was one of the great thinkers, organizers and strategists of the movement. How did he end up in a small room in the outskirts of Mexico City?

It was a time when a new revolutionary political philosophy was taking shape, along with a new artistic movement that defied convention — and reality. Many left-leaning artists were emphasizing the harsh realities of the modern world; now, the surrealists came to challenge reality head-on, juxtaposing the esoteric and the fantastic with the mundane and pedestrian. And in Mexico, realism and surrealism mixed with communism and socialism, Latin American politics with Soviet polemics. They all came together in sultry on of Coyoacan, the suburb that became the stage for this drama.

Coyoacan was home to Mexico's best-known artists of the time, including, intermittently, the now legendary couple of muralist Diego Rivera and his painter-wife Frida Kahlo. Another great Mexican muralist, David Alfaro Siqueiros, also a leftist, would likewise become a major player as the story unfolded.

In Mexico, social conflict was nothing new. Exploitation and abject poverty in a society that was still feudal in many respects drove many intellectuals, artists and politicians to seek a more equitable path. It was precisely because Mexico was profoundly acquainted with poverty that the intellectual upper crust closely followed the development of a philosophy that, to many, appeared tremendously promising. They became admirers of the revolutionaries who had seized power in Russia under the banner of Marxism, and followed the development of Soviet Russia as ideology and philosophy were crystallized into power.

These artists' beliefs were displayed in their works. Kahlo's surreal paintings are peppered with allusions to socialism. Her work, "Marxism will bring health to all the ill," for example, shows Karl Marx as a kind of angel hovering over Frida (who endured acute pain all her life, having had polio and then suffering major accidents). Symbols of American capitalism, illness, and peace mix on the canvas.

Even in the land of capitalism, Diego Rivera left his mark through politicized art. Excited about the prospect of working in the heartland of America's proletariat, he agreed to paint a mural in Detroit's Art Institute (even if it meant being paid by Henry Ford, a man whose anti-Semitic views he and Frida despised). When the mural was unveiled in Detroit in 1933, art critics, clerics and prominent citizens complained righteously that the city had been had, and by a communist, at that. Thrilled by the controversy, Rivera and Kahlo now advanced on the epicenter of capitalism.

Rivera set out to paint another mural at Rockefeller Center, but controversy this time wouldn't mean just publicity. High Society in New York kept a close eye on the work, and the polemic gathered an unstoppable momentum. When Rivera added Lenin's face to the nearly-completed work, Nelson Rockefeller himself told him he'd gone too far, and asked him to paint it over. Rivera refused, claiming that that would destroy the integrity of the work. The sponsors of the project resolutely shut him down: the mural was destroyed. (He recreated the design the following year on a wall of the Fine Arts Palace in Mexico City. This time it also featured a non-too-flattering likeness of John D. Rockefeller.)

During the years when Rivera and Kahlo lived in the U.S., the differences between Joseph Stalin and Leon Trotsky widened into an unbridgeable gulf. Trotsky started forming a separate faction within the Communist Party. Rivera, like other Mexican communists, followed the internal politics of Moscow; but unlike many others, he sympathized with Trotsky. (Trotsky also makes an appearance in the Mexico City mural.) Most communists in Mexico, like muralist David Alfaro Siqueiros, stuck with the mainstream of Soviet politics, supporting Stalin and considering Trotsky a traitor.

When Lenin's health began to deteriorate, the rift between his two most likely successors became a severe chasm in Russia and among followers of Marxist-Leninist doctrine around the world.

Diego Rivera supported Trotsky's view calling for less bureaucracy, for a state of "permanent revolution," and for an international approach to change. Stalin's preference — to focus on Russia, first — prevailed, largely because of the methods he used to elbow Trotsky out of power. Trotsky's fall was absolute. He was banished from the USSR in 1929 and began a pilgrimage from Turkey to France and then to Norway. Even the Norwegians couldn't resist the pressure from the giant to the East. Trotsky and his family were forced to flee, as Norway was under economic blackmail from Stalin; Norway could not afford to lose its valuable trade with the USSR.

Mexico had elected a president who, while hardly a communist, did have some leftist leanings. President Lazaro Cardenas, like many in Mexico, was an admirer of Diego Rivera. (For many years Kahlo's artistic reputation was largely overshadowed by that of her rotund and renowned husband.) The friendship between the president and the painter would prove critical in finding Leon Trotsky and his wandering family a new home.

When Norway told the Trotskys to hit the road, the situation became desperate. Rivera was contacted by a group of Trotsky supporters and was persuaded to intercede with the Mexican government. President Cardenas agreed to make the very controversial move of allowing Trotsky into Mexico. It is hard to imagine why (except for Rivera's friendship) Cardenas would grant Trotsky asylum. Trotsky was hated by communists and anti-communists alike.

With a promise of not participating in local politics, Trotsky arrived in Tampico, Mexico, on January 9, 1937. Fearing for her life, Trotsky's wife refused to leave the boat before seeing a friendly face. Frida Kahlo made her way up the plank and escorted the exiles to land.

Leon Trotsky began his Mexican exile in the now-legendary Blue House, the home where Kahlo was born and where she lived for several years with Rivera. For a couple of years the Trotskys, too, lived in the Blue House. There Leon enjoyed a new freedom, away from the Party that now considered him an abject traitor, and from Stalin who by then was show less and less concern for the value of individual lives. Coyoacan in those days had wide empty spaces, and Trotsky liked to go horseback riding; he is said to have pushed the horse as fast as it would go, in an exuberant attempt to enjoy his newfound freedom.

He also worked feverishly, both to clear his name and to articulate his views in writing. Trotsky organized a committee to review the evidence Stalin had used against him in the trial that had ended his life in Russia. The widely publicized review was carried out, before the press, by a group of distinguished leftists from several countries. Trotsky was exonerated. Meanwhile, his relationship with Rivera and Kahlo became profoundly strained.

Trotsky and his wife of 35 years, Natalia, spent a great deal of time with Rivera and Kahlo; it was perhaps the troubles between the latter two that eventually led to the tensions that followed. The relationship between the two artists had been both profound and excruciating for Frida. Diego was an incorrigible womanizer. His affairs were widely known, and were crushing for his wife. In fact, the two even divorced before deciding to remarry and accept what they seemed unable or unwilling to change.

They both had many affairs, she with men and women alike. But it was Rivera's affair with Frida's sister and confidante, Cristina, that was most painful for Frida. Perhaps in part to get even with Rivera, she allowed Trotsky's attraction for her to develop into an affair. Trotsky would slip letters into books that he would lend to Frida, and she would openly flirt him in front of Diego. The affair ended quickly, perhaps because of the dire consequences that would follow if they were discovered. Trotsky couldn't bare the sadness of his devoted wife, who had endured the travails of the revolutionary's life. Or, perhaps Frida had satisfied her need to get even with Diego.

Still, even after the affair Frida kept a special bond with Trotsky. On November 7, 1937, a date that was both Trotsky's birthday and the anniversary of the revolution he had helped bring about, Frida gave Trotsky a special gift — one of her many self-portraits. In most of her self-portraits, Frida appears with exaggerated features. She overstates her large eyebrows and deliberately seems to take away from the attractiveness that shows in photographs of her. But in the gift to Trotsky she makes no discernible effort to make herself less desirable, wearing an elegant dress and seductive make up, holding flowers in one hand and, in the other, a piece of paper that reads: "To Leon Trotsky, with all my love, I dedicate this painting on November 7, 1937."

Frida's professional reputation was beginning to grow, by now, and she was invited to hold exhibitions in major world capitals. In early 1939 she left for Paris, leaving both Trotsky and Rivera in Mexico. Her recognition as one of the major surrealist painters of her time was becoming complete. But her relationship with Rivera was falling apart, as would the friendship between Rivera and Trotsky.

Rivera seemed irritable without Kahlo, and his irritability magnified his political and personal differences with Trotsky. Trotsky was a purist, a profound theorist. Rivera was an artist. He had certain beliefs, but things seemed more relative to him. The differences exploded in a very public feud. Letters were written to and about one another. Finally, Trotsky wrote a letter to the Mexican newspapers wherein he stated his disagreements with Rivera and explained he could no longer accept his hospitality.

Trotsky found a new place for himself and his entourage, still in Coyoacan, just a few blocks from the Blue House which today houses the Frida Kahlo Museum. And that was the home where he would find his death.

By the end of 1939 Frida and Diego were divorced. (It was a rupture that would only survive 12 months.)

Barely one year after Trotsky and his family left the Blue House, the Stalinists made their first move against him. A group including David Alfaro Siqueiros broke into the bedroom shared by Leon and Natalia Trotsky. Incredibly, the two managed to survive by falling behind the bed and evading a spray of bullets. The bullet holes remain, all over the broken plaster walls near the couple's bed, just a few feet from Trotsky's study. Siqueiros went to jail for a short time, before President Cardenas released him to exile in Chile.

Riveras was considered a suspect for a short time, due to the well-publicized feud. After his close friend Paulette Goddard tipped him off that the police were searching for him, he left the country to avoid difficulties.

But Stalin was adamant in putting an end to Trotsky and his anti-Stalin writings. Three months after the first attempt, a man called Ramon Mercader befriended Frida and Trotsky's personal secretary. Through them, he gained acceptance into Trotsky's inner circle, a feat that had become increasingly difficult (especially after the assassination attempt). Mercader, inside Trotsky's home, managed to be left alone with him for just a moment — long enough to plunge an ice pick into his head.

Because of Frida's friendship with the assassin, she was taken in for interrogation and was jailed for a short time. Rivera was shaken by Frida's arrest and her deteriorating physical condition. The relationship that had never really ended was officially reestablished, and the two decided to remarry by the end of that year.

Trotsky's killer went to jail and after serving a lengthy term went to the Soviet Union, where he was received as a hero. Only when Gorbachev's *glasnost* took hold was it publicly admitted that the Soviet secret police had been responsible for the killing.

Trotsky's cremated remains, along with his wife's, now lie under a Soviet flag in the courtyard of his home in Coyoacan, Mexico, more than 6,000 miles away from the birthplace of his failed world revolution.

The Promise of a Global Era

The euphoria that followed the collapse of Communism came dressed in promises of freedom and prosperity for all. Eastern European nations began to convert their economies to the free market, often looking with anticipation at the booming Asian countries, hoping to mimic their exploding growth. Many in the Third World looked on and shook their heads. They had lived with their version of the market system for decades, and they knew prosperity would be uneven, unpredictable and, to a great degree, out of their control. As the world merged into one economic lane, the fortunes of each individual country would become tied to the rest of the world.

The word *market* began to take on a whole different meaning around the globe. Each year, fewer people would think of the market in the quaint sense of a place to go shopping for supplies and start to understand it instead as a complicated locus of financial transactions with the mysterious power to affect the lives of millions.

Another term began to take hold, describing the world's transformation: globalization. Globalization meant more than an economic process. Initially, it was a prescription for a system of free trade around the planet; but it became much more. A new alignment of ideologies was in the making.

The forces of globalization aimed to turn the planet into one big free trade zone. The markets, and not the bureaucrats, politicians or central planners, would decide what each country or region would produce. The fabled talents of the free market would unearth the unique gifts we each possessed, and skillfully match them to someone's needs, somewhere in the world. A little like the old Marxist promise — from each according to his ability, to each according to his need. Except this time, it would all be done for profit, and in freedom. Globalization, however, turned out to be much more complex than advertised.

The significance of globalization as a power in the emerging era was not evident in the early days of the New World Order. Democracy, freedom and trade somehow made their entrance onto the stage simultaneously, as if they were all leading actors in the same play. It was hard to see which would take the leading role, but gradually globalization became the most controversial performer, drawing standing ovations — during the first act — from most, and later inciting a chorus of boos.

Perhaps it was fitting that, as the victor in the Cold War, the United States would have the primary role in shaping the new world. It took on the role without a trace of humility and moved to make the world in its own image. The new world would be modeled to give everyone a chance at the American Dream. The picture, at first glance, shimmered with appeal. Each country would enjoy democracy and develop a huge middle class, living in a thriving vibrant economy. Workers' generous salaries would bring nice homes, cars, and vacations. Technology would play a major role, bringing high productivity to industry, entertainment to the home, and untold ease to the toils of daily life.

This vision gave signs of becoming everyone's dream, especially in the former East, where young people had always had a hankering for Rock & Roll and blue jeans. But the hints were coming that American-style Nirvana might be hard to reach, and that even if they reached it they might not like it as much as they thought.

That was all before the Asian Economic crisis of 1998. It was before the Battle of Seattle, where demonstrators protesting what they saw as the evils of globalization brought down a meeting of the World Trade Organization. It was before the protesters at the World Economic Forum in Davos stormed a McDonald's restaurant to vent their rage against the "global economy" (because in their minds nothing stood more for America-led globalization than McDonald's).

Protests against the International Monetary Fund and World Bank — symbols of the global trends — became the chic ideology by the late 1990s and into the new millennium. The global anti-globalization movement mustered protesters from Australia to the Czech republic, jetting in and out of summit towns and piling up the frequent-flyer miles in their search for justice. They railed against the rule of unrestricted free markets and they championed the rights of the poor with the iconoclastic passion of revolutionaries. But the movement could hardly be called revolutionary. In fact, the movement stood for a slowdown of the liberal trends sweeping the world after the Cold War. Rather than trying to overturn the existing order, they wanted to ameliorate its effects. Like people in a fishing village trying to stop a tidal wave with their bare hands, they tried to stop the inevitable, or at least to channel it so that fewer would drown.

In the early 1990s, the planet was still inebriated with the prospects of permanent world peace; it wasn't clear what type of trouble might lie ahead. By the mid-1990s, however, one of the U.S.'s long-time trade partners experience a devastating economic crisis with consequences that reached far from its borders. Like an ominous drumbeat, Mexico's collapse and the ensuing spillover (known as the "Tequila Effect") presaged the Asian crisis of 1998. Globalization increasingly meant that big financial institutions and investors gained greater ability to affect international markets. The story of how the actions of a single trader caused the downfall of the venerable Barings Bank foreshadowed what could happen to a country and a region left vulnerable to the whims of investors.

During the innocent days, the talk had been more about the Peace Dividend. As the prospect of all-out nuclear war vanished, the enormous sums that had been spent on weapons could be spent on programs to make the world a better place. (Or to cut taxes, thereby making it better yet, depending on your point of view.)

In the early weeks of 1994, Bill Clinton — barely one year into his presidency — visited the Czech capital, Prague. The Czechs, hoping the

West would now offer more protection than it had done when the Germans and then the Russians invaded, received the U.S. president with open arms. "Whitewater" was already roiling, and Clinton's sexual indiscretions were already haunting him, dominating the question-and-answer sessions of every press conference during his European tour. But in Prague, that didn't matter. Bill Clinton was still "Bubba." And the Czechs simply couldn't get enough of the cool sax-playing leader of the free world. They were fascinated with the president, and mystified by Americans' obsessive focus on his sex life.

As it happens, Clinton's European tour, dealing with potentially earth-shattering subjects — nuclear missiles, the war in the Balkans, and the future of NATO — came at the same time as another sort of historical news event in America. Lorena Bobbitt had cut off her husband's penis, and her trial was taking place while world leaders discussed the future of the planet. You need not wonder which story was more successful in capturing television viewers' attention.

News organizations had to decide what to give their viewers. CNN's Solomonic solution to this editorial quandary was a television production effect now commonly known as "Big Box, Little Box." The screen would show two pictures at the same time, each framed in a box: in one square, the president in session with world leaders, debating the dismantling of missiles; in another, Lorena Bobbitt in court. You can have two pictures, but you can't have two sets of sound; the trial won the audio war most of the time. Viewers heard, word for word, the description of how she cut off her husband's penis and then threw it away. As the world leaders continued their meetings, Lorena told her tale of woe.

Lorena's story might have been enthralling to U.S. viewers, but in Prague Bill Clinton was the ratings leader. The story that follows describes the reception the U.S. president was given in the new Czech Republic.

The Occidental Tourist:
A Western Leader Draws Cheers in the Former East
January 1994

(Prague) For the many Westernized people of Prague, the visit of President Clinton presented a terrible dilemma: should they act unimpressed, show their worldliness and sophistication by displaying a touch of cynicism as the White House circus rolled into town? Or should they make their excitement visible as the leader of a world so many of them want to emulate made a visit to the their homeland? The problem was a source of obvious anxiety for the thousands of Americans and Americaphiles living in the Czech capital.

To be fair, the preparations for the arrival of a U.S. president anywhere can make a cynic out of the biggest patriot. For the people of Prague, accustomed to casually running into their president (a man whose place in history was guaranteed long before anyone knew what a Hillary Rodham was), the whirlwind of activity was all the more baffling. Were all these great expectations well founded, or was it much ado about nothing?

Already in Prague several English-language newspapers betray a growing culture that is part MTV hip, part Beavis and Butt Head-nihilism, and part Peace Corps idealism. Even the native Czechs who have learned English from American movies and American immigrants (the "ex-pats") referred to Mr. Clinton's impending arrival as the "Coming of Bubba"

But the truth is that neither the new nor the old residents of this capital of old Bohemia could manage to conceal their excitement under their elaborate veneer of sarcasm. And in their effort to project hipness, they managed to debate some truly important issues that came into sharp focus precisely because this is Prague.

During the days leading up to Mr. Clinton's arrival, amid announcements of nuclear disarmament in Ukraine, possible air strikes in Bosnia and a NATO partnership for Eastern Europe, the U.S. media's focus remained on another matter of apparently great concern to the American people.

This was before the historical penis-severing trial. The Bobbitts, or for that matter Whitewater, had not yet moved the spotlight away from the allegations of Arkansas troopers that the President was as shamefully frisky as had been rumored — only more so.

For observers in Prague, this obsession with the President's hours between the sheets was a matter of great interest, even as the throngs of reporters that follow Mr. Clinton began making their way to the capital of the Czech Republic.

As the Czechs noted, Vaclav Havel, the president of their republic, a hero of anti-Communist resistance, has never claimed adherence to a "till death do us part" performance in his marriage. In fact, in one of his many books he declared, "I certainly have more than one sin in my heavenly tally sheet." People hardly noticed. In fact, Clinton and Havel have quite a few traits in common. But those traits couldn't have been treated more differently by their electorates.

They're both children of the 60s. Both have experimented with the substances of the times, and both have been known to engage in, shall we say, good living.

But only Mr. Clinton has had to carry his part like a burlap sack full of bowling balls up the mountain of power. Why is that, perplexed Prague residents inquired of each other? How come we don't care, and they seem to care little about anything else?

Their soul-searching yielded several possible explanations. The Czechs are too prudish to discuss the sex lives of leaders in print; or, perhaps the opposite. Czechs are so sexually liberated that they consider these matters only human and hardly relevant to public discourse.

Another self-critical theory said Czech journalists don't have the gumption to criticize the powerful. But the argument that seemed to carry the day maintained that the Czechs have far too many problems — important problems — and the sex lives of politicians will just have to wait for better post-Communist days.

Perhaps the matter that intrigued Czechs most of all was the sheer amount of money Americans were spending on this visit. They remembered other visits from American dignitaries, like the time Dan Quayle came to Prague in 1991 and President

Havel was nearly shoved back into the crowd by an overzealous security man who apparently had not been briefed on who was to be allowed near the all-important "Veep."

The White House reportedly brought a delegation of almost 800 people to the Czech Republic. We could not confirm that number, and we don't know if it included the large number of State Department personnel from U.S. diplomatic missions in other countries in the region who were redeployed for the Great Event.

The Czechs undoubtedly spent quite a few *krona* themselves to make the event come off smoothly, with battalions of Prague police, for one, conspiring with U.S. Secret Service agents to make it impossibly difficult to get from one place to another.

The U.S government reserved the gigantic Atrium Hotel and its 735 rooms. There slept Mr. Clinton. And there operated the press-filing center where some 500 journalists did their work.

For the longhaired Czech youngsters, speaking heavily-accented English laden with even heavier American slang, and for their ex-pat pals, the Atrium was the place to be.

Those who got access were abuzz with excitement. One moment they laughed at America and, munching on a Big Mac or a slice of Pizza Hut Supreme, they wondered if Dan Rather would be there (he was) and moments later tried not to choke on the pepperoni when Ted Koppel marched in.

In the end, the 24-hour visit produced no major *faux pas* by the President. That, in rough international affairs analysis, means it was a successful visit. Everyone got along famously.

The Czech president gave the President of the United States a saxophone; he played later in a jazz club during a pub-hopping spree. Everyone got great PR.

Rude Awakenings

The world was shrinking, especially for corporations and their shareholders. The longest economic expansion in the United States was underway — until the Asian Economic Crisis of 1998 sent one third of the globe's economies into a profound recession, and placed the world's entire financial system on the edge of catastrophe. President Clinton declared this the greatest threat to the world's economy in 50 years.

But the first economic crisis in the new era had already devastated millions of lives overnight — in Mexico, in the last few days of 1994 and 1995. The Federal Reserve Board Chairman said the Mexican crisis of the mid-90s was the first major economic crisis of the 21st century; Asia's 1998 collapse was the second he said, cheerlessly forecasting there would be many more.

Investors lost billions, in cities most of them had never seen. But the real suffering fell on the poor populations of the countries with the shattered economies. In the first 3 months of the Mexican crisis, a quarter of a million people were thrown out of work in an economy with no new jobs to offer. As the value of the peso sank from 3.45 to more than 8 to the dollar, and then even more, banks and businesses saw the value of their dollar-denominated debt nearly triple. Thousands of businesses closed. People were forced to rely on their savings, which had evaporated as well. Interest rates exploded. By March, rates on credit cards had topped 70%, and they would rise far more. New borrowing was out of the question, and impossibly high payments on existing debts meant economic ruin for thousands.

The United States and the international financial organizations set out to try to heal Mexico's economy. The treatment was quintessential Western medicine. It was sure to cure the patient, if it didn't kill him first.

Mexican President Ernesto Zedillo had been caught off guard, but as the extent of the crisis dawned on everyone he found he had no choice. Even Bill Clinton's emboldened opposition saw that the U.S. should intervene. As the value of retirement accounts for U.S. workers started feeling the effects of the plunging market in Mexico, the U.S. agreed to help out. The medicine for Mexicans was bitter, but it sure made the *Norteamericanos* feel better.

The government cut about 10% of public spending. Sales taxes went from 10 to 15%. Already gasoline prices had gone up 35% and electricity 20%. Economists said another million Mexicans would lose their jobs before the end of the summer of 1995. The economy, they warned, would sink into a recession, and inflation would exceed 40%

for the year. Meanwhile, salary increases — especially for the millions on minimum wage — would be kept to no more than 10% — Mexicans lucky enough to remain employed would effectively lose one-third of their purchasing power.

The idea was to keep inflation from spiraling out of control. Eventually, the theory went, the lower exchange rate would make Mexican products more affordable abroad and boost exports. The country would once again become the darling of investors, and a total collapse would be averted.

By some measures, the treatment was hugely successful. In 1995 Mexico's economy — its GNP or Gross National Product — shrank by more than 6%, but the next year it grew 5%. Between the lessons of 1995 and the propulsion of the North American Free Trade Agreement (NAFTA) put into effect in 1994, Mexico's trade-driven economy has made some impressive strides, tearing down obstacles to free trade like over-regulation and corruption. Others point to the size of Mexico's underclass as a sign that globalization has stripped away necessary protections. With about half of its people living in poverty, Mexico is firmly in the ranks of the developing world, which today means it is largely a supplier of cheap labor to a rich country. And, alarmingly, Mexico's economy is dependent on a thriving U.S. economy for its own survival. Still, the collapse did come to an end. It was an outcome that was far from assured in the early months of 1995.

Mexican Meltdown Can Burn U.S.
March 1995

(Mexico City) In this capital, housewives take to the streets to protest rising prices and political activists join in, shouting slogans against opposition parties. In the state of Tabasco riots break out, with protesters hurling bottles and burning garbage near the state house. In the state of Chiapas, Maya Indians nervously tap their weapons, debating what the Mexican government will do to correct inequalities and corruption. All the while, in the building known as "the Egg," — home of the Mexican *Bolsa* or stock exchange — traders tally up their losses from the financial bloodshed of the last few weeks. And the turmoil from the Mexican meltdown doesn't end there: in Washington D.C.

politicians and bankers, Republicans and Democrats, oppose President Clinton's $40 billion bailout, causing the President to give up on the plan, while in financial capitals around the world Mexican envoys struggle to reassure investors.

At the center of the Mexican drama totter two weak presidents with little support and little stature in their respective countries. First, President Ernesto Zedillo, who helped bring on the crisis and whose continuing indecision allowed it to worsen, is now the Captain of the floundering Mexican ship. The would-be rescuer, Bill Clinton, tries to steer a country whose rudder was just handed to his opposition in Congress.

This most recent Mexican crisis brings home the new reality of a world that seems smaller by the day. The actions of one president in a Third World country can have implications reaching all corners of the globe. When the country is a next-door neighbor, the implications are potentially much more serious.

The biggest losers in the Mexican morass are, as is tragically the norm, the poor in a poor country. But losses extend everywhere. In the U.S., it's likely millions of people don't realize they too have lost money. And the crisis — and the losses — are far from over. Billions of dollars in individual stocks and mutual funds have been invested in Mexico and in other so-called developing countries by private investors and retirement fund managers. Those funds have lost much of their value. American companies doing business in Mexico have lost and will lose money. In addition, the hundreds of thousands of workers making products for sale in Mexico will see their customers vanish, while in border states the flow of immigrants is likely to surge as impoverished Mexicans desperately look for work, any kind of work.

As President Clinton struggles to find a way to help Mexico, the reality is that his actions too will affect people around the planet. The world has become inextricably interdependent.

In the past few years, virtually the entire world has gone capitalist. Economies where the government used to control industry and labor have opened their markets, welcoming foreign investment. A recent report by the World Bank boasts that private in-

80

vestment in the Third World has reached a record $180 billion. That is triple the aid coming from governments. But much of that investment has gone to countries like Mexico, and much of it can be withdrawn by the tap of a keyboard. This philosophy of capitalist "self-sufficiency" leaves the impoverished people of the Third World at the mercy of Wall Street and Tokyo. If the Mexican market is allowed to collapse, investors will look at overseas markets, especially developing markets, with great trepidation. The billions that fled "the Egg" in the last few weeks will seem like chicken feed.

For the countries experiencing the crisis, it must seem like trying to swim in the tangles of many puppeteers' strings. Mexico tries to stay afloat — confronting the economic, political and social currents within the country — while the Federal Reserve in the United States continues to raise interest rates. That means Mexico has to offer even higher rates to attract investors. (A recent auction of government securities offered about 20% interest rates on short-term bills. Only 20 percent of the bills were sold.) The people of Mexico, half of whom live at or below the poverty level, are seeing their salaries swept away by the new tide of inflation, while many companies have begun laying off workers because shoppers are disappearing. The Zedillo government tries to keep from sinking by reasoning with investors, negotiating with opposition parties, talking to the rebels in Chiapas, and trying to diffuse the surge of indignation Mexicans experience when they hear the goings on across the border. American politicians, learning to work the ropes of the new balance of power, discuss the Mexican rescue as they might argue construction of an unneeded bridge across a forgotten river. Congressional debate on loan guarantees spill over into demands that Mexico drop contacts with Cuba, or that Democrats stop attacking Newt Gingrich's book deal — issues that have no place in the debate. But that hardly seems to matter.

When Foreign investors poured more than $70 billion dollars into Mexico, and when Mexican consumers buying American products created what the administration says are almost 800,000 jobs in the U.S., the benefits came to this country. The benefit to Mexico, according to some, was obvious. Others said it was questionable. During the years of the Mexican Miracle, the number of millionaires there surged. Astonishingly, Mexico now has one of the largest numbers of billionaires in the world. But for ordinary Mexicans, real wages continued their steady decline, leaving them with a 40% loss in purchasing power since 1982. In the United States, the financial losses of the poor in Mexico meant more illegal immigration and more instability south of the border, a worrying development so close to home.

When politicians debate whether to help solve the Mexican quandary, and when the rest of us ignore it as just another problem in another country, we make the mistake of believing that our borders are crossed only by people, and that our direct interests all lie at home. Most analysts believe Mexico will come out of this crisis. But if it doesn't? We have never seen a true refugee crisis, or felt the specter of intense political violence, at our doorstep. And we have never stopped to think that when we go cast our vote at the library down the street, our vote will be felt in a place called Chiapas, Tokyo or Tabasco.

Hell No, We Won't Go!

As the situation in Mexico deteriorated during 1995, protests against the government mounted, with massive demonstrations frequently erupting, blocking roads and buildings. But the most popular location in the entire country to hold a demonstration is the expansive Zocalo, the giant paved plaza in front of the ancient Metropolitan Cathedral and the National Palace. The Zocalo, one of the largest urban squares in the world, is the place to vent in Mexico. And in those days, there was plenty to vent about.

When I arrived in Mexico City in the spring of 1995, I went straight to El Zocalo. As expected, there was no shortage of protests. But there was something there I didn't expect. Much of the place had been taken over by a large number of peasants from the now-famous state of Chiapas. Perhaps the most amazing aspect of the protest was how little publicity it had received. The group had marched, on foot, for almost 700 miles to air its grievances, but their plight and their message were lost in Mexico's sea of troubles.

I spoke with organizers, and with average participants. They seemed determined to get a hearing. They all vowed they would not leave until the president gave them an audience.

The scene at El Zocalo in many ways was reminiscent of Tiananmen Square. The story was irresistible. I had come to Mexico on my own, not on assignment from CNN, so I called a newspaper editor in the U.S. to discuss an article about the peasants of Chiapas, determined to continue their protest until the president received them or until they were expelled by force. He loved the story and we agreed: I would take pictures and write a feature piece for the Sunday edition.

I finished the interviews, took pictures of the "Mexican Tiananmen," and wrote the story. Then I decided to pay one last visit to the valiant protesters who had risked life and limb for their cause, and would let nothing stand in their way. I arrived at El Zocalo. To my shock, the tents were being folded and the kitchen was being packed. Had the president given in? I rushed to ask one of the men who had talked to me before. No, he told me. He had not spoken to them and he wasn't going to. The president was too busy, and they too had work to do, back home.

The article, of course, had to be changed.

Little Tiananmen in Mexico
March 1995

(Mexico City) In the midst of the high drama of Mexico's current crisis, a passionate display of conviction became lost in the glare of competing news events. For weeks the Mayan version of a mini-Tiananmen Square came to life in the heart of Mexico City. The place, called El Zocalo, is the city's enormous main square.

The demonstrators departed Mexico's southern-most state in what they called "The Great Caravan March, Chiapas-Mexico." The trek began February 20, and reached the capital on March 8th.

Once they arrived, the Chiapanecos set up a tent city in the old colonial center of the town. Bright red, blue and black tarp tents housed the demonstrators as they tried to bring attention to their cause. They hoped to pressure Mexico's President Ernesto Zedillo to speak with them and meet their demands.

But the president never met with them, and the press relegated them to Section B. In today's Mexico, there is a great deal of competition for the front page.

Mexico is mired in a profound economic crisis with disastrous consequences for the poor and uncharacteristically difficult challenges for the rich. The state of the country's politics is little short of Shakespearean, with murders and conspiracies leaving analysts and citizens alike shaking their heads.

The plight of the protesters from Chiapas is hardly one to raise an eyebrow of curiosity in a Third World country. One more group of poor people complaining of exploitation in a world we all know is filled with misery . . . But Chiapas did manage to catch the eye of Mexico's government, and the lens of the world press, when a New Year's Day uprising there in 1994 left more than 150 people dead.

The Zapatista Army of National Liberation (EZLN) shot its way into the public arena.

Since that time, the government has alternated between bludgeoning the rebels and offering olive branches. Just last week the government again indicated that it wanted to negotiate, and the rebels said they too would engage in dialogue if the government redeployed its troops far enough away to give the peasants some room to breathe. If dialogue does take place, it's difficult to know how far the government would go in meeting the Zapatistas' demands in relation to land distribution and government corruption.

The masked leader of the Zapatistas, Sub-Commander Marcos, has become a pop icon in Mexico. Likenesses of the pipe-smoking *guerrillero* are a favorite with students, workers, and tourists. The man with the gun and his armed followers are the subject of great interest.

But that's not the case with the members of the Great Caravan. With little formal education and virtually no financial resources, the peasants of Chiapas managed to survive the chilly nights on the hard cobblestones of El Zocalo and the neglect of the press. Theirs is the cause of hope against hope and, as such, it drew support from idealists and dreamers. Amazingly, the tent city

84

remained a model of cleanliness and organization. The 14 political and civic groups who made up the Caravan, each settled on a section of the square, with a communal kitchen where at any given time one could see massive quantities of beans and tortillas in various stages of preparation. Men in bandanas and straw hats and women in brightly colored Indian wraps milled about, listening to speeches from their *compañeros*, preparing banners for their daily demonstrations or shaving — without any soap or water. Trash was miraculously picked up before it reached the ground, and everyone seemed to know exactly how to go about surviving in this peculiar world. A doctor was usually available, courtesy of a local healthcare advocacy organization. Labor unions and fringe political parties occasionally set up tents offering free haircuts. And university students, who regularly collect money for the Chiapanecos, could sometimes be seen helping in the communal kitchen.

But mainstream Mexico paid little attention to the group. Even as the president made widely publicized overtures to the Zapatistas in the impoverished south, the peaceful protestors failed to attract any attention from the executive.

When the group staged a march from EL Zocalo to the north gate of the president's residence at the Los Piños complex, a gaggle of Mexican journalists was already stalking the south gate. They stood ready to pounce on a sound-bite from the gray-suited politicians emerging from tax wrangling with the president, oblivious to what the peasants might be up to.

The president refused to meet with the group's representatives, but the government did not completely ignore the marchers. When the demonstrators reached the bottom of the hill leading up to Los Piños, they were met by hundreds of police in full riot gear blocking their way. At the sight of such a display of muscle, several cameras materialized. But there was no bloodshed, and they promptly left.

The protesters had vowed to remain in the capital until their grievances were resolved, but the futility of their efforts became too obvious to ignore. Their difficult days and nights away from their families and their land, in this massive city of more than 20 million people, were accomplishing nothing. So, finally, on

March 21, they took down their banners and rolled up their colorful tarps, ready to start the long way back.

In the meantime, the government appears genuinely worried about the armed Zapatistas — the ones who didn't march — and it may actually have made some progress towards restarting talks. With the people experiencing growing economic suffering, Zedillo would rather not have idealistic armed revolutionaries in plain view of the masses. But the sight of peaceful demonstrators seemed the least of his worries. The demonstrators, it seems, took notice. Nonviolence here is not gaining many new adherents.

Oceans of Money

The Zapatista rebellion that brought Chiapas to the forefront started on the day NAFTA went into effect, January 1, 1994, when armed followers of Sub-Commander Marcos took over the town of San Cristobal de las Casas. Marcos, with his trademark ski mask and pipe, managed to bring attention to the plight of the Indians. The Mexican government maintained an enormous military presence in the region, while a ceasefire continued without an outright resolution of the conflict. When President Vicente Fox came to power in December 2001, he vowed to bring down the number of troops, and negotiate a definitive peace agreement.

For intellectuals in the Zapatista movement, globalization — or the wave of neo-liberalism sweeping the world — has always been the enemy. For much of the world, it's still an open question.

The ideological battle (which seems to have replaced the left-right divide) centers on whether globalism is poison or panacea. Environmentalists expressed their views forcefully during the debates on NAFTA. In a globalized economy, they argued, the profit motive would easily trump the environment, as governments lowered standards to entice foreign investment, and as corporations readily shifted production to the country with the least restrictions. Preserving the environment generally requires regulations, and abiding by those regulations almost always has a price for industry. If businesses managed to dodge the regions that protect the environment, the price would be paid by all, in the form of dirty air, dirty water, and a poisoned, overheated planet. To make matters worse, say opponents of free trade, the globalization trend makes the world a less interesting place, diluting local cultures and replacing them with a marketing creation — a homogenous consumer culture that today looks very much like America, with identical chain stores and shopping malls and the same pop music everywhere.

Globalization, critics charge, makes the rich richer and the poor poorer. By some accounts, the average citizen of the "First World" is 74 times richer than the average resident of the Third World, a gap that has grown from a 10-to-1 ratio at the beginning of the century.

Labor groups maintain that the trend threatens hard-won gains for workers. Companies would close down factories in places where workers earned a decent salary and benefits, and reopen in countries with no protection against child labor and other forms of exploitation. The mere possibility that a plant might shut down, lay off workers and move to another country would put union and non-union workers at a disadvantage, lowering salaries across the globe and squeezing out greater profits for corporations and their shareholders.

Shareholders, investors, have the potential to cause devastating upheaval. Just as sales of finished products and raw materials enjoy easy access across national borders, investors can easily move their money from one country to another blurring lines on the map. A mutual fund that invests in Europe could be bought just as easily as one that invests in the U.S., Asia or Latin America; and withdrawals from a mutual fund based in Denver can cause unemployment in Thailand.

As early as 1997, before the crisis in Asia, financier George Soros warned of the dangers of unrestrained global capitalism, saying that global capitalism had taken the place of communism as the main threat to democracy. Soros declared, "There are collective interests that don't find expression in market values." Investors have a single motivation in mind: making money. If their actions bring prosperity or calamity to a nation, that is simply not relevant.

This fact would prove devastating for Asia in 1998.

The Mexican crisis in 1995 clearly indicated the danger of mas-

sive cash movements by foreign investors, but even as Mexico was beginning to stabilize, a single man managed to induce cold sweats across
several continents. His name was Nicholas Leeson.

Leeson's is the story of how one man can bring down an institution and send shockwaves crashing on the financial shores of distant
markets. Still, the Barings Bank incident barely seemed to flash a caution light to individual investors and financial institutions; very few
read it as a sign that someone could pull the plug on Asia's economies
just a few years later. Barings was considered a unique example of mis-
management and fraud.

Losing the Work of Centuries
February 1995

Back in the mid-1700s, before the French Revolution, around
the time the Colonies in North America declared their independence, a new bank came to life in England. It was Baring Brothers & Co. Over the years, the institution wove for itself a mantle
of venerability. It helped finance the wars against Napoleon and
the Louisiana Purchase in North America. Its bowler hat-
wearing, umbrella-carrying employees became the conservative,
reliable investment bankers to British blue bloods, including
Queen Elizabeth. But its real worldwide fame broke like thunder
in the waning years of the 20th century, in the year 1995.

It came like a shattering blast of heavy metal rock-and-roll in
the middle of a sedate chamber music concert. Barings Bank
went bankrupt maneuvering in the highflying world of computerized market derivatives. The actions of one young man practically destroying the work of centuries, sending a loud wake up
call to investors, managers and government regulators.

As the dust of the Barings debacle settles, what really matters
is how this happened. Could your money disappear overnight —
a modern-day magic trick that Barings' trader Nicholas Leeson
almost managed to pull with the funds of Barings' customers?

In reality, the astonishing feat took months to concoct and,
luckily, it seems the losses to investors and to the bank's employees will not be as devastating as it first seemed. (No need to
worry for a few of Her Majesty's endangered millions.) Now it

is becoming embarrassingly apparent, that the blame for this debacle falls on more shoulders than just Nick Leeson's, and that an incident like this could, indeed, happen anywhere.

Leeson was a Barings whiz kid. A rags to riches Brit, who made his way out of London's government subsidized housing, and joined the respected institution, quickly becoming manager of Barings Futures in Singapore. He was making about $300,000 a year, and bragged he would retire a wealthy man while still in his 20s. He had authorization to make low risk investments in complex investments known as derivatives. But instead of low-risk investments, his trading snowballed into the avalanche of losses that toppled the bank.

The bulk of his investments was in futures on the Tokyo Stock Exchange's Nikkei Average. The investment meant that Leeson agreed to buy a group of stocks at a pre-determined price, on a pre-determined future date. Convinced the market would go up, he believed the preset price would prove lower than the going rates for that future date. He would make a killing. But he lost, and then he lost some more. As his losses mounted, he frantically tried to make up for them by risking more and more of the bank's money. If his bet had proved right, Leeson would have been a hero. Instead, the plan failed miserably, the world found out about the investments, and Leeson wasted no time fleeing the scene of the disaster.

When police reached his luxury condominium in Singapore's fashionable Orchard neighborhood, they found shirts drying on the balcony and mail piling up by the front door; hardly signs of a long-planned escape. Until the end, it seems, Leeson thought he would pull it off.

The gamble had reached a staggering $27 billion, more than half the value of all the goods and services Singapore produces in a year. And the losses for the bank eventually exceeded its total worth. The bank was valued at about 900 million pounds, $1.4 billion, before the disaster.

On the weekend of Leeson's disappearance (the weekend he turned a ripe 28 years of age) the losses reached $800 million. But word of the scandal sent a tidal wave through world markets. The British Pound fell in European markets, stock prices dropped in Taiwan, Manila, Hong Kong, Seoul and — cruelly — in Tokyo. Despite pleas for calm from exchange officials, the market plummeted, sending the Nikkei even lower, and thus bringing even more losses to Barings. So far the losses have been calculated at $1.5 billion.

Following Leeson's capture at the Frankfurt airport, the search for the guilty began in earnest. He was the first target of the finger-pointers, who said this was simply a case of a "rogue trader, gone out of control." Then Peter Baring, head of the bank, said he thought Leeson may have been "encouraged" to bring down the company. Speculation was that Leeson and others invested so the bank would lose and they would gain. Then the damning evidence came to the surface. The bank received warnings — several times — that this could happen.

As far back as 1992 there were warnings of impending disaster over the way Leeson operated in Singapore. In August of 1994 an internal review showed Leeson had too much control in the office. Leeson was in charge of both trading and of keeping the documentation for the trades, an extremely unwise setup. In addition, regulators in Singapore, seeing the numbers on Barings trades mount, had also warned of catastrophe. But the bank failed to take action, perhaps also hoping Barings would ultimately win one large bet, or maybe just incapable of stomaching the implications of what was happening. Maybe it was plain incompetence.

In the U.S., government and financial industry officials rushed to reassure everyone that something like this would be nearly impossible here. But when pressed, they admitted there is no way to guarantee it will not.

And yet, the derivatives game sent into bankruptcy wealthy Orange County, Calif., a client of the prestigious firm Merrill Lynch. And Wall Street firms themselves have teetered and fallen before. In the 1980s, Drexel Burnham Lambert, once the Street's mightiest, collapsed under the weight of security violations indictments. More recently, Salomon Brothers was almost brought down by the antics of one trader in the supposedly super-safe market in U.S. Treasury securities. Last year's demise of the venerable Kidder, Peabody was also blamed by the company on the actions of one broker who, according to firm officials, recorded $350 million worth of phony profits in order to cover gigantic losses.

Calls for increased government scrutiny have met skepticism from a government now talking about lifting long-standing regulations of the banking industry to help it compete in the global market. Even Federal Reserve Chairman Alan Greenspan admits this world of instantaneous multi-million dollar computerized transactions cannot be effectively controlled by legislation.

With the wreckage of Barings now purchased by the Dutch ING Group, the legacy of the Leeson experience will undoubtedly mean stricter internal enforcements for investment firms. But investors should take heed and follow one of the most basic rules of survival in the risky world of finance: Don't put all your eggs in one basket. Even if it's a basket made by the finest weavers, practicing their craft for hundreds of years.

The Tigers, Tamed

Nick Leeson spent 4 ½ years in jail, finally returning to England in the summer of 1999. Former Barings executives moved on well with their lives, finding other jobs or, in the case of the bank's last chairman, Sir Peter Baring, retiring to the life of the British aristocracy. The Nicholas Leeson who left Singapore was a very different man from the ambitious, self-confident youngster who joined Barings a decade earlier. While he was in prison he developed colon cancer and his wife left him.

After Mexico's (and Leeson's) crisis, international institutions tried to improve the amount of information available to investors about what are known as "emerging markets" — the global economy term for what in Cold War parlance is called the Third World. But proposals from financial institutions and investor representatives did little to prepare the world — rich and poor — for what was about to take place in Asia.

Asian economies had been the envy of much of the world for years. The so-called Asian Tigers managed to reduce poverty and lift incomes with spectacular growth in their economies. Many of the poor did better, and many in government did great. There was an unspoken agreement. As long as some of the spoils went to the masses, the people would look the other way when it came to lack of democracy and corruption. In fact, some believed that too much democracy could spoil prosperity. The people tolerated the excesses of their leaders in exchange for a share of the wealth.

I visited Singapore when it was still in full expansion mode, several years before the crisis. It was clear even then this was a nation like no other. Reading the Singapore Times on the plane I thought someone had made a mistake. A new law was about to ban gum in Singapore. This had to be a typographical error. Perhaps they were talking about Gun control. But no, this was Singapore, and this was Gum Control. The authorities grew tired of messy, sticky chewing gum, the blight of urban beautification.

The newspaper detailed the stiff penalties in jail time or cash for transportation and possession of the illegal substance. In town, people chuckled a bit about it. Singaporeans understood their situation. Their country was routinely chastised as a violator of civil rights by international organizations. But the government maintained that prosperity was the most important human right. There's no question, prosperity ruled. The average income of a Singaporean was the same as that of an American, increased in a quarter century from $800 a year to $15,000.

For decades, growth in East Asia averaged some 8 percent per year, an astonishing figure by any region's standards. But much of it was built on excessive debt. Money was loaned and borrowed for unnecessary and costly construction projects. Thailand bragged that the national bird was the crane, the construction crane. The party lasted until the middle of 1997.

The official start of the Asian Economic Crisis of 1998 was July 2, 1997. On that date, authorities in Thailand decided to allow the country's currency, the Bhat, to float. That is, they decided to allow the market to set the value of the Bhat relative to the U.S. dollar and other currencies. Instead of sliding gently, the Bhat collapsed, plunging 15 percent in a matter of hours. For investors and speculators around the world it was a clarion call to take a close look at their investments, particularly in Asia. In the months that followed, countries like the Philippines, Malaysia, Indonesia, South Korea and others in Asia saw the value of their currency shrink, as their people saw the value of their savings vanish. Investors had lost confidence in Asia, and they took their money out en masse.

The economies of the regions crumbled. Stock markets around the world fell in what analysts call sympathy but was really a panic. Local populations and foreign investors put the countries' economies under the microscope. The situation looked grim. It had been an open secret that many of the Asian economies were run on a system of favoritism, rather than free market competition. Crony Capitalism jumped into the every day lexicon, and as it did, authoritarian regimes that had managed to maintain stability through economic growth found themselves in trouble. Indonesia exploded into riots that left hundreds dead and managed to push President Suharto out of power after 32 years of autocratic rule. Unrest visited other countries where growth had brought the promise of a better life before abruptly awakening them to the reality that their dreams were unlikely to come true.

As foreign investors saw their mutual funds crushed in the stampede, the people of Asia receded into deeper poverty in ever-growing numbers. Working feverishly to stop the free fall, the U.S. Federal Reserve Board aggressively lowered interest rates, and the IMF and World Bank poured money into the struggling region, persuading local governments to raise interest rates to prop their currencies. The IMF also gave up on its mandate for fiscal austerity that had brought it so much antagonism and resentment in other countries.

In Malaysia, Prime Minister Mahathir Mohammed reached into the closet of tools forbidden by the new rules of the game. He imposed restrictions on capital flows, vowing he would not let foreign investors determine the fate of his country. As he fought to keep his grip on power, the economy stabilized. And, critically important, the economy of the United States, the greatest beneficiary of globalization, continued its ravenous expansion. America's insatiable appetite for imports created a strong market for just about any product the world could put on the global market shelf. If the U.S. had not been in the middle of such a powerful economic expansion, history would have taken quite a different direction.

It had become clear that much of the economic miracle of Asia was built on quicksand. With the skeletons of unfinished skyscrapers towering in the skyline of formerly booming Asian cities, the people were told to tighten their already tight belts, and bear the pain.

The time had come, said the experts, for transparency in government, for better regulation of financial institutions, and for more accountability. With Asian currencies at all-time lows, and Third World workers even more desperate for work, the case for globalization came face to face with a wall of enraged opposition. At the same time, other voices — perhaps more influential voices — said the way out of recession for Asia was through crafting a better fit with the global economy. Reforms, they said, were clearly needed if Asia was to rejoin the boom. And yet, Asia rebounded strongly without implementing many of the prescribed changes. Was the world once again setting the stage for another catastrophe? Was Globalization the way in or out of trouble?

Columnist Thomas Friedman likes to explain the new political divide of the post-Cold War era as a matrix made up of a horizontal and a vertical axis. On the horizontal axis are global integrationists, those who favor free trade at one extreme, and those who oppose it, separatists, at the other. The vertical axis indicates positions on how the state should deal with those left behind in the globalized economy. At one end are those who believe the government should take an active role in protecting the down-trodden — Friedman calls them the safety-netters — contrasted with the other end of the vertical axis — the let-them-eat-cakers — who believe in survival of the fittest without government handouts.

The new ideological map is not a simple re-labeling of the old one. It creates a realignment; hence the otherwise unexplainable alliances that seem to pop up every time a trade-related issue comes to the fore. Politicians who believe in free trade but oppose heavy government spending on social programs may line up with globalists, who also support free trade but want more help for the poor. When the time comes to discuss social policy, the alliances shift to the other side of the vertical axis, with pro- and anti-globalization forces in favor of social programs banding together against those who would keep a tight leash on spending.

As the discussion matures, each side scores points of persuasion, and there are fewer people who stand on either extreme of the axis. Just as with Capitalism and Communism, where no nation practiced a pure form of the system without elements of the other, with Globalization, a consensus is emerging that some regulations are needed. Very few argue that the markets should rule without constraints of any kind.

The question is just how much participation individual nations will have in the new global economy. A world without government involvement, say critics of full globalization, is a world without a conscience. The markets, they say, don't always respond to the needs of society. They respond to the needs and the wants of corporations, and often leave the poor behind. In the field of health, for example, the market economy has created a system where pharmaceutical companies spend untold millions on research to discover a new drug to improve the sex lives of men in rich countries, while millions die of malaria every year. According to the World Health Organization, 500 million people suffer from the disease, and some two million die of it each year. Most of them are extraordinarily poor. That means that for pharmaceutical companies, committed to making profits for their shareholders, there is little if any incentive to spend research dollars on malaria. On the other hand, research into drugs to provide firmer erections for men, or drugs to help women loose weight, for example, receive generous funding in private industry.

The case with AIDS is perhaps more dramatic. The disease is ravaging entire continents where desperately poor people could never afford to buy expensive drugs. In wealthier nations, those drugs have turned the disease into a chronic condition rather than a death sentence. In Africa, the epidemic has reached such proportions that it isn't just destroying millions of lives, it's obliterating any hope for a better future for many countries, as it exterminates populations in their prime, taking away those who were supposed to be productive, and leaving behind a sea of orphans with little chance of receiving even a basic education.

In places with limited resources, there simply is no money to provide both health care and education. In fact, when expensive AIDS drugs are available, there's simply not enough of them to go around. A volunteer for the humanitarian group Doctors Without Borders recounted an incident in Guatemala, at the Luis Angel Garcia Clinic, where 90 patients with AIDS receive care. The clinic obtained enough medication for four patients. On June 29th, 1999, the patients gathered in the waiting room anxiously. A lottery was held, and four patients were declared the winners of a year's supply of AIDS medications. The 86 losers, in effect, received their death sentences.

When it comes to malaria, one of the best ways of preventing the disease is a simple, inexpensive mosquito net. With half the world's population living on less than two dollars a day, every expense can become an impossible burden. But the real answer to malaria is development of a vaccine. Since mostly poor people suffer from the disease, there is little incentive to fund research.

Pharmaceutical companies are not charity organizations. The solution, say free market advocates, is to find a way within the market system to encourage research for a vaccine, and to help AIDS victims gain access to medication. Harvard economist Jeffrey Sachs has suggested the creation of a fund by rich nations, providing one billion dollars a year. The money would be used to buy the drugs and the nets, and when the vaccine arrives, to pay for vaccinations. Sachs argues that the economic benefit of taking this route would far outweigh the economic cost of the plan.

In the meantime, pharmaceutical companies are under great pressure — and in some instances yielding to the pressure — to lower the price of life-saving drugs in poor countries or face widespread violations of their patent rights.

Proponents of free market economics and globalization say their way is not only the better way. It's the inevitable way. The trend toward open markets and trade driven economies is irreversible. And, they say, it's a trend that brings with it the seeds for curing the very ills that globalization's opponents worry about.

A global market will not ignore environmental concerns, human rights, corruption or poverty. The system will bring progressive forces to bear throughout the world. Globalization, they say, is forcing governments everywhere to open the books, to bring transparency to what used to be smoke-filled room decision-making that benefited only the rich and the powerful.

The market rewards skills. That means that in order to prosper, countries will find it necessary to invest in education. Globalization will create strong, educated middle classes that will not tolerate corruption and cronyism, and will demand accountability of their leaders. And with the critical role of advanced communications in the global economy, rulers will find it impossible to control the flow of information. Globalization, say the free-traders, will bring prosperity and will ensure freedom.

To ensure that the trend is, in fact, as beneficial as its promoters claim, many say it is necessary to build safeguards. They worry that corporations are gaining power at the expense of governments. They say governments will have to take decisive action to assert their authority, and international organizations will have to make and enforce fairness standards to make sure everyone plays by the same rules. Without some rules of fairness, for example, there would be nothing to stop nearly cost-free slave prison labor from competing with the work of those trying to earn a decent living.

Staking the middle ground of this debate are the "Third Way" advocates who say national governments have an important role to play in the new economy, promoting the creation and enforcement of rules of fairness, helping to prepare their population for the economy through training, and helping those left behind.

In the end, society seems to face a pretty clear choice. Most today agree that globalization creates prosperity, but it does it at a cost. A global economy brings uncertainty, workers are easily hired and fired, and whole industries can disappear at the hands of lower-cost competition. Societies must decide how much prosperity they're willing to sacrifice to lessen the harshness of globalization. As French President Jacques Chirac put it, globalization has come hand in hand with rising joblessness, job insecurity and poverty, "Here (in Europe)," he said, " the status of work is protected, but the unemployment rate stands high. There (in America), unemployment is lower but the precariousness of work is growing . . ."

It seems Europe and America have each made their decision as to what they're willing to sacrifice for prosperity. The decisions, of course, are not final. Each country, each society carries on a continuous debate about what the role of government is to achieve the well being of its people.

In the meantime, international organizations also struggle to find their role in the new world. Globalization seems to be expanding into areas beyond economics, and it seems all but certain that authority and responsibility will continue to flow to institutions that are responsible to more than one nation.

International legal tribunals, for example, are starting to dispense justice on crimes the world has determined are an affront to humanity as a whole. Individuals with controversial past, like Chilean General Augusto Pinochet, suddenly find that the entire world is a potential plaintiff.

Efforts to deal with the world's problems on an international level, like other aspects of globalization, tend to provoke resistance. Many view with suspicion any move towards a dreaded "world government." Those fears have stood in the way of the United Nations, often resulting in acrimony with politicians in donor countries.

In 1996, the U.N. held a conference in Istanbul to deal with the pressing problem of housing. The Habitat conference was an attempt to find solutions to one of the difficult side effects of the global economy. Globalization has accelerated the movement of people from small villages to big city, resulting in hundreds of millions of homeless, and even more people living in squalor as they try to jump on the new train of prosperity.

For the people of Istanbul, it was a chance to shine, and a chance to make some money catering to the expected avalanche of conference participants and journalists. City leaders saw the conference as a form of advertising for a city with great aspirations for an important place in the emerging world. But the conference presented one more target for those who view the United Nations with a great deal of mistrust, and even those who fully support the U.N. believed it might be time for the organization to find a different way of looking for solutions.

The World Comes to Istanbul, Sort of
June 1996

(Istanbul) Even before the delegates started arriving in Istanbul, it was clear the city had high expectations for its day in the spotlight. It was equally clear the world had developed a case of conference fatigue on the eve of the latest United Nations mega-meeting.

When Habitat II, the United Nations City Summit started, the ancient and mysterious city of Istanbul was all aglow. Many had complained about some of the methods of its clean up campaign. The killing of thousands of stray cat and dogs infuriated residents. Yet, proud residents of this exotic city with one foot on Europe and another on Asia remained optimistic. Carpet sellers, bazaar merchants, and generally proud Istanbul residents and Turkish government officials were sure the City Summit would bring not only dozens of heads of state, tens of thousands of delegates and hordes of journalists, but more importantly, they were convinced it would bring a lot of money — a payoff for the estimated $40 million the city spent getting ready to host the event. Quietly, they believed a triumphant conclusion to Habitat II would help the old Constantinople win its bid to host the 2004 Olympic games.

One would be hard pressed to find more important problems than the ones discussed at the meetings. The U.N. conference would deal with critical matters. With 600 million homeless people around the world, the issues facing cities are daunting: poverty, environmental devastation, water shortages, overpopulation, and unemployment. The list goes on, and the problems become more critical every day. The two weeks of meetings brought representatives of more than 140 countries, hundreds of mayors and local officials, and dozens of non-governmental agency activists. They discussed their problems and their solutions. They exchanged ideas in hopes that failures would not be repeated and successes would be emulated.

The setting was little short of spectacular. Delegates met in a conference center on a hill overlooking the Bosphorus, the narrow straits that separate Asia from Europe and connect the Mediterranean and Black Seas. The sounds of the Muslim calls to prayer could be heard wafting from the thousands of minarets that rise alongside mosques all over this city. Delegates worked feverishly to solve the problems of the world, anxiously awaiting the moment they could do some shopping at the 500-year-old Grand Bazaar.

But only a few days after the start of the meetings, bazaar merchants knew this conference was not what they had so eagerly anticipated. Like the rest of Istanbul, the alleyways underneath the twenty domes that cover the bazaar were swept and the shops restocked. But the caravans of shoppers did not materialize. Were there not as many people attending the conference, or was the work so arduous that the time for sightseeing and shopping was cut short?

Both. For thousands who came to historic Istanbul, the problems addressed by the conference represent a lifelong commitment to a better world. Undoubtedly, many of these people were energized and visibly excited about the contacts they made day after day in the course of the two weeks of Habitat II. Yet, the City Summit is the 6th major U.N. conference in four years. The United Nations is suffering profound financial difficulties under the weight of its peacekeeping operations around the world, combined with refusal from the United States to pay some two billion dollars in dues it owes to the U.N. American officials say the organization is overly bureaucratic and inefficient, and insist that the U.N. slash costs before the U.S. pays up. Against this background of criticism and a little tired after the Women's Conference in Beijing, the Environmental Summit in Rio, the Population Conference in Cairo, and all the others, many countries simply did not put much energy into Istanbul.

Just two days into the conference, Sen. Jesse Helms held hearings in Washington, attacking the conference. He said the meeting once again was a waste of taxpayer dollars. Conference officials angrily responded saying the meeting cost less than one fighter plane, and insisted that the world could ignore the problems of cities at its own peril.

To say these gatherings accomplish nothing is to deny the obvious. The meetings allow for exchanges of ideas and for development of solutions to problem that rule the lives of millions and affect the life of just about everyone on the planet. But it is precisely because these meetings are so important that they should occur less frequently. The events have become commonplace, and that is what caused the criticism and the disappointment.

The U.N. says Habitat II is the last of the great conferences this century. The Habitat II participants say millions will benefit from what happened here. Merchants in Istanbul now pin their hopes on the year 2004. Perhaps if their city gets to host the Olympics, then the shoppers will come.

After the Istanbul conference, donors seemed to abandon the U.N.'s Habitat agency. Contributions fell by half and the agency struggled to regain its stride.

All international agencies have had to look for their place in the new world as the Global economy reshapes all aspects of interaction between nations. International organizations, just as countries, are trying to define their role, to remain relevant to the changing world. It seems the Darwinian aspects of the global economy, survival of the fittest, applies as much to corporations and individuals, as it does to countries and international organizations.

Agencies dealing directly with trade and the economy, like the WTO, IMF and World Bank are the eye of the storm, accused of callousness and neocolonialism. And as the world adjusts to the new system, unexpected reactions are sprouting from the system that's uniting the world.

According to the U.N. Human Rights commission, globalization is one of the reasons for a new wave of nationalism and fascism erupting in Europe and around the world. The old systems included an ideology and values. The new one is shallow and uninspiring, and it's bringing a sense of insecurity and a fading sense of identity. It's all fertile ground for exploitation by clever politicians.

It's becoming a small world. But what kind of a world?

The New World Order

"You're crazy, Ackermann." That's what German Chancellor Helmut Kohl reportedly said to the man who brought him the news the Berlin Wall was falling on November 9, 1989. Eduard Ackermann, Kohl's long-time advisor, wasn't crazy. It was all true. Soon the disbelief would erupt into a wave of euphoria that would sweep much of the world. It was the end of the world as we knew it.

Nothing symbolized the ominous days of the Cold War better than the Berlin Wall. Now, the jubilant German people were reaching for any tool they could find to help them tear it down. No more Cold War. The time for peace was at hand.

Exhilarated world leaders, scholars and regular people the world over could barely comprehend the magnitude of the changes.

Francis Fukuyama called it "The End of History." Without competing ideologies, united by common values and stronger ties, the peoples of the world would grow closer. The reasons to fight were disappearing. The nations of the world would become intertwined through technology, democracy and commerce. The Good Old Days were just getting started.

But happily-ever-after didn't last very long. The gift-wrapped package of a new world contained some dangerous toys. Nationalism, ethnic hatred and religious extremism had not disappeared. In many cases, they were about to burst out of their Cold War dormancy.

Less than a year after the fall of the Wall, Saddam Hussein helped christen the new world with his invasion of Kuwait. When Iraq's forces rolled into the tiny oil-rich kingdom, U.S. president George Bush declared momentously that we had entered a "New World Order." Without the fear of dragging the Soviet Union into a world war, the U.S. led a massive coalition in a campaign to push Iraq out of Kuwait. The new order had rules. Nations could not invade nations without inciting the wrath and the might of the new world. Old partnerships were dead; the future was rapidly taking shape.

Germany began the massive effort of unbreaking the most visible split of the Cold War, and creating one nation from what for half a century had been two separate Germanys. The excitement was such that it seemed little else mattered. That, incidentally, was lucky for me.

On October 3, 1990 — German Reunification Day — I was returning from the Middle East for a break between operations Desert Shield and Desert Storm — the first major multinational military operations of the vaunted New World Order. I had been in Jordan for several weeks, and was headed back to the U.S. My flight from Amman to Frankfurt was delayed by several hours, as the overwhelmed Amman airport, swamped with a flood of refugees fleeing Kuwait and Iraq, struggled to keep a semblance of order. The scene at the airport had changed little from the eerie night in late August when I arrived, a few days after the invasion of Kuwait. The airport then was carpeted with human beings, desperate refugees sleeping on their bundles on the crowded floor. From the airport to the hotel, on that surreal August night, the roads were lined with Mercedes Benz cars, with whole families sleeping inside. The rich Kuwaitis had made it to safety.

A month and a half later, the airport was just as full, and so were the flights. Humanitarian agencies and governments were chartering planes and booking available seats, trying to get foreign workers who had escaped back to the impoverished countries they had earlier left looking for work. The airport was in chaos. My flight was delayed, cutting the originally scheduled 23-hour layover in Frankfurt by half, ruining my plans for a relaxing day of sightseeing.

I arrived in Frankfurt in the evening, and decided to get up early for a few hours of tourism before my noon flight. From the airport hotel I walked down to the train station beneath and looked at the train schedule. Platform 7, it said, the train going to downtown Frankfurt was scheduled to depart at 6:45am. It was 6:30am, I looked at platform 7, and the train was there, doors open, passengers walking in. I bought my ticket and walked in. The train doors closed and we left the station. I marveled at the elegance of a train making the short route from the airport into town. Then I marveled some more — with a twinge of apprehension — when I started noticing the luggage on racks over the seats. "Is this train going into town?" I asked the man next to me. "Town?" he asked. "Frankfurt . . ." I replied. He frowned and shook his head. "Das ist Westphalia Express."

And Express it was. I was on my way to Westphalia, not downtown Frankfurt. My flight was due to leave in about four hours. Vowing to get off as soon as the train stopped, I watched helplessly as village after village flew past our windows. This train had no intention of stopping anytime soon. I decided to relax and enjoy the scenery. I saw the gorgeous castles along the Rhine, and tried not to think about how I would explain my delay.

When the conductor came by to check tickets, everyone seemed to proudly display impressive documents. I took out my tiny little stub. "Was ist das?" inquired the man. "Mistake . . ." I said sheepishly. Everyone was in a great mood that day. "You pay when we arrive," were his instructions. I didn't exactly know when or where we'd arrive. But I agreed. We finally stopped in Koblenz, where, after standing in line at the ticket booth, I discovered that my credit card was no good for the return fare. Time was running out for the train whose schedule gave me the only chance of returning to Frankfurt with a few minutes to spare before my flight. I'd gotten this far without a ticket; I decided I'd do it again. I rushed to the train — this time making sure I didn't get on the one to Amsterdam — and hoped the joy of reunification would help me get home.

"You pay in Frankfurt," the conductor said with a broad smile. I smiled back. Everyone appeared to be in an exuberant 'reunification' mood. We arrived at the airport station; I rushed to my room at the hotel and picked up my luggage. Then I ran to the terminal. Every agent

along the way mentioned I was terribly late and then smiled gener-
ously. It was a happy day. I checked my suitcase and ran to the gate.
Walked into the plane, sat down, took a deep breath, and realized I
hadn't checked out of the hotel.

I made it home and spent a few weeks there before returning to
the Middle East where, amid the promises of the New World Order, a
new multi-nation war erupted. In the Cold War days, the U.S. would
have been reluctant to go to war against Iraq. Every battleground was a
potential for a dangerous slide into a war between the two superpowers. But now that danger was gone.

For a moment it looked as though the first major conflict of the
new era might portend the end of war as a way to resolve future disagreements. Iraq's overwhelming defeat at the hands of such a broad
coalition, the theory went, would tell other countries that the rules of
the New World Order would be so effectively enforced that soon no
nation would get away with breaking them. But that was a short-lived
fantasy. Wars were breaking out all over the globe.

From Hatred to War

Old nationalist passions were resurfacing, and the world again
looked like a dangerous place. Wars were now more about nationalism
and greed and less about ideology.

By the end of the first decade after the end of the Cold War, one
third of the nations on the planet found themselves besieged by violent
conflict, according to the National Defense Council Foundation. The
Council said 65 conflicts, border wars, civil wars, and major insurgencies raged in the last year of the century. By contrast, the number just
before the end of the Cold War was 35, almost half. The Cold War was
replaced by scores of hot wars.

The number of conflicts around the world is not simple to count.
Different organizations use different thresholds. The CIA, for instance,
counts the conflicts it describes as having "high levels of organized violence." Their list of conflicts numbers in the 30s. By another count, the
United Nations says the number of conflicts has, in fact, declined in
recent years, from 55 in 1992, to 36 in 1998. Either way, it is clear that

peace didn't automatically blanket the world when the Cold War ended.

The superpowers had great skills at keeping their war on ice. The danger of all-out nuclear war made both sides keep the countries under their umbrella on a short leash, sometimes preventing wars or working to keep them from expanding. Nations that tried to stay out of the purview of the superpowers had to contain internal conflicts in an effort to keep the global giants away.

In many Third World countries, repressive regimes had a strong grip on the levers of power, because the USSR or the U.S. armed them and financed them in exchange for their allegiance. Now the superpowers no longer needed the allegiance of the despots, and the hatred that had simmered for years finally exploded.

Many of the "small wars" around the world today are of little consequence to powerful nations, even as they ravage millions of human beings and destroy countries. In fact, the more ravaged the nation, the less ability it has to participate in the world economy, and the less it tends to matter to the rest of the world. Except, that is, on humanitarian grounds, when extreme conditions steal the world's attention.

After the Cold War, two trends developed side by side. Countries were joining with each other, trading together, and uniting in alliances that aimed to erase national borders and bring prosperity and peace to entire regions. At the same time, some nations began to disintegrate, with old ethnic animosities fanned by the winds of freedom; freedom to declare independence, freedom to hate openly; freedom to kill.

Before the Cold War, Europe had experienced the corrosive, destructive power of nationalism. Nationalism had given birth to two world wars. The world wars had given way to the Cold War. Now, Europe and the world were going to do it differently.

Even in Europe, unintended consequences sprouted from good intentions. The United Nations Commission on Human Rights noted ominously that "Neo-Fascism and neo-Nazism are gaining ground in many countries, especially in Europe." Ironically, the U.N. attributed the trend partly to what were supposed to be unifying forces. Globalization, it said, had created an economic climate of fear, along with a loss of identity. As countries became more alike, skilled politicians were reaching for the differences, and using them as a club for beating scapegoats.

In Austria, Hitler apologist Joerg Heider made strides on the political stage. In Switzerland, the anti-immigrant Christopher Blocher moved his party up in the polls, even as he praised the work of a Holocaust denier. In eastern Germany, support for Neo-Fascist parties gained enormous strength among a large percentage of the young, who struggled after reunification. The extreme nationalist right also gained ground in France, Belgium, and Norway.

Still, Western Europe appeared to benefit from global changes, despite the worrying trends. In other areas, the collapse of Communism proved utterly disastrous virtually as soon as it happened.

Suicidal Nations

Just as the Wall fell and the prospects for peace and prosperity for Europe seemed better than ever, Yugoslavia took the road to self-destruction.

Perhaps no country was in a better position to benefit from the changing face of Europe than Yugoslavia. Against all odds, Yugoslavia had managed to remain unaligned, neither a Soviet-dominated state, nor a Western nation. The country's leader, Josip Broz "Tito" had managed to keep old animosities under control, lest they give the rest of the world, the Soviets in particular, an excuse to roll in with their tanks, as they had done in other Eastern European nations. Yugoslavia, a peaceful confederation of six distinct nationalities with a long and complex history, had maintained a standard of living that was the envy of its Eastern neighbors, along with a degree of freedom astounding by Communist standards.

But without the charisma of Tito and the powerful forces of the Cold War, the place quite simply fell apart.

As early as 1990, Yugoslavian tanks were dispatched to Kosovo to put an end to protests by ethnic Albanians. The following year, Slovenia and Croatia broke away from Belgrade. The year after that, 1992, Bosnia and Macedonia also split away from Yugoslavia. The bloodshed and suffering of the old Yugoslavia intensified, as nationalism was fueled by manipulative politicians. The 1990s was the decade of the Yugo-slavian wars of self-destruction, and of the world's mostly timid efforts to put an end to the slaughter.

When U.S Secretary of State James Baker declared in 1991 that the U.S. would not support the disintegration of Yugoslavia, Serb leader Slobodan Milosevic launched an attack on independent-minded Croatia. The Yugoslav army bombed the cities of Vukovar and Dubrovnik. Civilian massacres became the order of the day, as the term "ethnic cleansing" entered the vernacular. Spurred on by their leaders, the people who had made up Yugoslavia were saying they no longer wanted to live with each other. They would remove, or kill if necessary, the member of other ethnic groups, so that they could live in a space "cleansed" of people of other nationalities, people who until recently had been their neighbors.

Nationalist leaders like Slobodan Milosevic in Serbia, Franjo Tudjman in Croatia and Radovan Karadzic in Bosnia, fine-tuned their populist techniques, instilling a mixture of nationalist pride and ethnic fear in their followers. As each side intensified the rhetoric and backed it with actions, the other sides felt more justified in their stance. The politicians' supporters grew more numerous and more passionate. The mixture exploded into the worst tragedy Europe had seen since World War II. The joyous visions from the days of the Wall's collapse seemed a distant memory as the United Nations sent the first peacekeeping troops into Croatia and later Bosnia. The war in Kosovo was still a few years away.

Ethnic hatred had its horrific heyday in Africa in 1994, when the world took one step back and watched hundreds of thousands of ethnic Tutsis in Rwanda massacred by ethnic Hutus. What transpired in Rwanda, the former Belgian colony, sent a sobering message to the world that had — once again — been naïve in believing that the globe could now count on some sort of international system to maintain peace. The new world, as it turned out, was much more confusing than the old.

When was war in a distant land a reason for concern — for involvement — by the rest of the world? It was more difficult to figure out who the enemies were, and it was catastrophically difficult to decide who was responsible for taking action. Rwanda became the symbol of one of the most profound moral and foreign policy dilemmas of the post-Cold War era.

The minority Tutsi, about 15 percent of the population, had dominated Rwanda's Hutus from the 1600s, when the Tutsi herdsmen from North Africa arrived and conquered the Hutus. In 1959, just three years before independence, the Hutus lead what they called a "social revolution," resulting in a half million Tutsis leaving the central African country to become refugees. The remaining Tutsis, even after the uprising, were the dominant economic force in the country. An undercurrent of resentment ran below the surface, and outbreaks of violence occasionally erupted between the two groups. Africans charge their former European colonial powers with encouraging the mistrust in order to help them maintain control.

As in Yugoslavia, there had been a degree of harmony in Rwanda for many years. Despite the mistrust, Hutus and Tutsis, for the most part, lived together in peace. Tutsis and Hutus shared the same language, the same land, and essentially the same culture. Still, Hutu rulers, with memories of centuries of Tutsi oppression, made no effort to integrate the two groups. Schools, for example, were required to keep separate lists of their students based on their ethnicity.

In 1990, a Tutsi-led force made up largely of descendants from the 1959 refugee crisis entered Rwanda under the banner of the Rwanda Patriotic Front. The conflict received some international attention, and mediation helped yield a power-sharing agreement. But by April of 1994, tensions had flared again. A United Nations peacekeeping force was on the ground. Signs that something terrible was going to happen were far from concealed.

While the world was busy brooding over its role in Bosnia, something ominous was brewing in Africa. And everyone knew it.

According to Human Rights Watch, the U.N. Security Council, the U.S., Belgium and France "received dozens of warnings in the months before the genocide." The ruling Hutus were preparing lists of Tutsis and of moderate Hutus, preparing for a massacre in which more people would be killed in a shorter time than perhaps at any time in history. Months before the massacres, the head of the U.N. peace keeping force in Rwanda Canadian Lieutenant-General Romeo Dallaire, sent a secret message to the U.N., warning that extremists in the Hutu military had a plan to exterminate the country's Tutsi population.

As preparations for the slaughter proceeded, the U.N. did nothing.

On April 6, 1994, a plane carrying the country's military ruler, President Juvenal Habyarimana, crashed in the jungle. Within hours, an orgy of killing was unleashed by Hutus. In the first hours of the massacre, ten Belgian peacekeepers were killed. The U.N. peacekeeping force withdrew.

During the next three months, Hutus armed mostly with machetes hacked to death anywhere between 500,000 and one million mostly Rwandans Tutsis. The enthusiasm for a world with uniform values, ready to stand up to infamy — as it proudly did when Iraq invaded Kuwait — somehow did not materialize. When U.N. commanders in the field beseeched the U.N. Security Council for reinforcements, as the brutality unfolded, the Security Council instead voted to cut back its presence. It was a clear signal that the international community would not step in to stop the brutality. Neighbors were killing neighbors; children were being forced to kill their families; the wealthy were paying cash to buy death by a bullet rather than machete. At the United Nations, in New York, the new world order was nowhere to be found.

The massacres finally ended in July, when a Tutsi force overpowered the ruling Hutus. In the rest of the world, the idea of going to war for reasons unrelated to the Cold War, was a work in progress.

For the United States, the images of a humanitarian mission gone disastrously wrong remained vivid in the nation's collective memory. Eighteen dead, and the mutilated body of an American serviceman through the streets of the Somali capital in 1993 killed all interest in any further African adventures.

People were killing one another in places called Kigali, Rwanda and Goradze, Bosnia. In the prosperous Western world, people were reaping the riches of the end of the millennium. Americans thought hard about where to go on vacation, or what new car to buy. (They decided on a sports utility vehicle.) There was no time to think unpleasant thoughts of massacres or ethnic cleansing. In Atlanta, the local baseball team, the Atlanta Braves, was on a hot winning streak. From the perspective of most Americans, these were good times.

A Time of Terror — and Hope
April 1994

(Atlanta) As we eagerly watched Tuesday night to see if the local baseball team, the Atlanta Braves would keep their winning streak alive, the people of a town called Goradze remained hidden in terror in their cellars.

Bosnian Serb artillery continued the slaughter in a town already overflowing with people who moved there to escape killings in their hometowns. Shells landed in hospitals and apartments where young children shivered in their mothers' arms.

Even as the people of Goradze saw their town turn into a slaughterhouse, a civil war in Rwanda brought new levels of inhumanity to the last decade of the lurid 20th century. In the capital Kigali, thousands had taken refuge from the bullets and the machetes in a soccer stadium whose name means "Peace."

The unstoppable wave of killing reached the stadium, too. By some accounts, the civil war in Rwanda has left 100,000 dead in just two weeks. In Bosnia, peacekeepers from the United Nations were taken hostage by the Serbs, and in Rwanda, U.N. soldiers ran for their lives along with everyone else.

There isn't much peace to be kept in either place. It was a bad day.

Every time we turn on the television, when our attention is captured for a brief moment at discovering that Arsenio is going off the air or that Roseanne is getting a divorce, during that exact moment people are killing each other in many corners of the world, including our own. That's why sometimes instead of watching the news we turn to a rerun of Cheers. It's too hard to even conceive of what is happening. Are we wrong for worrying about our trivial lives? Should we drop everything and head to Washington to picket, to tell the government to stop the war in Bosnia, to do something about Rwanda? Would it do any good?

Maybe the world is just a lost cause, and the best thing to do is enjoy our own lives, pay as little attention as possible to tragedies in faraway lands, so that the dull ache of guilt won't interfere with our own existence.

But maybe not. Let's look for just another moment at what else happened on the day the Braves lost their second game of the season.

In South Africa the prospects for peace greatly improved when the Inkatha Freedom Party agreed to participate in the process of bringing democracy to the country. After much bloodshed, suddenly it looks as though peace has a much better chance in that troubled land.

In the Middle East, where it looks like every silver lining is nothing but the cruel packaging for another dark cloud, negotiators from the Palestinian Liberation Organization and Israel took a break from their peace negotiations in order to brief their leaders. They said they would go back to the table on Wednesday.

All over the world, at least in part because people have complained that things need to change, things are changing. A long boycott of South Africa helped persuade that country's government to reconsider its policy of keeping blacks separate and oppressed.

In the Middle East, at least in part due to pressure from people at home and from governments and citizens abroad, all sides are making statements that would have seemed unthinkable only a few years ago, back in the days when the Braves were the worst team in baseball, back when the issue was whether Nelson Mandela would be let out of prison, not whether he would become the president of his country.

It would be a strange world if we all dropped the small, perhaps trivial parts of our lives because important issues need to be dealt with. In fact, many of those important issues are about people wanting to have lives in which they too can concentrate on some of the smaller things, rather than on sheer survival. But we all make a choice about how much responsibility we take for our world.

After all, with the billions that populate the earth, there is room for pitchers and catchers and presidents and soldiers, and actors, and sports fanatics. But in our lives too there is room for a little baseball, for work, and for more. The actions of common people may not always succeed but sometimes they change the world.

Tangled in Hatred's Web

Ethnic mistrust can be one of the most puzzling emotions to understand for outsiders. Often, journalists trying hard to untangle the logic that leads to carnage yield to frustration, and late at night, unwinding at hotel bars, they simply describe it all as just stupid. In generations of killings, demagoguery, religious dogma, and twisted versions of history, the ability to reason becomes secondary. In the end, the issue in contention is often pure power. But it's generally much more complicated, and much simpler than that.

Tell two sides of a centuries-old dispute that their battle is useless, accomplishes nothing, and is destroying their future. In all likelihood, they already know that. It makes no difference. To outsiders, it can be baffling.

Hoping that all conflict would end with the end of the Cold War was plainly beyond optimistic. A good predictor of some of the conflicts to come could have been found in the Turkish-Greek conflict with Cyprus at its epicenter. Greece and Turkey had both been on the same side of the Cold War — they were both members of NATO — and yet, they had managed to maintain their enmity. The two countries, facing similar threats from inside and outside their borders, had not been able to resolve their differences. Pushed and prodded by the U.S., which saw everything through the prism of the Soviet threat, they had resisted efforts to place their common interests ahead of their regional and internal ones. Alliance did not guarantee friendship.

Many of the roots that sprouted into Balkan hatred and mistrust had also grown across the water, emerging miles away to plunge themselves in the heart of the small Mediterranean island of Cyprus.

The island was settled by the ancient Greeks. Christianity was introduced by the Romans, and later the Turkish Ottoman Empire of the 16th century brought Islam. When Greece gained independence from the Ottomans in 1821, Cypriot Greeks started advocating Enosis — union with Greece. In 1878 the British gained control of the island. In the 1950s the Enosis activities grew into a guerrilla revolt against the British, and the Turkish population started to call for Taksim, or partition. The dispute between the two ethnic groups lead neighboring Greece and Turkey to become involved on the side of their respective communities, exacerbating centuries of animosity.

In 1960, a settlement was reached by all sides, including Turkey and Greece, which had both joined NATO in 1952. It granted independence to the Republic of Cyprus. The Greek Cypriot leader, Archbishop Makarios became president, and the Turkish Cypriot leader became vice-president. But the arrangement did not succeed. Interpretations of the constitution lead to political stalemate, and by 1963 violence between the two communities became so extensive that the U.N. sent in peacekeeping forces. By then, the two groups had become completely separate from each other, and their supporting countries on the European mainland, Greece and Turkey, had seen their relations become more and more acrimonious. On more than one occasion, the two countries almost went to war over Cyprus.

Ethnic killings continued even after the U.N. forces arrived. The minority Turks — 18 percent of the population — were pushed into small enclaves.

The Greek government — a right-wing military junta — worried about the left-leaning Archbishop Makarios, and in 1974 it sponsored a successful coup against him. Turkey sent troops to restore order. The Turkish military took control of the north of the island, declaring on its 38 percent the territory the "Turkish Republic of Northern Cyprus."

Only Turkey recognized the republic. The small island was divided by a buffer zone patrolled by U.N. peacekeepers. The bullet-riddled buildings in the zone remained standing as ghostly witnesses to a Mediterranean paradise turned into a forerunner of the Balkans' ethnically cleansed territory, a testament to the power of hatred over reason.

I had my own bizarre encounter with the logic of this hatred when, during a working trip to Cyprus, I decided to cross from the Greek part of Nicosia, where I had come to help establish a CNN office, to the northern, Turkish side.

The migration officer on the Greek side of the Green Line stamped my passport, asking me with disdain what reason I could possibly have for wanting to visit the Turkish side. He reluctantly forgave my journalistic curiosity and warned me, in the most certain of terms, about the general unpleasantness of being among Turks.

I walked across no-man's-land to the immigration booth of the Turkish Republic of Northern Cyprus. I showed my U.S. passport to the woman on duty. She examined it thoughtfully before walking over to a colleague and conferring with him. Then she returned to me and inquired, "From where you are?" I pointed to my passport and said "U. S. citizen." Yes, yes, she said impatiently. But from where you are?"

"I was born in South America. I'm a U.S. citizen." For some reason, my answer was not satisfactory.

"From where your father, your grandfather" she persevered.

"Also from South America." I said. "Is there a problem?"

"You are Greek," she snarled. "Ghitis. You are Greek."

I couldn't believe it. I'm not Greek. I'm a U.S. citizen. I don't have any Greek relatives anywhere in my ancestry.

Perhaps what amazed me most is how emphatic I had become about not being Greek. As if it were a terrible flaw or a crime. She took my denial and savored it, looking me deep in the eye, as if to uncover the seat of truthfulness in my soul.

"Okay. You wait. I will check."

She walked into the office of the person who seemed to be in charge. I saw through the open door the conversation. The man tilted his head to glance at me before again examining my passport. The two officials spoke heatedly in Turkish. Then he picked up the phone. A moment later she came out of his office with the verdict.

"It is confirmed," she said. "You are Greek."

Apparently the ending of my last name — "is," sounded Greek enough to offer definitive proof for the authorities.

There is no Greek blood in my veins (unless Greek olives and feta cheese have altered my DNA). But I wondered, what if there were? What if a great grandparent had come from Athens. Somehow, that would turn me into an automatic enemy, into a person not to be trusted.

After long discussions and explanations, I was finally allowed to go north, but on the condition that I go in the company of a government information office representative. That meant I would take the Indoctrination Tour.

I walked into the Turkish side, was invited to a detailed exhibit of Greek atrocities against Turks as part of my "special" tour and somehow managed to squeeze in some standard tourist sites along with my official host, who ended up as my guest.

Allies of both Turkey and Greece tried in vain for decades to find a way to bring an end to the simmering conflict in Cyprus — to no avail. In fact, some say that Western acquiescence to the partition of Cyprus was interpreted by nationalist movements in other places as tacit international approval for forced secession as a way to deal with competing nationalist aspirations.

Divided at Dayton

The forced separation of the two communities there was a faint, distant prelude to the ethnic cleansing that became the hallmark of the Yugoslavian wars. In fact, when the agreement to halt the war in Bosnia was reached in Dayton in 1995, many in the Bosnian capital Sarajevo worried aloud that their city would resemble Cold War Berlin, and their small country would end up like Cyprus. Their fears were not far off the mark. The Dayton peace accord was a thinly veiled partition document.

The agreement in Dayton created two separate entities within Bosnia, each with its own government and administration. It provided the avenues for reversing partition, calling for the return of refugees and national elections. At the very least for the short term Dayton was a partition of Bosnia along ethnic lines, a defeat for the forces of multi-ethnicity in the country.

Defenders of partition say it is the best, sometimes the only, solution to this type of conflict, especially when it has advanced — or regressed — to the point where the war in Bosnia had in 1995. They say it is the only way of salvaging the country and defending the rights of all sides, while — perhaps most important — stopping the bloodshed.

What to do with a raging multi-ethnic conflict? What to do to keep these conflicts from reaching the "raging" point? In the new world, where every situation is no longer viewed as a battle between East and West, between the Soviets and the Americans, or even between good and evil, the question has been the subject of much debate. And the discussion will continue, since contending ethnic groups have in many cases become emboldened since the end of the Cold War.

The Dayton deal stopped the fighting in Bosnia (after NATO decided to bomb Milosevic's forces, bringing him at last to the negotiating table). But partition has no stellar record in world history. Partition did not resolve the conflict in Cyprus, leaving instead a volatile situation that has required an extended U.N. presence. It didn't bring peace to the Middle East, and it certainly did not stop the bloodshed between Hindus and Muslims in the Indian subcontinent. Instead, it created lingering resentments, continuing violence, and some of the greatest mass migrations in history.

Globalization has united the world on economic and technological grounds, but it has done nothing to diminish ethnic or religious differences. In some cases, it has actually intensified them.

The idea of multi-ethnic harmony was never defended with such ardor as it was during the Bosnian war in cosmopolitan Sarajevo. Although ethnic extremism was hardly absent in the Bosnian capital controlled by a Muslim government, many residents spoke proudly of their town's efforts to avoid the wave of ethnic division sweeping the country. Bosnia, like the rest of Yugoslavia, had managed multi-ethnic peace under the Habsburgs and under Tito, but with the end of the Cold War ethnic fury was unleashed by ultra-nationalists throughout the disintegrating Yugoslavia. Sarajevo's defenders, Muslims along with thousand of Serbs, said they were resisting in the name of the multi-ethnic ideal. The city's leaders repeatedly proclaimed their commitment to a "sovereign, democratic, and multi-ethnic Bosnia-Herzegovina." In reality, even the Muslim government of Bosnia wavered in its commitments to the ideal.

As the war progressed, even Bosnia saw Muslim extremists and nationalists gain influence. Still, the ideal of a truly mixed state, of a genuinely multi-ethnic Bosnia, did not die.

After the Dayton agreement was signed, the Serbs, who had controlled a number of neighborhoods in Sarajevo, left and took everything with them — including, in some cases, their dead.

Another Bosnian town that proudly brandished the flag of ethnic tolerance was Tuzla.

When the Dayton agreement was signed, Tuzla became the center of operations for the American contingent of IFOR, the implementation force that would ensure that the commitments made in Dayton would materialize on the ground in Bosnia. The U.S. would send 20,000 troops, leading a 60,000-strong force from NATO and some 24 more countries, including its old adversary, Russia, and several of its former allies like Hungary and Poland.

Nobody was free of guilt in Bosnia. But the people of Tuzla liked to think of themselves as enlightened. The town's polluted air, a badge of honor earned by housing Bosnia's biggest power plant, gave Tuzla strategic importance. The town's reformist politicians had stood up against the government in Sarajevo. Local leaders continued to support multi-ethnicity, even as the Bosnian president Alia Izetbegovic and his supporters considered the notion of a Serb- and Croat-free Muslim state.

Tuzla had survived, but it had suffered mightily during almost four years of war. There had been relentless shelling, a siege, and a flood of refugees. The economy was devastated, the mountains had lost their trees to the need for fuel, and the city had lost thousands who had escaped to safety. Graffiti on the wall of a downtown building summed up the mood: "Sick of it all."

But now, after Dayton, Tuzla prepared to host the Americans. The Americans who had taken so long to show up were finally coming to Bosnia. Many were too afraid to be hopeful.

Tuzla — An Oasis in Bosnia

December 1995

(Tuzla, Bosnia) — Military fatigues flutter in the cold polluted air of Tuzla, waiting to dry on the balconies of this industrial city in northeastern Bosnia. Traffic on the city roads is made up mostly of white U.N. vehicles and the only good jobs belong to those who managed to land a position with a foreign relief agency, or with the journalists preparing to cover the impending display of U.S. military might.

Tuzla has somehow held on until now, although many of its people have died and its population has more than doubled because of an avalanche of refugees who lost their homes in the country's epidemic of so-called ethnic cleansing. Not only has Tuzla avoided falling to enemy armies, it has — incredibly — escaped the poisonous air of hatred that has left Bosnia physically and morally devastated after a three-and-a half year war. "I hope Tuzla will be an embryo," says George Ristich, a Serbian resident of Tuzla who fought in the Bosnian army to defend his city. He is one of thousands of ethnic Serbs who live here, among a majority of Muslims, and alongside thousands of ethnic Croats. Defying the logic that explains the darkest places in the human heart, Tuzla offers what is perhaps the only hope that peace will succeed in this once-beautiful land.

Except for a one-day battle at the edge of town, Tuzla has not been an open battlefield in the years of what Ristich always calls "this bloody war," using the term in the British sense that denotes his hatred for the conflict, although bloody applies in every sense of the word. He pauses to shake hands with a young Gipsy boy, and then he reaches in his pocket to give him a coin. With the seldom-seen sun hitting the horizon (it's not yet 4 p.m.), the boy smiles and runs off in the direction of the memorial to the worst tragedy to hit Tuzla since the war began.

Just 7 months ago, a single artillery blast fired by Bosnian Serbs from the mountains nearby fell on the worst possible place, at the worst possible time. A cobblestone street, a favorite evening hangout of young people, became a scene of horror. Seventy-one people whose average age was 22 were literally torn apart by the shell. The small crater in the ground is filled with flowers, and the wall next to it has a photograph of every one of the people killed. The locals explain that, unlike what normally takes place in shelling incidents, many of the windows of surrounding buildings did not break. Instead of flying far in all directions, the shrapnel lodged itself in the victims.

For the town's ethnically — and peacefully — mixed population, the war hasn't quite remained at bay. The fighting came to Tuzla's doorstep, and the fighters settled just a few miles away. The city that will now be the center of operations for the 20,000

American forces has endured sporadic shelling and more than a year of total isolation, as its enemies surrounded it on all sides. Perhaps Tuzla was not an important place in the war, but it can become one for peace.

For approximately one year during the war against the Croats, the city survived a tight blockade. To the north, Bosnian Serbs drew the line, and to the south Bosnian Croat forces locked in the people of Tuzla. Food, cigarettes, virtually everything was in extremely short supply. A pack of cigarettes cost $20, if you could find it. Eventually, the Bosnian government and Bosnian Croats made peace. The blockade was lifted and refugees started flowing again to this city that started the war with a population of only 100,000. The Croats, mortal enemies of the Bosnian army earlier in the war, are now their partners, united in the Bosnian Federation with the Bosnian Muslims.

The majority of the people here are Muslim. Like most Serbs, George's heritage is Christian Orthodox. His wife is Muslim. But religion, he says, is not the point. The word Muslim here refers to ethnic background more than to religion, he explains. For his part he claims to be an atheist. His rejection of all faiths suggests that perhaps religion does play a part in the war he hates.

Whether religion or ethnicity, this is the former Yugoslavia, and even in Tuzla prejudice has a way of creeping in. Sometimes it's in the language that people don't even notice. Rasim, an English teacher in a local elementary school, proudly explains he has students of all ethnic groups. "Not even a single class-room in the school is 'clean,'" he declares. It takes an outsider to point out the insidiousness and the subtlety of the poison in his words. He finally acknowledges that to say an ethnically mixed class is not clean is to say it is dirty.

The shelling has stopped for now, and preparations are under-way for the arrival of NATO and U.S. troops. For the people of Tuzla, the optimism is muted, at best. There's no dancing in the streets where shells fell leaving ugly pockmarked walls, lest anyone forget the enemy waits within artillery range. Everyone wants peace right now, they say, because they are tired of the war. But what will happen after the fighters and their families get a good rest from the fighting? The people here hope they will become the example Bosnia needs to remember what it was like to live in peace. George says Tuzla is an oasis. Somehow, he holds out hope that its uncommon waters will spill over the rest of Bosnia. Perhaps the mothers of the fighters will be able to fold their fatigues and years from now show them to their children and grandchildren, to tell them the story of the time their country was torn apart and their city held together.

The Mighty Force Arrives

As soon as the Dayton agreement was announced, we were preparing for the big deployment. Journalists from all over the world made the tortuous journey to the dismal town of Tuzla, prepared for a massive display of American muscle. We arrived with visions of the Gulf War, huge cargo planes disgorging waves of burly soldiers. Our imaginations even added some cheering locals ready to embrace their saviors. But the merciless Balkan winter had other plans, even as the bosses held on to their Nielsen ratings fantasies.

This was no Saudi Arabia. A blue sky never made an appearance, held far in the distance by a combination of dense fog and even more dense pollution. From the top levels of management in Atlanta we received our marching orders: live shots around the clock, whether we had something to report or not. The motto was, "Show the flag." We all shook our heads in disbelief. We called for reinforcements to staff our operations for the largely news-less coverage, around the clock. Ours was not to ask, but to bring extensive live coverage of the arriving troops. The only problem was, the troops were nowhere in sight.

Day after day, night after night, we heard the roar of the invisible planes approach and fade away, as pilots repeatedly concluded that it was impossible to land with no visibility. Reporters went on the air time and time again to tell the world something was about to happen. But not much happened. A trickle of men arrived, including the military's public information officers, ready to be besieged by the hungry press. And they worked valiantly to satisfy that hunger.

On one occasion a press bus took a full load of journalists to the end of the runway at Tuzla air base, to show military specialists "upgrading" the landing strip. The reporters and cameramen and women streamed out of the bus, only to find a young soldier changing some lights along the runway. In his report, CNN's inimitable Richard Blystone showed the press engulfing the bewildered soldier and asked "How many journalists does it take to change a light bulb?"

Eventually, the troops made it in, but the drama of their arrival was quite different from what anyone had anticipated. They came by land, across the muddy Sava River. As a reporter for the (London) *Daily Telegraph* explained, the John Wayne script for the deployment had to be rewritten, and it looked like the Marx brothers did the writing.

NATO forces took their positions throughout Bosnia, while the Americans built pontoon bridges to try to cross the river and make their march to Tuzla. The muscle of military engineering was repeatedly overpowered by high winds and floodwaters. On one occasion the entire camp was washed away by a surge of muddy waters, but at last, after 10 days, the bridge was ready, and U.S. troops started streaming to their positions.

Somehow, the battalions of reporters managed to get to Tuzla long before the soldiers did. (I flew from Zagreb, Croatia, to the coastal city of Split. From there I drove — was driven, rather — to Tuzla).

One afternoon, after working for weeks from our place just outside the Tuzla Air Base, a small group of soldiers exited the gate, looking strikingly determined to achieve its mission. We rushed with cameras to see what, exactly, was happening. They didn't go very far before they set to their task: pulling out small pieces of equipment and lowering themselves to the ground, covering a small area of land near where the media had been gathering.

They were looking for mines. The cameras followed them up close. Their eyes shone with the intensity of men whose work is a matter of life and death. Suddenly, with a camera just inches from his face, one of the soldiers lost patience and shouted, "Do you mind? We're trying to clear a mine field here!" We'd been walking on their minefield for weeks.

Initially, the small number of troops had remained largely confined to its base, awaiting the arrival of the bulk of the forces. Foot patrols were limited to the little village of Dubrave, just outside Tuzla.

The first military foray into the city itself came and went little noticed. I happened upon it accidentally, and still wonder why the military's public relations people let it pass, missing a perfect opportunity. Maybe it was a simple case of compassion.

Love and War in Bosnia

December 1995

(Tuzla) The colors were familiar enough. It was the vehicles that baffled the locals on Christmas Eve. A small group of American soldiers driving their green Humvees were venturing into the city of Tuzla for the first time since U.S. troops started arriving in Bosnia. Until then, the Americans had confined themselves to the area near their base in Dubrave, about a half-hour away from Tuzla. Only the folks there had started adjusting their lives to the presence of these larger-than-life soldiers.

The people in this area have made adjustments before. For years the people of Tuzla have tried to carry on with their lives, despite sporadic shelling from the front lines just a few miles away, despite the knowledge that their country was collapsing around them in the worst fighting Europe has seen since the 1940s, in a war that involved at least three armies and that brought in military men and women from around the world. Now a new force is starting to show up. This time the new army vows it brings peace. But in Tuzla, as in the rest of Bosnia, they have heard all that before from other generals and politicians.

Camouflage fatigues in carefully chaotic designs of green, black and brown are quite a familiar sight against the blinding white snow of Bosnia. It has become another symbol of the war, marking men as soldiers. These are the shades the people of Bosnia see when they look at American troops who now make regular patrols in the small town that is home to their base of operations. They swagger out of their compound, striding with decisive steps, betraying no fear underneath the helmets and bulletproof vests they never seem to take off. For now, it's a sight that inspires confidence among the people of the village.

Rather than helping blend the soldiers into the landscape, this camouflage will make them stand out against the stark white background in the snowy hills around Tuzla. But for a moment, perhaps as a welcome to Bosnia from Mother Nature, the snow has melted and the hills changed their colors to match the soldiers in the days leading up to Christmas in this mainly Muslim land.

It was against the green and brown hills and the puffs of smoke in the sky that American troops ventured outside the relative safety of their headquarters, and made the first road trip into the City. It was the first time the people of Tuzla saw the G.I.s in their peculiar looking vehicles. And it was totally unplanned.

The half-hour drive from Dubrave happened in the afternoon hours of Christmas Eve. It came with no publicity, no glare of cameras, and no advance warning to the local population or to the scores of journalists that eagerly await any morsel of information. It was an operation of the military's Civil Affairs officers, rather than a strategic "recon" mission. The mission for Civil Affairs is to deal with the civilian side of the equation, trying to get the people on their side. This first foray into Tuzla received the kind of welcome that warms the heart of a Civil Affairs officer.

The military had agreed to transport a young boy with leukemia back to Bosnia, so he could die with his family after doctors in Germany couldn't save him. The plan had never been to drive him all the way home, but when relatives were unable to make it to the gate of the air base, the vehicles that escorted him from the transport plane kept on driving into town.

The small convoy of three humvees rolled along the tortuous road that connects Dubrave and Tuzla. One soldier stood with half his body showing above the armor of the vehicle. While the man at the wheel was busy maneuvering through the potholes, the one standing seemed even busier keeping up with the children who waved with broad smiles on their faces. Older people working in their cabbage gardens all stopped what they were doing, mesmerized by this miniature show of force. Those who were old enough recalled the day German tanks rolled in during World War II, beginning the Nazi occupation. They did not wave hello to this soldier.

Throughout the drive in the hills, and all the way into the city, the response was the same: children nearly jumping with excitement; young adults observing, many waving; almost all smiling approvingly. All, except the other men in camouflage, the Bosnian Army soldiers who eyed the convoy suspiciously. They too stopped what they were doing and keenly gazed at the Americans, trying to look unfazed. The Americans appeared to be elated. With few exceptions the local population clearly loved them.

The people of Dubrave, who now know the Americans better than just about anyone in Bosnia does, say they are thrilled to have them. They don't mind that C-130s and C-17s from the U. S. Air Force constantly roar above their heads. They say they don't mind the noise. They say they don't care if the streets get jammed, or if the American tanks destroy their roads. Bring them on, they say. Even the old now speak that way, even the ones who remember the German invasion. For now, the Americans make them feel safe. The village is only about 5 miles from the Serb lines, and nerves are still frayed from enduring shelling and from trying to stay safe while walking in an area where landmines are all around.

And yet, a few people dare to remember the day United Nations peacekeeping forces arrived. They too were received as saviors. But their glow quickly dimmed when they did not stop the shelling or the killing or the raping. The true test of this love affair has not yet come. The welcome-to-Bosnia warm up from Mother Nature has given way to the cold, snowy days of Bosnian winter. Things are now returning to normal and that means that sooner or later, chances are that somebody will challenge the soldiers of IFOR, the implementation force of the Bosnian peace agreement. The moment of truth will come when these soldiers have to shoot. Will they shoot? And if they do, what will the other side do? And then, what will the people in America say?

That is when the people of Tuzla will know if the Christmas Eve visit from the American troops was only a public relations act, or if the U.S. troops here are really different from all the other soldiers in camouflage fatigues.

Hail to the Visitor

Once the troops had arrived, the Commander-in-Chief decided he would pay them a visit. When some 8,000 American soldiers had slogged their way to the Soviet-built Tuzla Air Base, President Clinton decided it was time for a morale-boosting visit.

He chose what turned out to be one of the coldest days of the winter to make his appearance. The weather, as usual, refused to cooperate. Nobody warned the fog that it was Air Force One trying to land. The President had to be diverted to Hungary, to the staging ground from where the troops had made their way to Bosnia.

Security concerns forced a planned visit to Sarajevo to be scrapped, but the President finally made it to the tarmac in Tuzla. By the time he finally arrived, the soldiers' patience had been wearing thin. The troops had much to do preparing for the arrival of the rest of the American contingent. Many resented spending a day out standing in the cold while their tasks remained undone. When the President finally made his appearance, wearing a leather bomber jacket and bearing 200 cases of Coca-Cola and some 5,000 Hershey bars, the level of enthusiasm did rise. But on that particular day, Bill Clinton was not the most popular person on the base. Many soldiers had brought their cameras for the occasion. Requests to have a picture taken with Christiane Amanpour seemed to outnumber those for the photos with the President.

Amanpour had been a fixture in Bosnia for years, challenging the West, and Bill Clinton in particular, to do something to stop the bloodshed. Knowing that those early events in Bosnia could land them in the Balkans, many American soldiers had kept a close eye on Amanpour. When formation broke and the President started mingling with the troops, many of them turned their back on the President to get the shot with Christiane.

Another Balkan War

Few people believed that bringing NATO forces into Bosnia would mark the end of the troubles in the Balkans. Indeed, the troubles were far from over. Political leaders continued shaking up the volatile brew that was Yugoslavia. By 1999, NATO went to war against Slobodan Milosevic over the tiny Serbian province of Kosovo.

The troubles in Kosovo started to intensify just as NATO — the alliance created to keep the Russians out of Europe — pondered what its role would be in the post-Soviet world. As they prepared to celebrate the organization's 50th anniversary and made plans to expand its membership to include some former allies of the Soviets — and even a consultative role for Moscow — NATO leaders nervously watched developments in the former Yugoslavia.

The Russians, meanwhile, were trying to claw their way out of the 1998 economic crisis that had plunged them, along with much of the world, into a grimmer post-Soviet reality.

The ailing Russian leader, Boris Yeltsin, was becoming increasingly unpredictable, leaving the people of the once respected nation with a bitter sense of powerlessness. The Kosovo conflict would come to galvanize those feelings and severely test the bonds that the West had tried to forge with Yeltsin's Russia.

Kosovo, a province whose population is 90 percent ethnic Albanian, had enjoyed a special status within Serbia and Yugoslavia for 15 years. The province had been granted autonomy in 1974, back in the days when Tito was keeping Yugoslavia together as one nation.

Slobodan Milosevic saw the province and its history as an ideal place to detonate a nationalist hand grenade. In April of 1987, while he was still an emerging politician, Milosevic came to the historic town of Kosovo Polje. That was the place where, in 1389, according to varying versions of history, the Serbs had lost the decisive battle against the Turkish Ottomans, bringing their land 500 years of Muslim domination.

Nationalist Serbs reportedly prepared for the Milosevic appearance by staging an attack on the local police, prompting them to respond by beating them back. With Serbs under attack by Kosovo's police, Milosevic jumped into the fray and proclaimed to the local Serb minority and to a large television audience throughout Serbia, "No one should dare to beat you." He became an instant hero of the nationalists. When Milosevic took power, he quickly revoked Kosovo's autonomous status, and an increasingly repressive regime in Kosovo ignited the passions of separatist Kosovar Albanians.

Hard line proponents of Kosovo's independence joined forces in a guerrilla movement that became the Kosovo Liberation Army. Moderate ethnic Albanians, pragmatists who sought autonomy within Serbia, aligned behind the scholarly Ibrahim Rugova. KLA guerrillas and the Yugoslavian Army clashed repeatedly while the world tried to figure out how to avert yet another all-out war in what was left of Yugoslavia. In the end, mediation proved fruitless, and NATO went to war for the first time in its history. Russia protested with all its (verbal) might.

Hearing the Russians and NATO simultaneously describe the war, it was hard to believe they were talking about the same conflict.

The pictures of refugees streaming out of Kosovo made Muscovites shake their heads in sorrow and disbelief. In the West, the images, coupled with numerous interviews with the refugees, made it clear the mass exodus was the direct result of a Serb plan to expel all Albanians from the province. In Russia, viewers saw civilians fleeing the bombs of a foreign nation. NATO was the root of this evil. NATO was attacking the Serbs, interfering with a sovereign nation's justified efforts to defend its territory. (From Moscow, Kosovo looked disturbingly like Chechnya trying to break away from the Russian Motherland.)

With bombs falling in Serbia, rhetorical explosions reverberated in Moscow in the Duma (the Russian parliament), in the Foreign Ministry, and in the streets. Anti-U.S. sentiment grew exponentially. There were calls for Russia to arm Yugoslavia. Communists and nationalists spoke out in favor of their Slavic brothers, the victimized Serbs.

As the bombing of Kosovo continued, over loud Russian objections, Yeltsin reportedly asked his generals, "Why are they not afraid of us?" Every bomb in the Balkans added to the humiliation of Russia. On a CNN interview heard with insulting clarity in Moscow, Senator John McCain declared, "Russia is a basket case." His message, that Moscow was too weak to be taken into consideration, stung Russian viewers.

Boris Yeltsin's days in power were numbered and the direction of relations between the United States and Russia wouldn't soon return to its former course. For now, however, Russia would find its way to a key role in the drama that was Kosovo.

Kosovo Bombs Exploding in Moscow
April 1999

(Moscow)   On an unusually sunny Saturday afternoon in Moscow, the crowds at the trendy Manezh shopping center compete for the handful of outside tables at Sbarro, the Italian eatery overlooking the Kremlin walls. "New Russians" in their fashionable European sunglasses sit under the red and green umbrellas, munching on pizza and sipping bottled water between calls on their cell phones.

Suddenly, an old man in faded military fatigues approaches along the sidewalk. He walks slowly, with the help of a cane, his eyes fixed on the steaming slice of pizza on a plate in front of a handsome young man wearing a ponytail. The old soldier comes closer, a number of medals visible on his chest, a dirty plastic bag filled with who-knows-what hanging from his shoulder. He stops in front of the pizza, swallows hard and stares at it, scratching his unshaven face. The young man in the ponytail shifts in his chair and looks the other way. The soldier looks away and takes a couple of steps from the fence that separates the pizza-eaters from the passers-by. Then he looks again, before scratching his beard one last time and limping away with his dignity barely salvaged.

This is the Russia that has trouble paying its soldiers — some of the same soldiers that kept the United States in a constant state of alert during the days of Cold War. This is the Russia where the average worker lives on about $30 per month. It is also the Russia that is infuriated at the U.S. for the attack it is leading against Yugoslavia.

A couple of hundred yards away from this very spot, at Red Square, anti-U.S. demonstrations have become an almost daily occurrence. Russians say what NATO is doing to the Serbs over Kosovo could be a sign of things to come. A weak Russia feels vulnerable to a swaggering North Atlantic Alliance and a powerful U.S., its ambitions unchecked in a world with just one superpower.

When the bombing began, the first reaction in Russia to the sense of powerlessness was almost a temper tantrum. Muscovites took to the streets and shouted insults at the United States. On one occasion, a grenade launcher was unsuccessfully targeted at the embassy. Now the embassy stands surrounded by Russian troops. But the demonstrations have become smaller, and the Russian strategy has not only changed. It has started to yield results.

The early stages of the conflict were salt in the wound of Russia's injured pride. The West was launching a major military operation at Russia's doorstep, and the formerly formidable adversary was being largely ignored. That prompted the rage. It prompted talk of sending weapons to Belgrade, and brought back the specter of Russian missiles re-targeted at the United States. The threats worked. The United States suddenly seemed to remember that Moscow still controls enough weapons to destroy the world a few times over. A quick meeting was called in Oslo, where Secretary of State Madeleine Albright and Foreign Minister Igor Ivanov discussed their differences.

Russia discovered it was in a position to do more than spoil America's plans. By offering itself as an intermediary in the conflict, Moscow could emerge as a key player, scoring important points in the contest for international recognition and prestige. Now Russia has placed itself in an enviable position. By taking on the steep challenge of finding a solution to the crisis, it has little to lose, and much to gain. Already Moscow has become one of the principal stops along the diplomatic road traveled by those seeking a solution to the Balkan conflict.

In the early raging days of the air war, Russia spoke out consistently in favor of its historical allies, the Yugoslavian Serbs. Now the tone has changed. Moscow still demands an end to the bombings, but now it's leaning on Slobodan Milosevic to accept an international peacekeeping force. To the world, Russia says: We can help. We have a close relationship with Belgrade and we may be the only ones who can come up with a solution acceptable to both sides.

The tough talk has done wonders for the troubled fortunes of Boris Yeltsin. Before the bombing started, the Russian president was on the verge of being impeached by the Communist-dominated Duma, the lower house of the parliament. His political enemies started to monopolize the conversation, urging the President to send help to Belgrade. But Yeltsin — much like Bill Clinton — is at his best in a crisis. Invigorated by the crisis, he has taken control of the Kremlin, and few doubt he's the one calling the shots.

Whatever happens in Kosovo, the United States blundered in ignoring Moscow early on. Russian public opinion is firmly positioned now, not only against NATO actions, but also against the United States. Perhaps Kosovo was partly an excuse for Russians to vent some of their frustrations. After great expectations for prosperity following the fall of Communism, the economy has collapsed. Many Russians feel betrayed on that score. Whatever the reason, this conflict has changed the political landscape here. Politicians friendly to the U.S. will have trouble succeeding in the next elections, and that will spell trouble for U.S.-Russia relations for years to come.

A successful strategy for the U.S. will require treating Russia with a measure of respect during this crisis and beyond, and trying to regain the trust of old soldiers and new Russians.

In the end, or at least the end of the Bombing of Kosovo chapter of Balkan history, the United States brought the Russians in to help find an end to the war. President Yeltsin named his ex-prime minister Viktor Chernomyrdin as a special envoy for the Balkans.

Chernomyrdin initially castigated the West for its attack on the Serbs, likening the action to the Soviet invasion of Czechoslovakia in 1968. But eventually the tone changed.

The U.S. brought in the president of Finland, Martti Ahtisaari, as a diplomatic resource, and sent the State Department's Russian expert, Deputy Secretary Strobe Talbott, to manage negotiations. Talbott was careful to treat the Russians with deference, even referring to the crumbling nation as a "Great Power."

The three men met outside of Moscow, in Joseph's Stalin's old dacha. After intense talks — keeping always an empty chair to remind the group that Slobodan Milosevic was ultimately the man who would be presented with the product of their work — they hammered out what was, in effect, an ultimatum for an end to the bombing.

Ahtisaari and Chernomyrdin went to Belgrade and read the document to Milosevic. Losing the war on the ground, and now seeing that Russia was no longer standing by its side, Milosevic agreed to the deal and Serbian troops withdrew from Kosovo, leaving the province in the hands of the international community.

The bruises in the relationship between the West and Russia did not fade fast. Yeltsin withdrew from power six months after the end of the Kosovo conflict and Vladimir Putin, a former KGB spy, took the reins of a Russia weakened but still in possession of a massive nuclear arsenal. A decade after the fall of the Berlin Wall, a new era in relations between Washington and Moscow was about to begin. Russia would deal with nationalism within its borders with the firmest of hands, raining destruction on Chechnya. (Many human rights activists would argue the actions of the Russians under Putin in Chechnya deserved as much scorn as those of the Serbs under Milosevic in Kosovo.)

What had started as a promising convergence of ideologies between two former adversaries was taking a new direction. It wasn't clear exactly which way Russia, determined to regain its self-respect, would move under Putin. Clearly, the goal wasn't another "dictatorship of the proletariat." But what was it?

There were no longer two competing, diametrically opposed ideologies threatening the planet with nuclear extinction. Still, the world had hardly blossomed into a harmonious landscape of eternal tranquility. In the aftermath of the Cold War, nations found themselves searching for identity. On many occasions that meant defining themselves in such a way that they excluded people who had been living in their midst. The madness of ethnic hatred burned viciously in some places, while in others the embers remained hot, and politicians played dangerous games, fanning them with their rhetoric.

With the end of the battle between the two dominant ideologies, the world had become a more unpredictable place, and for many individuals a much more dangerous one.

The New Game

What a simple world it used to be. It was dangerous, the stakes were high, but it was all much easier to understand. East and West stared each other down. The Soviets and the Americans, along with their allies, played the planet like it was a gigantic chess match, taking each other's pieces, conquering and defending. The two big players viewed everything that happened in the world as part of their chess game. Then, somebody picked up the board and spilled all the pieces. After all the noise was over, the game didn't look like chess any more. The pieces weren't just black and white. There were dozens of colors, and the board wasn't a simple square with each side trying to overtake the other to win.

The face-off was over, but people had not stopped killing one another; instability in one place remained a threat to peace in entire regions. What, then, were the powerful to do? When were they supposed to get involved? When did killings in one country matter to the people of other countries? Without a clear enemy, countries, and leaders, didn't know which way to glance when they looked over their shoulder.

During the Cold War, if the shadow of leftist revolution-in-the-making appeared anywhere, it concerned Washington. Direct intervention — with the possibility of drawing a dangerous face-to-face confrontation with Moscow — was highly unlikely, but some type of action to influence the course of events was almost guaranteed. Often, smaller countries went to war as the proxies of their superpower sponsors.

Now, with world revolution dead in its tracks, America and its European allies had to decide when other countries' problems merited their attention.

In the U.S., the mantra for foreign intervention was, as it had been for decades, the "National Interest." America would become involved beyond its borders when its interests were at stake, whatever that meant. The definition was extraordinarily flexible. To those with the widest view of U.S. concerns, America had an interest in seeing its values upheld around the world. That could include defending democracy and human rights, stopping genocide, or feeding the hungry in defense of humanitarian principles. In the narrowest sense, the U.S. should only intervene when physically attacked by its enemies.

Many whimsical notions have been uttered in an effort to describe the so-called National Interest. But that devolved into a grand intellectual exercise, and in the end it seemed each situation was taken on its own, handled by the political leaders of the day, looking at the political realities of the day.

There was a consensus that prosperity was a national interest; little argument there. With the United States solidly in place as the most powerful nation on earth, gorging itself on economic globalization, world prosperity meant U.S. prosperity. And prosperity required stability. The question was, how much instability would it take to get the mighty American Goliath to suit up and go to war?

During the Gulf War, America mustered massive international support to stand up to Saddam Hussein. President George Bush stood on high principle. It was easy to explain why the U.S and its allies, with the Soviet Union losing superpower status and standing out of the way, would not tolerate a regime that crossed borders and brazenly took over another country. The moral merits of the argument raised to higher ground a war designed essentially to protect the oil supply and the prosperity of the West.

Gradually, an amazing transformation took place. The old Hawks, right wing Republicans determined to match Soviet military adventures at any cost, were becoming the doves of the new world. The old left, the anti-war protesters of the Vietnam days, all grown up now, were gradually becoming the new hawks, eager to take on injustice by force far away from U.S. shores.

With the last U.S. government of the Cold War era coming to an end, the debate over the future of U.S. foreign policy started to shape the choices for the new era. George Bush's place in the White House was being challenged by people inside and outside his Republican party. By the end of 1991, odd new alignments were taking shape.

A Democratic presidential candidate from Arkansas, Bill Clinton, picking up a theme from the Carter administration, argued the U.S. should have an active role in the world in defense of human rights. At the same time, Republican Pat Buchanan became the candidate of isolationism, arguing against using human rights as a factor in foreign policy. In many ways, the Republican challenger had less in common with the Republican president than did the Democratic candidate. Other Democrats, like Tom Harkin of Iowa, aligned themselves on this issue more closely with the isolationists' wings of Republicanism than with internationalists like Bill Clinton.

Clinton focused his campaign sharply on domestic economic issues, in stark contrast to President Bush's well-known preference for foreign matters. Still, Clinton spoke forcefully about the need to rethink foreign policy for the new times. He outlined a global view that envisioned a strengthened United Nations, with military muscle in the service of humanitarian causes. He highlighted his willingness to take on "tyrants," and he sharply criticized the previous administration for its policy of "coddling dictators" in China. Clinton articulated his perspective of what was in the interest of the U.S.: "The defense of freedom and the promotion of democracy around the world are not merely a reflection of our deepest values; they are vital to our national interests. . ."

Clinton's policy on China would come to resemble his predecessor's, but in other parts of the world, the national interest in the new president's view would bring a new set of principles and a new threshold for intervention. In Bill Clinton's world, Americans soldiers would find they were their brothers' keepers much more frequently than they had been in the old days.

The transition came gradually. In fact, American intervention on purely humanitarian grounds came even before the new president took office. Just a few weeks after losing the election, President Bush announced a humanitarian mission to Somalia. Twenty eight thousand American soldiers would go to Africa with the mission of helping bring an end to suffering. Hundreds of thousands were dying of starvation, caught in the middle of fighting between rival warlords in an anarchic country where drought was conspiring with human viciousness to bring tragedy for millions.

Intervention in Somalia was one of the early examples of what came to be known as the "CNN Effect," a twist of democratization in foreign policy by televised tragedy. World leaders began finding it more difficult to keep their arms crossed in inaction while millions of viewers (voters) were brought to tears by close-ups of dying children.

In some ways, the power of the CNN Effect — which could be set in motion by news organizations other than CNN — brought more responsibility to journalists. If showing a tragedy had such a potential to change the course of events, perhaps even bringing an end to the suffering, journalists had a greater burden than ever when they placed their mirror before the world.

Critics charged that the CNN Effect resulted in less thoughtful foreign policy, one that reacted to emotionalism rather than strategic thinking. Many said it was the CNN Effect that brought the U.S. to Somalia, and later, when American forces withdrew from Somalia in humiliation ten months after arriving, the CNN Effect was also blamed. Pictures of a dead American soldier, his mutilated body being dragged through the streets of Mogadishu, sparked a public outcry just as pictures of dying children had stirred emotions earlier.

The political fallout of the Somalia disaster, incidentally, resulted in Defense Secretary Les Aspin losing his job. Colin Powell, who had demonstrated a remarkable skill at polishing his own image, was left unscathed. Powell had left office just a few days before the disastrous operation to try to capture warlord Mohammed Aidid. But the operation had been his idea, and the decision denying a request for AC-130 gun ships had also been his.

In the field, the presence of the best-known CNN journalists has a similar effect. In Haiti, for example, the military had deposed an elected president to the loud objections of the international community. The media had gathered amid rumors of possible military action from the U.S. When Peter Arnett arrived in Port-au-Prince to cover the crisis, the restaurant at the Montana Hotel, where most of the media were based, was abuzz. Arnett was one of the journalists whose name had become well known in households around the world after the Gulf War. Along with people like Wolf Blitzer, Christiane Amanpour, Bernard Shaw, and many others, they had helped make CNN an international force in journalism. After the war they had become better known than many of the newsmakers they covered.

The name Arnett had become synonymous with the U.S. bombing of Baghdad during the Gulf War. With Arnett in town, the word among journalists and residents was that the U.S. military couldn't be far behind. In fact, the soldiers were still nowhere near. When Arnett was replaced by Christiane Amanpour, journalists dropped their forks. They thought they could already hear the helicopters approaching. Wrong again. With no military intervention, Amanpour decided to leave for Africa where the Rwandan massacres were giving way to more devastation in refugee camps across the border in Zaire.

Writing the New Rules

After announcing its intervention in Somalia, the Bush administration in its final weeks took pains to defend the decision to act there in light of inaction in other places.

Why Somalia and not Bosnia? The question was being asked more and more frequently by editorial writers, television viewers and international observers.

Secretary of Defense Dick Cheney explained with certainty that the Bosnia conflict was largely intractable, and its solution beyond American intervention. "If I had 200,000 troops on the ground in Bosnia today," he declared, "I'm not sure what I would tell them to do."

Clinton had said during the campaign that he did have some ideas about what could be done. But it would take some time.

Clinton, as President, kept Colin Powell in place as America's top military man, Chairman of the Joint Chiefs of Staff. Powell's cool and confident demeanor had helped make him a national hero after leading the war against Iraq. In a memorably dramatic press briefing, Powell had explained the U.S. plan against Saddam Hussein's army. "We will cut them off," he said, "and then we will kill them." But Powell wasn't all that interested in cutting off and killing Serbian forces in the complicated, history-drenched Balkan battlefields. He had been a vocal opponent of intervention to help the Bosnian government, even as massacres and ethnic cleansing created some of the most gruesome scenes in Europe since World War II. The word "genocide" was now being used to describe what was happening to the Muslims of Bosnia. Still, Powell believed a mission in Bosnia did not make sense.

If it didn't make sense in Bosnia, it was even less warranted in Haiti. The despotic military rulers that overthrew Jean-Bertrand Aristide in September 1991 led an army that couldn't march straight. The soldiers terrorized the population, leading many to take to the seas in a life-threatening effort to reach U.S. soil. Candidate Clinton had also called this one of the situations the United States should address more effectively, since U.S. policy against the tiny destitute nation had accomplished little, and the flood of refugees threatened to rage out of control.

Gen. Powell's view prevailed for almost nine months, keeping the idealistic vision of a president (who had come to office under a cloud of contempt for his avoidance of military service in Vietnam) from materializing on the world stage; the new president, with virtually no experience in foreign policy, struggled to find direction.

Powell's view, which came to be known as the Powell Doctrine, held that U.S. forces should go into foreign missions only in the face of a direct threat to the national interest; only with the benefit of such an overwhelming military advantage that success was virtually guaranteed; with absolute support at home; and with a clear goal and well-defined exit strategy. Limited interventions with limited resources for a broadly defined national interest simply did not meet the standard.

Clinton's early days had been little short of disastrous in dealing with the military. His clumsy attempts to allow gays to serve legally in the military, combined with his own much-maligned efforts to avoid the draft, made his reputation sink to new depths with the military. His push for a more aggressive U.S. policy in the former Yugoslavia was seen by many as naïve and amateurish. Already the Bush team, with Powell as a potent advocate against intervention, had said it would take as many as 400,000 troops to bring peace to Bosnia.

United Nations peacekeeping forces had taken positions in Bosnia, but their presence had not stopped the fighting. The international community seemed more concerned with protecting the U.N. soldiers than with stopping the massacres.

News reports were full of quotes from named and unnamed Defense Department officials explaining why a war in Bosnia could not be won. Analysts, soldiers and pundits explained how a conflict dating back hundreds of years had neither a solution nor a role for the U.S. In the meantime, hundreds of thousands were being killed or forced out of their homes. The people of Sarajevo managed to survive under constant shelling, gaining emotional sustenance from unfounded rumors that American and NATO forces were about to come to their rescue.

When former British Prime Minister Margaret Thatcher suggested the West engage in limited air strikes to stop the Serb shelling of Sarajevo, Powell dismissed the idea, saying "As soon as they tell me it is limited, it means they do not care whether you achieve a result or not. As soon as they me tell me 'surgical,' I head for the bunker."

At the end of September 1993, Colin Powell bowed out of the Clinton administration and retired from active duty in the military. By then, President Clinton had done little to cool the conflict in the Balkans, and the carnage had intensified. The reluctance to intervene for anything less than the narrowest definition of the national interest remained long after Powell's departure. The new liberal definition of national interest was slow to gain converts, and Clinton's efforts to gain the respect of the military continued throughout his presidency.

Before Clinton was out of office, in the year 2000, the foreign policy establishment was preparing for the return of the hero of the Gulf War. Colin Powell was returning to public service as Secretary of State under the newly elected George W. Bush, promising a strengthened military, ready to fight only in the face of a threat to national interest. The words were not new, but their meaning in the new Bush administration would be sharply different. The new American government would endeavor to move away from humanitarian interventions. It would develop a foreign policy where the national interest would be much closer to simple self interest, angering many in the international community who accused him of being, if not an isolationist, at the very least a unilateralist, leading the U.S. to act without much regard for the views of other nations. America's allies had come to expect a far more active role from the world's only superpower. Less than a decade before, it had been the Clinton administration that had found itself under pressure to bring the country's newfound power into action.

An Empty Epilogue to the Cold War Victory
(1994)

The mission was a success. The United States managed to build the mightiest military machine in the history of the world. Why is it, then, that Bosnian Serbs continue to humiliate the U.S. and its allies? Why is it, then, that for years the military leaders of the pathetic Haitian Army thumbed their noses at the Colossus of the North, despite repeated threats from the Leader of the Free World and Commander-in-Chief of the earth's mightiest army in history?

Neither the Serbs nor the Haitians ever had any illusions that they could defeat the unchallenged superpower of the world. But they were privy to that well-known secret about American military power today: the U.S. military does not want to fight. And it is not only the military that doesn't want to use force to resolve conflict, the entire political equation that propels the use of military force has been turned on its head since the end of the Cold War.

Long ago and far away, back in those days of U.S. vs. USSR icy non-combat, the Liberals generally opposed the use of force. The Conservatives were the tough guys. The Liberals wanted to negotiate; to use diplomacy to solve problems like civilized adults (or like cowards, depending on your point of view). The Hawks, usually Conservative, usually Republican, said first bludgeon your enemy, then sit down and talk. You'll have a much more fruitful talks that way, they said.

Liberals put flowers in their hair to march against Vietnam, and piled into their VW vans to lobby against intervention in Nicaragua and El Salvador. Conservatives showed little hesitation to fight not only a perceived or real Red Menace; they also used force unabashedly whenever American commercial interests were threatened.

Has the world changed! During the years of the Haitian standoff, it was the most liberal wing of the Democratic power that persistently pushed for military intervention. Conservatives in the House and Senate maintained that there was nothing about Haiti that made it worth fighting for.

And the soldiers? Leaks from the Pentagon spilled out a consistent message, which held that the folks in uniform opposed intervention. They didn't think it was worth it. It is much like what the leaks on Bosnia have brought. Unnamed but, of course, respected sources in the military tell us that the tide in Bosnia would be difficult to turn. Casualties would be many, and the outcome remains uncertain. The rationale for not intervening forcefully in Bosnia has been at times astonishing. A frequently proffered explanation for NOT bombing the Serbs while they engage in the genocide of civilians has been that bombing would endanger the U.N. forces on the ground. Imagine that: we can't protect civilians because soldiers might get hurt. It is a well-known fact that soldiers, by profession, undertake risks. Just as it is a well-known fact that wars always entail risk. But, politicians and soldiers made it clear that they opposed military action, because it was risky!

The "paradigm" — to use a term in vogue — is that the U.S. will fight wars by bringing to bear overwhelming military power. From now on, a defeat at the hands of the U.S. military will be absolute, and it will be a foregone conclusion. It's a good thing Europe is not now under the heel of the Nazi invaders. It would be too risky to get involved. We might have casualties.

The equation of military intervention now has Liberals asking for intervention on humanitarian grounds, and commercial disputes being handled through hand-to-hand combat at the negotiating table. With President Clinton in power, the U.S. tried valiantly, perhaps futilely, to bring democracy to Haiti, and sent soldiers to feed starving Rwandan refugees. Under President Reagan force was used to fight the Communism threat in the tiny Caribbean island of Grenada, and to retaliate against terrorism and show who's tougher, with the bombing of Libya. George Bush was the transitional Commander-in-Chief. He fought for oil in the Middle East, and he got the troops into Somalia.

It is fitting, perhaps, that a country that now has a liberal president with a conservative Congress is trying to decide what justifies the use of American military power. It is, after all, a time of transition in the world, too. What is not acceptable is to have the members of the military tell the civilian government what situations warrant risking their lives. They can, of course, offer their wisdom in tactical and strategic matters. The question of when and why they will go into combat is not for them to decide.

The Senator and the General vs. the President and the Secretary

Eventually, Clinton did use his military. The activist vision of his secretary of state, Madeleine Albright, helped tilt the balance towards more intervention overseas. During a legendary confrontation with Colin Powell on the subject of using military might to end the siege of Sarajevo in 1993, she had shot, "What's the point of having this superb military that you're always talking about if we can't use it?" At the time of the discussion, which Powell later recalled made him "so angry he thought he would have an aneurysm," Albright held the post of Ambassador to the United Nations. Her influence was such that in 1996 Bill Clinton named her Secretary of State, the first woman to hold that job in the history of the U.S.

Albright, a native of Czechoslovakia, was among the most committed internationalists to hold that influential office. She proudly explained that, in sharp contrast to many in the U.S. foreign establishment, the guiding history in her philosophy was the failed appeasement of Hitler in Munich, rather than the disastrous U.S. intervention in Vietnam, which shaped the views of men like Colin Powell.

Just a few weeks after Powell's departure from the administration, President Clinton ordered half a dozen U.S. naval warships into action. The ships constituted a new show of force from an administration whose foreign policy was under attack from all sides for its inaction in Bosnia and Haiti, and its action in Somalia.

The situation in Haiti had become a major embarrassment for Washington and for Bill Clinton. The military coup against Aristide had come under the watch of President Bush, but the Clinton administration had promised action and showed no results. This highlighted Clinton's problems in foreign affairs, especially when the military was involved. Candidate Clinton had vowed to pursue "assertive multilateralism," active involvement in the world, under the auspices of the United Nations.

Madeleine Albright at the U.N. had successfully involved the world community in targeting the military rulers in Port-au-Prince, but the results had been laughable. In the summer of 1993, the Security Council imposed an oil and arms embargo on Haiti, along with a freeze on the government's financial assets. The embargo would be lifted if the junta leaders, Lt. Gen. Raoul Cedras and his cohorts, agreed to allow Aristide's return to power. Albright had persuaded the Security Council to act on what many believed was an internal Haitian matter, explaining that instability could lead to a massive exodus which would have international repercussions.

When the Clinton administration eventually sent forces into Haiti, it referred to the need to stop the flood of refugees as one of the elements of the national interest justifying intervention. Clinton spoke of the need for stability and the promotion of democracy in the Western hemisphere as other factors warranting American involvement in Haitian affairs.

All along, as the Clinton administration labored feverishly to craft a path back to democracy in Haiti, Republicans in Congress and their supporters inside the CIA and the Pentagon seemed determined to undermine official government policy.

It was clear much of the U.S. military and intelligence establishments, brought up in the Cold War philosophy of opposing anything with the smell of socialism, resisted the Clinton approach on Haiti. An anonymous official told a reporter that Aristide "represents everything that that CIA, DOD and FBI think they have been trying to protect this country against for the past 50 years."

Senator Jesse Helms, on the floor of the U.S. Senate, called Aristide a psychopath. The majority of the country opposed the use of American military forces to restore Aristide to power. The CIA leaked a report, which was later discredited, claiming Aristide suffered from a severe mental illness. Later, it was revealed that the National Security Agency had been listening in on telephone conversations of the man Washington was ostensibly trying to help return to power.

Aristide, a priest-turned-politician, had won the first free democratic election held in Haiti with an overwhelming majority. But critics charged the fiery orator with encouraging brutality against his opponents. They said he advocated the practice of a barbaric ritual known as "necklacing," practiced by his supporters, in which a tire would be placed around a person's neck and then set on fire. Aristide denied he encouraged necklacing. Clinton defended Aristide, making his reinstatement as President the guiding objective of his Haiti policy.

Within weeks of the imposition of the U.N. embargo, on July 3, Lt. Gen. Raoul Cedras came to Governors Island, New York, and signed an agreement promising to surrender power. Aristide, according to the agreement, could return by the end of October 1993. It seemed a great success for U.S. foreign policy and for U.N. efforts. The United Nations lifted the embargo. It was the very first time since the end of the Cold War the economic sanctions had been withdrawn after seemingly succeeding.

The moment the embargo was lifted, the military regime started stockpiling oil as fast as it could. The U.S. and the U.N. started preparing for Aristide's return and for the deployment of the international force of monitors who would help guarantee a peaceful return to democracy.

The agreement with Cedras collapsed. The General started demanding new conditions for his promised resignation, and when international monitors tried to reach Haiti to take their positions, one of the most humiliating episodes yet for the U.S. military ensued.

On October 11, 1993, the U.S.S. Harlan approached land in Port-au-Prince carrying 218 Canadian and American soldiers ready to help implement the Governors Island agreement. A frightening mob at the port ominously and loudly warned of another Somalia for U.S. forces. The mob beat foreign journalists and pounded the cars of waiting diplomats in plain view of Haitian soldiers — who did nothing to stop them. Waving guns and machetes, the ragtag platoon managed to turn the ship away when U.S. authorities, traumatized by events in Mogadishu, ordered the ship to leave Haitian waters. This came barely one week after Americans had been shocked by pictures of U.S. servicemen being dragged through the dusty streets of Somalia's capital. Clinton had decided to pull American troops out of Africa. Now American forces were again backing away, intimidated by thugs in another destitute Third World country. Clinton vowed the Haitian junta would not prevail.

Two days later, the United Nations re-imposed sanctions, and the U.S. sent a small armada to help enforce the embargo.

During the time between the two sets of sanctions, the Haitian military managed to build up oil reserves. But the sanctions dragged on, and the stockpiles started to dwindle. In the evenings, Port-au-Prince was completely dark. Or at least that's how it looked from our perch up on the hill at the Hotel Montana, in Pétionville, Haiti's upscale neighborhood. Not far from there, the city's wealthy elite kept power generators running, satellite dishes tuned to their favorite American television shows, and swimming pools filled — in a country where the vast majority had no access to running water.

The sound of gunshots regularly rang through the night, often coming from the slums of Cité Soleil, where Aristide supporters lived in filth and terror. Gangs of soldiers and thugs from the group known as FRAPH (Haitian Front for Advancement and Progress, whose name sounds like the French word for "hit") roamed poor areas, killing a few people every night, just to remind them who was in charge. The name Aristide was never uttered by the former priest's supporters. It was too dangerous.

The local economy started to shrivel. The only business that seemed to be booming was the black market for gasoline, in what was probably one of the most dangerous places on earth, or at least on the

Caribbean. It was known as Kuwait City, a stretch of road in Port-au-Prince where the overpowering smell of oil mixed with the sweat of hundreds of vendors selling gasoline smuggled from neighboring Dominican Republic. The road on which Kuwait City precariously thrived was thick with a sticky coat of spilled fuel. Wiry men stood by their containers, selling gas to the brave and the needy who came to this place that was an explosion waiting to happen. Children stood between their parents' legs, while mango vendors tried to make a sale as pigs squealed in the background.

Haiti's Kuwait City stood near the grounds of an old military barracks where scores of people — nobody knows how many — lay buried, victims of the brutality of the two Duvalier governments, the infamous dictators François Duvalier (Papa Doc) and later his son, Jean-Claude, known as Baby Doc. Life in Haiti had always been about survival. During this crisis, survival for many was found in Kuwait City.

The entrepreneurs stood by the containers with small hoses. When a buyer came to one of them, he would put one end of the hose in his mouth and suck until he got a mouthful of gas. With the flow of fuel started, after a quick spit he would dispense the liquid into the smaller containers provided by the buyer, often filtering dirt out of the fuel by pouring it through his own shirt.

The longer the crisis dragged on, the more the refugee crisis intensified.

With opposition to military intervention at home, Clinton tightened the sanctions, raising the stakes. Still, life in Port-au-Prince went on — at least for the rich. The city's best restaurants remained crowded with the well off, the ones who had not yet escaped to their Florida condominiums. New sanctions started targeting the elites, who were believed to support the junta's hold on power. Being a target of international sanctions suddenly became a point of pride and prestige for Haiti's upper crust.

Swindlers' List
(July 1994)

(Port-au-Prince) The soft, spicy sounds of the two-man band play in the background, as if providing the beat for the exchanges of pleasantries under the full moon of Port-au-Prince. Everybody knows everybody at this trendy restaurant in the Haitian capital. Light-skinned couples slip into the restaurant and away from the begging children in the street, to be greeted by the American owner with a kiss on the cheek for the ladies, a handshake and a light slap on the back for the men. As they are led to tables around the open courtyard, customers slow down to say hello to friends already seated. After a few laughs and a little gossip, the conversation quickly moves in one direction: The List.

The List is the latest arbiter of social status in a country where status these days brings a measure of pain. The black waiters in starched white shirts, black ties and red suspenders take orders with elegant subservience from people who address them by their first names. The multilingual clientele gracefully gravitates toward The List. A fashionable couple has brought a faxed copy tonight, and many who had not yet seen it buzz about their table, waiting their turn to closely examine the hottest best seller among the Haitian elite.

The List comes on U.S. Department of Treasury letterhead. Below the Treasury's name, the word "Urgent" is written three times across the top. The more than 200 people named are wealthy Haitians whose assets, the Treasury Department explains in this urgent letter to financial institutions, must be blocked and frozen.

Those listed, many of whom are represented tonight at Café des Arts, belong to what is cynically known these days as MREs — Morally Repugnant Elites. The term is catching on in Haiti, a country where the majority live without running water or electricity, while a tiny minority avidly follows every detail of life in the United States through the satellite dishes in the back yards of their lavish homes. As one observer explains, wealthy Haitians spend so much of their time in their condos in Miami or watching American television from their homes on the hills around Port-au-Prince that they can't believe Uncle Sam could possibly do this to them.

The Haitian elite has always played a prominent, if controversial, role in public life. Though they don't directly hold power, they have for years influenced the country's government by virtue of their wealth. In a country where military coups have been the principal means of changing administrations, the rich have always had the money to rule the rulers. Ironically, at the very time when the U.S. administration is basing its strategy on influencing the elite, the elite appears to be losing sway over the government in this country where money has always meant power without the dirty work of government.

Since the U.S. sanctions against Haiti began in 1991, the military rulers have developed their own sources of illicit income. Even U.S. government officials admit that the embargo — which is designed to exploit the influence of the rich — has made the rich less influential. Lighter-skinned Haitians, mulattos and whites, have always had higher social status and greater influence in Haiti. That goes back to before Haiti became the first free black republic in the world in 1804.

Even before the slaves revolted against the French, the mulatto offspring of white slave owners and black slaves already received special treatment. After the revolution, the class distinctions did not diminish, and the lighter-skinned Haitians, more educated and wealthier, only broadened the gap with the rest of the population. It was only during the decades of the Duvalier dictatorship that black Haitians attempted to wrest power from their mulatto countrymen. Despite the official anti-white and anti-mulatto policy of Duvalier, the lighter skinned Haitians kept their financial pre-eminence, with ownership of the factories and the land and with U.S. and European educations. In the poorest country in the Western hemisphere, with one of the most unequal distributions of wealth anywhere, the money of the rich could buy virtually anything, even coups and official government policy. Their money also bought a lifestyle that included frequent shopping trips to Miami and a cultural allegiance to the country just a few hundred miles north, the very country that now threatens their lifestyle.

Still, mixed in with the shock of Uncle Sam's betrayal, the financial troubles, and the simmering fear, is a certain amount of pride. If you belong on The List, you are clearly Somebody in this country. The List is a Who's Who of business, industry and, above all, high society. Some are upset at seeing their names on The List, others are upset at not seeing them. For practical purposes the List is rather meaningless.

Following the names is a summary of the policy, which explains that the sanctions also apply to "All Haitians living in Haiti." But many people express fears that those listed will be targeted for violence by supporters of exiled President Jean-Bertrand Aristide. Others say the military will punish those whose names are not spelled out, assuming they are supporters of the government in exile. For its part, the U.S. government expects the List to pressure members of the Haitian elite into persuading the military to return power to the democratically elected government of Aristide.

Divining the political future is at best an imprecise science in this land of voodoo, but many here say this particular American strategy will backfire. Rather than turning the rich against the military, they say, it will turn them against Bill Clinton. The poor may be enduring their sad lot with a quiet, means-justify-ends resignation, but the rich are quite vocal in their outrage. Undoubtedly, there are problems for the wealthy now in Haiti, much to the amusement of the poor. Not that the Clinton administration is about to slow down tonight's Seafood Night at the Café des Arts. But nobody likes to have a bank account taken out of reach. And the end of flights to Miami does complicate life quite a bit. Even more painful, the embargo for many wealthy Haitians has meant a total shutdown of their local businesses. The $50-a-month employees have also lost their jobs, but that is "collateral damage;" the real targets of the embargo are the wealthy.

Nobody is untouched by the international strangulation of Haiti's economy. But everybody agrees, if your name is on The List, you can weather this storm in style. After all, this is Haiti. People here have always suffered. And the lobster is truly exquisite tonight.

Clinton's Crisis

The crisis in Haiti became Bill Clinton's crisis. The President seemed caught in a no-win trap, enduring sharp attacks from just about every possible angle. Less than two years into his presidency, the consensus in the streets of the United States and among the sharpest political analysts was that Clinton would undoubtedly be a one-term president. Republicans, including former president George Bush, declared it was time to change the policy on Haiti and stand for democracy without Aristide. Clinton came under attack even by Aristide, who declared the policy of returning refugees to Haiti another example of American racism. Civil rights activist Randall Robinson went on a hunger strike to protest refugee policy.

Immigration authorities, regularly welcoming Cuban refugees to U.S. shores, sent Haitians back to their island unless they could prove they were fleeing political persecution rather than poverty. The State Department set up an office in Haiti, encouraging Haitians who feared for their lives because of their political views to apply for refugee status. The problem was that Aristide's supporters were virtually all poor and their support for the deposed President placed them in danger. It was practically impossible to separate economic from political refugees. Boats bursting with fleeing Haitians kept taking to sea, frequently capsizing in open waters.

At the same time, Clinton's approach to intervention was coming under attack for his handling of other world crises. The U.N. envoy for Bosnia, Yasushi Akashi, called it "timid and tentative."

As Clinton continued to insist all options were on the table, the cries for and against intervention became louder. Former President Bush said American lives were not at risk in Haiti, and hence, no intervention was warranted. Experts warned intervention guaranteed an American military presence in Haiti for many years. Randall Robinson, the activist on hunger strike, had to be hospitalized. He favored military action. Other observers now complained that three years after Aristide's overthrow, it was time to either take action or move on.

Some started to suggest a new factor to be considered as part of the national interest: credibility. If Washington had said it would not let the military coup succeed, its standing in the world and its ability to deter aggression suffered if it failed to act. It wasn't just the President's credibility at stake. It was also the nation's. The flexible standard of national interest in the post-Cold War days was growing even more elastic.

Also flexible was public opinion. Americans seemed torn on the subject of Haiti. Was it another Somalia, where lives would be lost dealing with other people's problems? Or, was it more like Rwanda, where the biblical proportions of the catastrophe had become apparent? Something that looked suspiciously like remorse started stirring in Western hearts. By the time a decision was made to invade Haiti, President Clinton had persuaded a narrow majority of Americans that the action was justified.

The coup leaders, meanwhile, had mustered little support around the world. Astonishingly, only the Vatican recognized Haiti's leaders after the 1991 coup against the former Roman Catholic priest. No other government did. When the Cedras government named 81-year-old Emile Jonaissant President of Haiti, the entire world acknowledged the maneuver was a sham. The Vatican sent a representative to Jonaissant's inauguration. Rome had never had any fondness for Aristide and his brand of liberation theology and class struggle. Aristide had been expelled from his order in 1988. Two years later, he'd won two-thirds of the vote in the presidential election.

In August of 1994, the United Nations gave the U.S. the diplomatic legitimacy it wanted for intervention in Haiti. The Security Council, in a 12-to-0 vote, authorized the use of "all necessary means" to remove the Junta from power. It was the same language that had preceded the war against Saddam Hussein's forces in the Gulf. The international consensus helped build support abroad and at home for intervention.

When the "national interest" had to do with vague issues of decency, human rights and democracy, Americans seemed to want other nations to take part in the decision-making. If the stakes were more narrowly defined, Americans appeared to favor action with less regard for international opinion. It looked like American and Haitian uniforms would not be the only ones on the ground in Haiti.

When the United States went after Panamanian strongman Manuel Antonio Noriega in 1989, the United Nations played virtually no role. In fact, U.N. approval would have been impossible, since the USSR, with a permanent seat on the Security Council, would never have agreed to authorize an invasion. The Soviets declared the action a reprehensible violation of the U.N. charter.

We, in Port-au-Prince, were summoned to an important speech by the new president, Jonaissant. The press corps filed into the modest home where the elderly man sat sternly before a small desk placed in a living room lit dimly by a single light bulb hanging from a naked chord. Television technicians crawled all around him, laying cable and lighting to televise the address, often asking the new President to move a bit so he could make room for the equipment. On the air, Jonnaisant declared a state of siege. It was clear that the military regime was not going to back down in response to the U.N. vote. Supporters of the military vowed a "fight to the death."

The level of violence and intimidation was worsening. The people were obviously terrified to speak. People showed up dead in the streets of Port-au-Prince with eerie regularity. The authorities concocted the most extraordinary charges against the press. We were once accused of going to the morgue and taking bodies out to the streets to photograph them. Some claimed they could tell we were showing the same corpse in different places. Harassment of journalists became commonplace. CNN and CBS crews were detained; another American television crew was unceremoniously taken to the Dominican border and expelled from the country after being paraded through Port-au-Prince in a pick-up truck.

As the invasion loomed closer, we were squeezed even tighter by functionaries of the military regime whose moneymaking positions were about to disappear. Suddenly, there were more license fees and special charges for transmissions.

By now, President Clinton's Haiti policy was starting to get caught in the storm of electoral politics at home. The mid-term elections that would give Republicans control of Congress were approaching and Clinton's opponents were not only attacking his Haiti policy, they started worrying aloud about the prospect of an "October Surprise," a military victory for the President just in time to help the Democrats at the polls.

Newt Gingrich, then Republican minority whip, proclaimed, "The American people are not going to risk the lives of their sons and daughters to solve this administration's domestic political problems." Senator Robert Dole told an audience the U.S. had no national interest in Haiti, adding that he would not rule out military intervention in Cuba to depose Fidel Castro.

The Pentagon's military brass showed reluctance to use force. The diplomats at the State Department were the ones beating the drums for war. Critics called the new activism the "Colonialism of Compassion," or a new form of "Liberal Imperialism."

In Haiti, the smooth Raoul Cedras didn't exactly go into hiding in response to the threats of imminent military action. He occasionally granted interviews to foreign journalists, who generally walked away impressed. Haiti's strongman remained defiant, appearing in public surrounded by a terrifying platoon of men in black hoods carrying automatic weapons, nicknamed the "Ninjas."

Clinton tightened the noose. As a number of Caribbean nations agreed they would join an invasion force and Britain said its forces stood ready to help, Cedras and his cohorts received a warning from Washington: They would face arrest and trial if they didn't leave the country. The threat sounded even more menacing when the human rights arm of the State Department released a report calling the regime one of the worst human rights violators in the world, and detailing a grisly account of murders, mutilation, torture and rape. Still, Aristide supporters continued turning up dead in the streets of Port-au-Prince, and the General, along with his top deputies, the feared police chief Michel François and Brigadier Gen. Philippe Biamby, remained in power.

Some of the Junta's men could be seen through the thick smoke in the bustling casino of the hotel El Rancho. A loud power generator kept the casino lit just enough to allow patrons to examine their Blackjack cards. Gun handles peaked out under the shirts of the casino's shady patrons when they leaned down to take a drink from the dwarf waiter who roamed the large room in his tuxedo. Graham Greene would have been at home in the Port-au-Prince of 1994.

Details of the upcoming invasion were telegraphed to the world. Military exercises were held, and plans for the future of a post-Junta Haiti were made public. Everyone expected the invasion. Even some critics now said it was time to do it. But opposition at home was hardly silenced. Republicans dismissed the talk, and analysts declared Clinton was "dancing with political death."

The Haitian military was reportedly getting ready for the "Battle of Haiti." Nobody claimed this would be the "Mother of All Battles," as Saddam Hussein proclaimed when facing the U.S.-led alliance. But the Haitian military was supposedly getting ready to face its powerful neighbor. Alas, Haiti's preparations left something to be desired. The Supreme Commander of the country's military worked roughly from noon until 2pm. The Air Force had practically all of its equipment in pieces, and the soldiers didn't look very well fed.

The military's civilian supporters, on the other hand, managed to talk a good game. People like Emmanuel Constant, known as "Toto," warned that American G.I.s would endure mass poisonings and unspeakable voodoo-spun suffering. A young Haitian working with us in Port au Prince in the months leading up to the intervention once spoke to me in fear, pointing to the Mississippi floods in the U.S., as proof that anti-Aristide voodoo tactics were yielding results.

Toto's eyes widened ominously when he promised the invasion would bring hell on earth to U.S. forces. The head of FRAPH, the paramilitary group believed responsible for perhaps thousands of murders of Aristide supporters, later claimed to be on the payroll of the CIA. The CIA has never denied it. (He now lives in the United States, where the government has declined requests to extradite him for trial in Haiti.)

Everyone waited anxiously for the advertised surprise. The landing would come at any moment. One night we heard the hum of airplanes overhead. Something was clearly there. Because of the embargo, there had been no flights in and out of Haiti for some time, and it couldn't possibly be the Haitian military. Then we saw it, through the clouds: parachutes descending over the city. As everyone prepared for this great televised war, CBS had just scored a major victory with an interview with Gen. Cedras. But on its evening of triumph, CBS overplayed its hand. Dan Rather cut into programming to suggest — hedging a little — that the invasion had started.

One of the parachutes landed in the brush near the Montana Hotel balcony from where we did most of our live transmissions. We rushed over, sliding down the embankment, and found a box filled with Radio Shack transistor radios. The destitute Haitians would now have radios to listen to U.S. radio broadcasts, if they could find a way to pay for batteries when the parachuted ones ran out.

Port-au-Prince was the ideal place for a live, televised war. At our perch in Pétionville, we could install a receiver to catch transmissions from our portable microwaves just about anywhere in the city. We were ready for the invasion.

And then, after diplomats had declared the talking was over and U.S. guns were virtually cocked in the direction of Haiti, came a last chance for diplomacy, a last ditch effort to persuade the Junta. President Clinton sent Jimmy Carter, Sen. Sam Nunn, and Gen. Colin Powell to talk to Cedras.

Carter was the man with the message for peace; Powell would talk soldier to soldier, explaining just how overwhelming a force Haiti would face; Nunn would demonstrate that Clinton had the power to make this happen, even if Congress had sounded less than supportive.

We assembled in the streets in front of the military headquarters, along with thousands of supporters of the military, watching Jimmy Carter at work. From the ground we could see the former president walk from one room to the other, talking to Cedras in one room, then communicating with Washington from the other.

The U.S. mission to invade Haiti had already started when the agreement was reached. Planes had already departed their bases and had to be pulled back after the agreement was signed. Cedras and his associates would leave, and a large international contingent, including some 15,000 American troops, would come to Haiti.

Bill Clinton had somehow managed to avoid a war, thanks in large part to efforts of the peacemaker ex-President. But victory in Haiti was not enough to bring his party a success in the November elections, and it was not enough to bring prosperity to the Haitian people — except, perhaps, to Lt. Gen. Raoul Cedras.

Haiti, the Loser in U.S. Elections
(December 1994)

(Port-au-Prince, Haiti) As the sun rose over the tense streets of Port-au-Prince on September 19, a low hum could be heard in the distance. People looked skyward. Suddenly, you could see it: a line of helicopters making its way from an aircraft carrier in the bay. The Americans were coming, at last. Finally, U.S. President Bill Clinton had delivered on his promise to remove the military from power in Haiti and restore the democratically elected President, Jean-Bertrand Aristide. It was the beginning of a new era. Little did the people of Haiti — or, for that matter, Clinton — know that in a few months, Aristide's enemies in the Republican Party would take control of much of the power structure in Washington in the November mid-term elections.

The first group of helicopters landed at the International Airport, which was quickly secured by U.S. soldiers. Then the helicopters raised an explosion of sand over the port area. It was a show like no one had ever seen on this land. The crowds gathered around the port wall to watch in awe. For the first several hours of the U.S. intervention, they just watched silently.

It was only in the hours of the early afternoon that an amazing transformation took place. It happened there, at the gate of the port. One man said it quietly: "Vive Aristide!" The other people gazed at him, puzzled, and then looked at the Haitian police, the old foes of the poor, standing outside the gates. The police, confused, glanced over at the towering American soldiers standing guard on the other side. The Americans looked like giants. The Haitian police said nothing. And, suddenly, the crowd discovered its new freedom. After years of repression, after years of killings, they could now shout, "Vive Aristide!"

It had been almost exactly three years since Aristide was overthrown and forced to flee by a bloody military coup. After the coup, his supporters had known the fear of roaming death squads and late-night assassinations. The bodies of Aristide supporters frequently were found dumped in the middle of busy intersections, for all to see. It was a successful campaign of intimidation that continued even in the face of international efforts designed to force the military leaders out of power.

The people of Haiti had suspected, and privately accused, the Bush administration of supporting the coup. After all, they knew that George Bush once had headed the CIA, the intelligence agency many of them feared. More important, the people of Haiti, who had brought Aristide to power in a landslide election, knew that the tiny elite of millionaires who controlled their country's destiny had close ties to powerful American interests. Washington, however, publicly led the campaign to oust the coup leaders. Under Bush, an embargo was imposed. And then Clinton began to turn the screws.

But while the administration embraced Aristide's cause, the CIA was reporting that the deposed President had a history of serious mental illness. Perhaps no one person in Washington did more to publicize the leaked CIA report than Senator Jesse Helms, the man now slated to chair the powerful Foreign Relations Committee. Speaking on the Senate floor, Helms expressed his visceral dislike of Clinton and of U.S. policy on Haiti. Helms declared of Aristide, "This man is a psychopath."

Less than a week after the mid-term elections, Senator Robert Dole was calling for a quick U.S. withdrawal. The fact that information provided by Aristide's opponents had underpinned the CIA report was ignored, as was a subsequent news item that Emanuel Constant, the top leader of a violent paramilitary group, had been on the CIA payroll. Clinton continued to push for Aristide, even in the face of strong opposition, particularly from outspoken Republicans like Newt Gingrich, the incoming Speaker of the House, and Senator Robert Dole, the new Majority Leader in the Senate.

Clinton maintained that the administration would rely on its own experience with Aristide rather than on reports from questionable sources. He insisted that the United States had an interest in seeing democracy survive in Latin America, and proceeded with the intervention. But after the elections that put both houses of the U.S. Congress under Republican control, pressure is mounting to wrap up the mission, even while the Aristide government enjoys little support among those Haitians who control the money and the guns.

So, Haiti could yet become one of the biggest losers of the U.S. election. Aristide's opponents in Washington have gained power, while his strongest support in the Congress, the Congressional Black Caucus, has lost much of its clout. In Haiti, American soldiers are still treated like heroes. Walls along the streets of Port-au-Prince carry spray-painted messages of gratitude. One near the military airport reads: "Thank you, United States. We will never forget." But the final paragraphs of this chapter in Haiti's history have yet to be written.

After the Storm

Anyone who had looked at Haiti's history of injustice, insult and injury would have known better than to expect much improvement in the situation.

On October 14, 1994, journalists willing to forego a night of sleep were rewarded with an amazing sight. For hours U.S. Ambassador William Swing held talks with Gen Raoul Cedras, until he persuaded — or bribed — the former strongman to leave the country. By 3 o'clock in the morning, Cedras and his entourage were ready for exile. At the Port-au-Prince airport, U.S. soldiers performed baggage-handling duties, loading box after box of the Cedras family's belongings into an American government airplane. The General and his former Chief of Staff and co-coup leader, Philippe Biamby, boarded the plane that took them to Panama under the generous auspices of U.S. taxpayers.

Not only were millions of dollars in stolen money released for the coup leaders' enjoyment, but Washington's largesse included renting Cedras' three homes in Haiti for an amount estimated at as much as $12,000 per month.

The third leader of the coup, Police Chief Michel François, perhaps the most hated man in Haiti, rented his palatial estate to the government of the neighboring Dominican Republic, which would host him in exile. He is believed to have amassed enormous holdings in the Dominican Republic.

The three men helped by Washington into luxurious retirement were the same of whom President Clinton had said only one month ear-

lier, "(They) have conducted a reign of terror, executing children, raping women, killing priests . . ."

In November 2000, a Haitian jury sentenced more than 30 former
top army officers in one of the many massacres that marked the three-
year regime of Gen. Cedras. Among those sentenced *in absentia* to life in
prison and hard labor were Cedras, Biamby, François, and "Toto" Constant, the leader of the paramilitary group FRAPH.

The trial focused on the massacre at the slum of Rabouteau in the
city of Gonaive, where in April 1994 paramilitaries and soldiers burst
into private homes and started a savage wave of beatings and arrests,
shooting those who fled. Relatives were not allowed to retrieve the
bodies, and stray dogs ended up eating what remained of the victims.
Nobody knows how many died in Raboteau.

Cedras, Biamby and François remain in exile in Latin America.
Constant is still in the U.S., living with an aunt in Queens. Human
rights groups have repeatedly demanded his extradition, but the government maintains his return to Haiti would be
"destabilizing." (Constant was, in fact, held at a detention center in
Maryland in 1995, under a judge's orders that he be extradited to Haiti.
He appealed, and threatened to reveal details of his involvement with
U.S. intelligence. He was later released in less-than-clear circumstances, and is now working as a real estate agent in New York.)

The day Aristide returned to Haiti, people dressed in their best
clothes. In the streets of Cité Soleil, the slum with the name befitting a
Club Med, they built small altars to the man they adored, and raised
their arms to the sky as they saw the airplane approach bringing their
savior down from the skies. But the promise of a better life didn't materialize. Aristide stepped down from power in 1996, at the end of the
term interrupted by the coup. His handpicked successor, René Préval,
held office until the end of 2000, although most observers are convinced that Aristide never stopped being the power behind the throne.

When Préval shut down Congress, foreign aid for the destitute
nation was frozen by donor countries. All signs of democracy started to
fade, and political violence and corruption reappeared.

Haiti remains by far the poorest country in the Western hemisphere, and one of the poorest in the world, ranked 170 out of 174 in the

U.N.'s human development index. Most people live on less than $1 a day and half the children under 5 are malnourished. At the same time, the country has become a major haven for cocaine traffickers.

Aristide was elected president again in Dec. 2000, in an election boycotted by all opposition parties, several months after a congressional election declared unfair by international organizations. Still, despite the low turnout and the lack of participation by his opponents, he remains a beloved figure for the poor, who expect him at last to fulfill the promises of a better life that stirred their passions in the early 1990s. To meet those expectations, Aristide needs to get access to more than $500 million in international aid. He has promised significant reforms to satisfy the international community.

Still, President George W. Bush has little interest in seeing the U.S. involved in countries like Haiti. The national interest, in the view of George Bush the younger, does not include "nation-building." But if abject poverty or violence a few hundred miles from U.S. shores prompts a new flood of refugees, the first Republican president of the new millennium could find it is time yet again to redefine the national interest.

What About Africa?

Unlike Haiti, Rwanda did not seem to fall under anyone's definition of national interest when one of the worst massacres in history came to its grotesque conclusion. When the magnitude of the massacres became apparent, some in the foreign policy establishment found the disaster a strong argument for including humanitarian considerations in the definition of the U.S. national interest. It is in our interest, they said, to avoid genocide; to promote democracy; to further human rights. That, of course, was much too late for the victims of the killings.

The Tutsis had managed to stop the slaughter by Hutus and send them on the run. The rout unleashed a river of humanity of biblical proportions, with refugees pouring across the dusty border into Zaire. As the world found out more details of the horrific events that had transpired in Rwanda, the situation for Hutu refugees in what was the world's biggest refugee camp in Goma, Zaire, was quickly deteriorating. The world leapt into action, sending massive aid to stave off calamity in the camps.

Among the hundreds of thousands of Hutus saved by international efforts were many of the people responsible for the massacres of Tutsis. Having permitted the first slaughter to take place, the Western world now felt responsible for the survival of people in the heart of Africa, sending troops and spending tens of millions to help the refugees spawned by the crisis it had failed to avert.

In the year 2000, candidate Bush was clear in stating his preference for a much narrower standard for intervention: "We should not send our troops to stop ethnic cleansing outside of our national strategic interest," Bush said, ". . . I would not send United States troops into Rwanda."

On Rwanda, Bill Clinton had done more — or less — than not stop the genocide. He and other Western leaders had refused to send their own countries' troops, and had actively blocked U.N. efforts to intervene. "We just didn't want to touch it after Somalia, and we were prepared to see the people killed rather than get involved in an operation to try to prevent it," is how James L. Woods explained it to a reporter years later. He was Deputy Assistant Secretary of Defense for Africa when the Rwanda massacres began.

Clinton, in retrospect, had found the outcome of his Rwanda decision unacceptable, and he later said he regretted his decision. Presumably, under Clinton's new evolved worldview, the U.S. would have found it in its national interest to prevent another Rwanda.

The United States may not be able to make up its mind about what role it should have played in Rwanda. But for the people of that country, there is little doubt that the world had a responsibility to do its part in preventing the killings. As far as Rwandans are concerned, we are all our brothers' keepers.

That point was made powerfully to U.N. Secretary General Kofi Annan, the respected African diplomat who was head of U.N. peacekeeping operations when the killings began.

Annan visited Rwanda in 1998, riding a crest of popularity as Secretary General. He had managed to avert a U.S. bombing of Baghdad by brokering a deal with Saddam Hussein over access for U.N. weapons inspectors. Modestly triumphant, the soft-spoken Secretary General arrived in Kigali, the Rwandan capital, four years after the African bloodshed. The reception was not exactly what he had expected.

Dishonesty Follows Bloodshed in Rwanda
(May, 1998)

Kofi Annan arrived on time at the Kigali club where he was to be the government's Guest of Honor during his official visit to Rwanda. When the Secretary General of the United Nations reached the club, his hosts had not arrived. Annan waited, and waited. The President and Prime Minister never showed up. The Secretary General got back into his car and left.

It was all part of an ice-cold reception the country gave to a man who recently seemed in danger of falling victim to pernicious adulation after his negotiations in Baghdad to avert armed confrontation between Saddam Hussein and the United States.

The Rwandan leaders boycotted the reception while many in of the African nation pointed an accusing finger at Annan for the inaction of the United Nations during the slaughter of 1994.

Clearly, the Rwandans who massacred other Rwandans between April and July of 1994 are directly responsible for what is one of the most unspeakable crimes of recent times. Rwandan Hutus killed more than 500,000, perhaps as many as one million Rwandan Tutsis, in the space of a few months. It was human slaughter on a scale that would have made Hitler envious. Month for month, the Hutus outdid Hitler's industrialized killing.

But that is hardly the entire story. The people of Rwanda say the United Nations — and Kofi Annan, head of U.N. peacekeeping operations at the time — failed to stop the genocide, despite having full knowledge that it was about to start. In fact, the U. N. pulled out most of its troops as soon as the machetes started their orgy of carnage.

A spokesman for the government said the country's leaders were offended by Annan's statements, made earlier to the country's parliament, in which he spoke of the need for atonement by the Rwandan people. The Rwandans wanted to hear some atonement from him. Annan explained he had done all he could under the circumstances, explaining the organization suffered from a lack of resources and, perhaps more important, a lack of political will to act. The Rwandans say the United Nations is guilty of the most immoral form of negligence.

Annan is right in saying Rwanda must look within. The country must look openly at what happened so that it will find a way to stop itself from self-destructing in the future.

But the rest of the world too has cause to look within. There is a reason why we call these atrocities Crimes Against Humanity. Humanity itself is the victim. The world failed to even try to stop the bloodshed. The world failed.

If we failed to prevent the Rwandan catastrophe, we still have one crucial responsibility: we must shine a probing light on what occurred, and see where we — all of us — went wrong. Hundreds of thousands were slaughtered and we did nothing to stop it. We failed as our brothers' keepers.

Even for those callous enough not to care about Rwanda, the stakes are high. It's almost a cliché now that if we don't learn the lessons of the past we are destined to repeat them. Some say if we had looked more honestly at the genocidal massacre of more than a million Armenians in 1915, we would never have allowed the holocaust of World War II.

The United Nations has established an international war crimes tribunal in Rwanda to seek out and punish those guilty for the bloodshed. The first-ever confession to the crime of genocide was recently presented by the country's former prime minister, the leader of the extremist Hutus who carried out the killings.

Before the confession, the tribunal had been harshly criticized for its slow and ineffective pace. The Rwandan system of justice, for its part, has also been at the center of controversy. There are two systems of justice at work. The U.N. tribunal can impose a maximum sentence of life in prison, and has so far indicted 35 people for the killings of more than half a million. It is currently holding two dozen people on suspicion of participating in the killing. The Rwandan government meanwhile is holding 130,000 suspects in squalid conditions of hideously over-crowded jails. Last month the government executed 22 people convicted of genocide. The executions evoked an outcry around the world — including United Nations officials — accusing the government of shedding the blood of men who had not been given the benefit of due process.

Plainly, revenge and justice are two very different actions. Revenge will only sow the seeds of more revenge, while true justice will help ensure peace for the future.

On the same day that Kofi Annan completed his rebuke-filled tour of Rwanda, the country's government announced the expulsion of the U.N. human rights spokesman because of statements made in criticism of the last month's executions.

The Rwandan events of 1994 remain some of the darkest hours of a very bloody twentieth century. Sadly, in the aftermath of the massacres, neither Rwanda nor the rest of the world seems to be taking this opportunity to engage in the self-examination needed to learn from those dark hours' terrible mistakes.

The Bosnia Dilemma

Like Rwanda and Haiti, intervention in the Balkans posed a challenge to a long-held tradition in international affairs, which gave countries a right to handle internal matters without outside interference. The rule dated back hundreds of years. The Great Powers who dominated the world until World War I had pledged to let each one run its own affairs, in a 17th-century agreement.

Of course, the flow of refugees across international borders provided easy cover. Practically any domestic situation causing extreme misery at home had the potential of bringing a refugee crisis to its neighbors, and instability to a region.

In the case of the Balkans, Europe and the United States were baffled. When Bosnia and Croatia declared their independence and Slobodan Milosevic went to war refusing to accept their independence, it was unclear whether the conflict was a civil war or an international dispute pitting sovereign nations against each other.

In the case of Kosovo, there was little doubt that the confrontation between ethnic Albanians, the overwhelming majority of Kosovo's population, and Belgrade was a domestic matter. Kosovo was a province of Serbia and no nation recognized it as an independent country.

After much wavering, Europe and the U.S. eventually intervened in both Bosnia and Kosovo, but only after the magnitude of atrocities committed by the authorities had come to light. A new doctrine for intervention was taking shape for the post-Cold War era. If there was enough cruelty and the cruelty was publicized well enough to elicit public outrage, intervention was a possibility. It was even more likely if the victims were of a distinct ethnic group and if the majority of the people rejected the authority of the government carrying out the violence.

This, of course, was not enough. Africa was still very much outside the sphere of even the most widely defined national interest. The nation in question had to be geographically positioned to be of interest to the intervening power. Haiti and the Balkans qualified for intervention; Sudan and the Congo did not.

When East Timor declared its independence from Indonesia and its people were butchered by Indonesian thugs, Australia, in the same neighborhood, took the lead in intervening.

The civil war in Sudan received scant attention in the West, despite its enormous toll on the civilian population. By the beginning of the new millennium, the religious angle of the conflict caught the attention of Christian leaders who realized that the principal victims of the 18-year-old war were Christian and were dying partly because of that. By the year 2000, the war in Sudan had left about 2 million dead and some 4 million displaced. The conflict, pitting the Muslim government against the Christian and animist rebels, saw the use of starvation as a key weapon of war. Relief agencies and international government contributions did move in force into the area, falling prey to military tactics of the government. Khartoum manipulated relief efforts to achieve goals of de-populating oil-rich areas.

As eighty percent of the population of the south was displaced and the death toll from war-related starvation and disease rose into the millions, oil companies competed for access to the disputed territory and its 2 million barrels of oil. Then, adding one more deadly ingredient to the recipe for tragedy, a threatening famine raised the specter of even greater devastation. The United States contributed hundreds of millions of dollars in food aid, and attempted to isolate the Muslim regime in the international community. But the diplomatic strategy in this low priority conflict achieved practically no results.

By the time the new Bush administration came to power, it appeared that the only possibility for more direct U.S. involvement would be in the form of political pressure. The prospect of pressure from Christian conservatives concerned with an attack on Christians in Sudan, combined with pressure from Black constituencies arguing for action in the face of another African genocide-in-the-making, provided a glimmer of hope for bringing a resolution of the Sudan conflict into the U.S. national interest; that, 18 years and 2 million dead after the start of a war largely invisible to West's foreign policy.

For Europe, the moment of greatest foreign policy shame came in the former Yugoslavia. The name of the place whose memory remains burned into Europe's conscience is Srebrenica, in Bosnia. In July of 1995, the town had been designated as a "safe haven" by the United Nations, a place where Bosnian Muslims would be protected from Serbs by U.N. peacekeepers. Tens of thousands of displaced Bosnians had fled to Srebrenica, seeking the protection of U.N. troops. But when Serb forces arrived, the Dutch peacekeepers did little to stop them. Serb troops ordered the men separated from the women and the children. By many accounts, the peacekeepers — outgunned and outnumbered by the Serbs — actually helped the Serbs separate the population. Many who tried to flee were shot; others were lured back by Serbs pretending to be Dutch peacekeepers. People seeking protection within the U.N. compound were forced out despite their pleas. While the women and their U.N. protectors watched in horror, the men where hauled away in trucks. They were later shot at close range.

The massacre of 8,000 men from Srebrenica, the worst in Europe since the end of World War II, became a turning point for intervention. Within weeks, NATO began a two-week bombing campaign against Serb positions. The bombing, combined with a successful ground operation by Bosnian and Croatian troops, which recaptured territory controlled by the Serbs, finally brought Milosevic to the bargaining table.

In November 1995, four months after Srebrenica, all the parties in the conflict signed the Dayton Peace Agreement. Soon after that, a multinational force entered Bosnia to enforce the agreement. Before international intervention helped end the Bosnian war, some 200,000 people had died and 2 million had been displaced.

When the crackdown by Serb authorities in Kosovo intensified three years later, the memories and the shame of Srebrenica still loomed darkly on the conscience of the West. Intervention came much more quickly.

Nations of the West still discussed the national interest and whether it was at stake in Kosovo. Again, the word "genocide" was brought into the debate, a word with its emotional link to the holocaust and its historical imperative for decisive action against ruthlessness.

Holocaust survivor and author Elie Wiesel disagreed with the use of the term, but agreed the world should take action. In a *Newsweek* essay, Wiesel acknowledged that Serbian actions and intentions in Bosnia and Kosovo might qualify under a legal definition of genocide, but were simply not comparable to the German plans for the total extermination of the Jewish people. Milosevic's ethnic cleansing of non-Serbs from Serbian areas was despicable, Wiesel agreed, but he pointed out that what has happening in Bosnia was not a repeat of Hitler's final solution. He objected to the comparison, but he found a compelling reason for forceful intervention. The rhetoric had always had strategic value on the political arena, but the horrors on the ground were undeniable.

When NATO went into action in Kosovo, in 1999, a permeating sense of international responsibility had taken hold in many sectors of society throughout the world.

When the Serbs were driven out, and Kosovo became a province without a country, the entire world took it on as a project. The powers that had driven Serb forces out were not calling for independence for the tiny province. The people of Kosovo stayed in a twilight zone of political limbo, with an international government running its affairs, and a future filled with uncertainty.

One year later, the place was crawling with do-gooders, as donors everywhere emptied their pockets to help the newly liberated people.

Test Tube Nation:
The World in Kosovo
(May 2000)

(Pristina) The traffic on Mother Teresa road in central Pristina is barely moving, clogged bumper to bumper with 4-wheel drive vehicles bearing colorful logos on their hoods. The logos are a veritable alphabet soup of acronyms and noble-sounding names: AGAPE (Association for Generosity and Active Promotion of Empathy,) ECHO (European Community Humanitarian Organization,) DOW (Doctors of the World,) AFPIC (Action for People in Conflict.)

The Kosovar capital has been invaded by an army of humanitarian workers — that's in addition to the real army or KFOR, the NATO lead force made up of some 39,000 soldiers, armed to the teeth, who also contribute to the ever-present traffic jam. The world has made Kosovo its number one cause. At least for now.

The international community wants to defy history in a quixotic effort to turn this tiny Balkan region into a most un-Balkan ideal: a tolerant, democratic society, where minorities enjoy dignity, respect and justice.

After the decade-long crackdown by Serb authorities, which left some 10,000 Kosovar Albanians dead — and just about everybody else here traumatized and overflowing with resentment — the enormity of the task is impossible to overstate. The world is not so much tilting at windmills as trying to reverse the wind altogether. After all, the crackdown from Belgrade that lead to NATO's 78-day war against Yugoslavia was just one more explosion in the centuries of hatred, division, and destruction that made the Balkans a symbol of hatred, division and destruction for the entire world.

No one knows exactly how many people have descended on Kosovo to do good deeds. The number of non-governmental organizations, or NGOs, is estimated at somewhere between 400 and 500. Their missions range from medical assistance, as in Doctors Without Borders and handfuls of other groups whose name includes the word Doctors, to mine removal, as in the

Mine Action Group, or MAG — the organization whose skull and crossbones logo is either frightening or comical — to scores of refugee aid and economic development organizations.

But perhaps the most daunting of all missions is the one assigned to the Organization for Security and Cooperation in Europe, or OSCE. The OSCE is one of four so-called pillars of the United Nations in Kosovo, or UNMIK. The other three are Civil Administration, Humanitarian Affairs — run by UNHCR — and Reconstruction — the job of the European Union.

OSCE's mandate is to build a "democratic and civil society" in Kosovo. In a land where revenge is the order of the day, and conflict is often resolved by shooting not just the offender but anyone in his family, in this or the coming generations, the task of the OSCE is akin to emptying the ocean drop by drop.

Consider a few typical days in Kosovo. On the first Sunday in May, four Kosovo Serbs — including an eight-year-old girl — were shot and wounded by ethnic Albanians in a village southeast of Pristina. The next day, a Kosovar Albanian, a former rebel commander, was killed by Kosovo Serbs. That Saturday, a 67-year old Serb man was killed in the same area.

On May 22, according to UNMIK police, a 53-year-old woman stopped to talk with a couple of men along a road in a Pristina neighborhood. After the conversation, the men left, only to return later with a gun. They shot her four times. Police say she was shot because her first language was Serbo-Croatian. When asked about the reason for such an attack, a friendly young Kosovar explained it very clearly: "She was probably a Serb." Perfectly logical.

Still, the world keeps trying, and the optimists — along with the spin doctors — say progress is being made. A year ago, some 50 revenge killings took place here every week. The number now has dropped to just a few every week, but a police official explains it under his breath, half-joking, saying there aren't many people left to kill. At least half of the estimated 200,000 Serbs who lived in Kosovo before the war have left the province.

Forging ahead, the massive effort to register all Kosovars has begun, and OSCE officials maintain it's moving along at an encouraging clip. The process will produce a much-needed assessment of how many Kosovars live in and out of the territory; how many need the services of the sprawling community of helpers. Perhaps most important, registration will help set the stage for democracy, producing voter lists for municipal elections to be held in October.

OSCE is turning Kosovo into a laboratory for democracy, helping develop the political infrastructure that took hundreds if not thousands of years to build in other countries. The international community is hoping for, and trying to nurture, a healthy political climate with respect for human rights. It is also trying to build a responsible police force, and working to create a fair judiciary out of the ruins of old Yugoslavia in Kosovo. Trainers from the West are working with the local media to create a free and responsible press where there was none, and endeavoring to instill the almost-unheard-of concept of the rule of law. First, of course, you need laws, and distilling the usable laws from the Yugoslavian books is another Herculean task.

As the world works to eventually turn over the administration of Kosovo to the Kosovars, signs from local politicians show sporadic flashes of encouragement. At least one guerrilla-turned-politician says Albanians and Serbs must learn to live together. Ramush Haradinaj, a 31-year-old retired leader of the Kosovo Liberation Army, does not advocate the creation of a multi-ethnic state. But in some way, the efforts to build tolerance here may be paying off: Haradinaj says Albanians and Serbs will have to live together, if they want to continue receiving aid from the West; perhaps not the most noble of motivations, but a motivation nonetheless.

Still, with all the efforts by the NGOs and the international organizations trying to build a new Kosovo, there is one important detail whose absence makes almost everything a mirage. The world — today's protector of Kosovo — has not decided if Kosovo will be an independent nation or will continue to be part of Yugoslavia. The Kosovars know what they want; they consider independence a non-negotiable fact, but political leaders in Washington, Brussels and Moscow have been unable or unwilling to tackle that question. Without that decision, the work of thousands in Pristina and in the rest of this tiny province lacks crucial direction.

But the work continues undeterred. The gleaming SUVs climb the dusty hills of Pristina, carrying aid workers to meetings with other aid workers, all focused on Kosovo until the money runs out or until they move on to the next emergency. After that, it will be up to the people of Kosovo, and to the forces of history.

Heroes, Generals and Jails

The doctrine for intervention, despite the emergence of some unspoken rules, remained very much a make-it-up-as-you-go exercise in the new era. In many places, regimes governed destructively, against the wishes of the governed, attacking ethnic minorities, and without the slightest threat of outside intervention.

Take, for example, the old Burma, renamed Myanmar by a despotic military regime. The country, positioned between India and China, occupies a strategic location in Asia.

In 1988, the country's economic system, in theory leading to a Burmese Socialist utopia, was in a free fall. Every measure the military government took, including suddenly abolishing the largest denomination paper currency (which caused people's savings to vanish without warning), made things much worse. Every single business had been expropriated without compensation to the owners, causing shortages of just about everything. After three decades of enduring hardship and dictatorship, the people finally rose up.

A woman named Aung San Suu Kyi just happened to be in the capital, Rangoon, when the troubles started. Suu Kyi, daughter of the country's revered founding father, Bogyoke Aung San, lived in Great Britain at the time. She was married to a British professor of Tibetan studies. She lived a quiet and comfortable life, far from the world of politics. While her husband taught, she pursued an advanced degree in Asian studies and cared for the couple's two children. Then one day a call came: her mother had suffered a stroke. She rushed to Rangoon, and just happened to be there when the people took to the streets. Suu Kyi emerged as the popular leader of the uprising, and her life, as well as that of her country, changed forever.

The military faced the protesters with bullets. Soldiers fired into crowds, killing thousands. When journalists tried to report the events, they found telephone lines cut. After two months of relentless anti-government protests, a new military regime took over, promising to hold power temporarily and to promptly hold elections to choose a new government.

The Junta, known as the State Law and Order Restoration Council, or SLORC, stalled on elections. It placed Suu Kyi under house arrest and gave up on Burma's Communist revolution. It also changed the names of the country and of several cities, labeling the old names legacies of colonialism. Burma became Myanmar, Rangoon became Yangon.

By 1990, the SLORC thought it had regained the support of the population, and allowed elections to proceed. The military profoundly misjudged the depth of the people's hatred for the Junta, as well as the popularity of Suu Kyi and her National League for Democracy (NLD).

The 1990 vote gave the NLD more than 80 percent of the seats in parliament. The Junta simply refused to accept the results.

The turmoil in Burma came at a time of cataclysmic change in the world as a whole. The world didn't pay very much attention. In fact, a superficial glance at events in Rangoon might have indicated another victory for the West; another defeat for the Communist revolution.

But Suu Kyi and Myanmar's plight gradually drew the world's attention, despite efforts by the military to cut off the country from the rest of the world. Six years after being placed under house arrest, Suu Kyi was freed in 1995. By then she had become an international celebrity. She had won the Nobel Peace Prize in 1991, bringing a great deal of attention to her cause and placing greater international pressure on authorities.

When the military decided to free her, four years after the Nobel Prize, it thought Suu Kyi had been relegated to an unimportant place in the Burmese people's lives. But again the government had miscalculated. Suu Kyi's popularity was undiminished.

The SLORC renamed itself a more benevolent-sounding State Peace and Development Committee. It was the same regime, one of the most vicious and repressive on the planet, with economic policies that brought disaster. A network of informers, believed by some to include one in ten households, managed to keep everyone in fear. The authorities forced entire villages to move with almost no notice, to keep the population off balance. Crimes now punishable by long prison terms in tightly isolated Myanmar include sending unauthorized emails, owning a fax machine without authorization from the government, gathering with more than four people, and welcoming a foreigner into one's home. The military routinely uses forced (unpaid) labor by hundreds of thousands of Burmese, particularly ethnic minorities, to carry out some of the most grueling tasks. Those refusing to work, or to bribe soldiers to avoid the labor gangs are often shot.

Some ethnic minorities are still actively fighting the central government with small resistance armies. That singles out members of those groups for the harshest punishments, with homes and villages routinely set on fire by soldiers, and residents, by their own accounts, enduring rape, torture and, one of the most feared practices, forced to walk on minefields.

After once being one of the more prosperous nations in Asia, Myanmar is one of the poorest countries in the world. Barely any health care or education is offered for children, as the nation's budget is devoted increasingly to military expenditures. Malnutrition and homelessness are rampant, and most of the population barely manages to survive on less than one dollar a day. At the same time, some military chiefs have grown rich, and the armed forces have doubled in size.

The world has responded to the tyrants, but with little vigor. In 1992, the European Union withdrew some of its diplomatic personnel and suspended non-humanitarian aid, but trade continued, despite protests by activists urging a full embargo against the regime, an embargo supported by Suu Kyi.

Sanctions were strengthened in 1997, when the United States imposed its own embargo on new investments in Myanmar. Europe approved a non-binding resolution urging EU members not to trade with the regime. The same year, Asian nations welcomed Myanmar's government into the regional South East Asian association, ASEAN.

Aung San Suu Kyi remains an icon of her people, even though the reality is that her movement has so far achieved little, if anything, for them. Perhaps her greatest contribution is helping keep Myanmar's plight in the consciousness of the rest of the world, and providing a measure of hope, however distant, to the people of her country. An exiled Burmese woman tells the story of her elderly mother who succumbed to Alzheimer's disease late in life. Towards the end, her mother couldn't recognize her, her own child. But she still asked about Suu Kyi, whose name she remembered well.

In the decade since the election, Beijing became the generals' number one friend. China provided weapons to Myanmar and intensified trade with its neighbor. In exchange, the friendship with the Junta gave China strategic access to the Indian Ocean.

Even though Western leaders have made calls for democracy in Myanmar, at no time has military intervention received serious consideration. No matter how despicable the regime, no matter how hated by its people, the world does not consider the national interest, even on humanitarian grounds, to warrant the risk.

The risk, besides the obvious possibility of loss of life, involves challenging China, just as during the Cold War the U.S. and NATO where held in check by fear of drawing in the Soviets. The new world order has China as a restraint for Western action. And it isn't only the fear of military confrontation that pre-empts intervention. China's most powerful weapon today is its enormous economy. The national interest, far above the protection of human rights and democracy, is the protection of economic concerns. China's economy is as powerful as a nuclear arsenal in guiding U.S. and European foreign policy.

The Woman Who Would Bring Democracy
(Aug. 2000)

(Yangon) The taxi driver was suddenly refusing to accept the fare we had agreed on. I would pay 400 kyat to University Road. That was our deal. But, as we approached the area, I told him my exact destination: I wanted to go to Aung San Suu Kyi's house. Visibly frightened, he looked at me in the rear view mirror, pulled over to a side street, and stopped the car. "I can't go there," he said in broken English, "big problem for me." Then he pulled his umbrella from under the seat. "It's starting to rain. Take it." I declined, and reached over with the 400 kyat, trying to pay. "No," he said, "No pay. Please take my umbrella. You go see our leader. No charge."

A few weeks later, Aung San Suu Kyi left her home with 14 members of her National League for Democracy (NLLD) party, and headed for a meeting outside the capital, Yangon. Their journey came to an abrupt stop when uniformed men blocked their way. The air was let out of her tires and a nine-day test of wills ensued. The group camped by the side of the road in sweltering heat, refusing to give up their efforts. The military finally took them back by force to Yangon. The party leaders — including Suu Kyi — were taken to their homes, locked up and placed under heavy guard. NLD offices were ransacked, and what is perhaps the final crackdown on Myanmar's efforts at democracy was set in motion.

For the impoverished and frightened people of Myanmar, and for the international community who supports them, the critical time has arrived. What strategy, if any, will allow Myanmar — the once prosperous land known before military rule as Burma — to join the world in the global march to open, responsible government?

In a country where millions live in the military's two-handed strangling grip of wretched poverty and vicious repression, Suu Kyi, the leader of Myanmar's democracy movement, and winner of the 1991 Nobel Peace Prize, is a figure of hope — fading hope. She is revered by malnourished mothers sleeping under bridges with their emaciated babies, by taxi drivers eking out a living in cities with stagnant economies, and by students kept by the military from attending classes and forging a better future.

But Suu Kyi, the winner of a landslide election victory in 1990, has spent most of the time since winning the election living under house arrest or confined to such restrictions by the ruling military junta as to have virtually no possibility of affecting her country's future. Ten years after her electoral victory, life could hardly be more painful for the people of the legendary land of towering teak forests.

The taxi, by the way, left me a few blocks from Suu Kyi's home. I walked until I reached a military roadblock. After a low-key discussion with a soldier and an officer in plain clothes, it was made clear I would not be allowed to walk down the wide thoroughfare in front of the deserted university. No explanation given. Yangon's traffic is completely disrupted to keep it from passing in front of the 55 year-old-woman's home.

After the nine-day standoff, nobody was allowed in Suu Kyi's home. Not diplomats, not supporters, not servants. Food was passed to her over the padlocked gate, allowing for some sustenance. That's more than can be said of the pro-democracy movement.

A leading member of the military junta has vowed to "crush" the party.

Demands by diplomats to see Suu Kyi and other NLD leaders were futile. The junta dismissed calls by Bill Clinton, Tony Blair, and other world figures for their release. Officially known as the State Peace and Development Council, the ruling military conclave maintains its rule is needed to keep the peace and maintain the nation united in the face of ethnic divisions. The government accuses the NLD of planning terrorist activities, and insists the matter with Suu Kyi and her party is an internal affair. The international community, it says, should stay out of it.

Internal affairs in Burma are resolved through intimidation, incarceration and worse. The junta routinely uses the population, especially members of tribes seeking independence, as slave labor for unpaid road construction and other grueling projects. People who resist the brutal forced labor are routinely shot. Gross violations of human rights are commonplace. Freedom of the press is such an alien concept in Myanmar that the local version of newspapers and television news could easily pass for comedy in the West.

The streets are filled with billboards describing what the government audaciously calls "People's Desires," a litany of government objectives aimed at maintaining the Junta's tight leash on society. Among the so-called People's Desires: "Oppose those trying to jeopardize stability of the State and progress of the nation; "Crush all internal and external destructive elements as the common enemy." It is clear that such "destructive elements" include Suu Kyi, who is regularly referred to in the press as a prostitute, a stooge of the West and a number of other disparaging labels.

In 1997, the United States imposed a ban on new trade with the country. But the same year, Asian countries welcomed Yangon into the regional South East Asian association, ASEAN, sending conflicting messages to the Junta. The European Parliament has urged EU members to refrain from trading with the generals and Suu Kyi has urged foreigners to stay away from Burma, to keep their money from flowing into the coffers of the supremely corrupt military regime.

All international and domestic efforts to persuade the military to negotiate with the winners of the 1990 election have proved either useless or counter-productive. Life for the people of Myanmar has descended from purgatory to hell.

In frustration, some former allies of Suu Kyi have called for an end to the sanctions, hoping an increase in trade will bring a trickle of money for the impoverished Burmese.

And yet, it's hard to see exactly which strategy has failed. Is it the isolation brought by countries like the U.S., or is it the engagement policy of Myanmar's neighbors?

The key to the destruction of Myanmar and the survival of its military's power may be found in Beijing and in South East Asia. China has supported and armed the junta, providing it with the resources to keep the people under its heel. The influence of Asia neighbors carries the moral authority of cultural understanding. According to the SPDC, all criticism of the regime is based on the colonial aspirations of the West. Incidentally, neither China nor India — the other Asian power aiming to gain ascendancy in Myanmar — made any open complaints about the junta's recent displays of despotism.

Isolation by the West will accomplish nothing without pressure on China, the behemoth of human rights violations. Beijing may not want to relent on its atrocities against Tibet or against religious minorities in China, but it might consider interceding for a political solution in Burma, as a concession to Western powers continually harping on human rights.

Whether economic sanctions are effective or not, one thing is clear. Sanctions followed by silence achieve nothing. If the United States and Europe want change in Myanmar, simple economic isolation is not sufficient. The generals urgently need hard currency to keep their country from a total economic collapse. They should know that any possibility of trade or assistance will not come without political change. Show them a carrot and remind them of the stick. The United States, with the exception of the last couple of weeks, has been much too silent on the tragedy of the Burmese people.

For the people of Myanmar, options appear to be running out. Suu Kyi's latest effort achieved success on the international front. Major world figures chose to shine a spotlight on her plight. But within her country's borders, the situation is now even more critical. For the people of Myanmar, the struggle may be reduced to a simple desperate gesture: not charging taxi fare to a foreigner hoping to visit Aung San Suu Kyi.

The world's timid reaction to the tyrants of Yangon resembles its all-words, little-action approach to China's wholesale destruction of Tibet's culture. Were it not for the star-status achieved by the Dalai Lama, another Nobel Peace Prize recipient, Tibet would be in the same category as other Chinese regions struggling to survive.

Still, for all the spiritual force of the Tibetans' political arguments, and for all the financial clout of Tibet's supporters in Hollywood and in academia, the Himalayan nation's plight remains one where reasons for optimism are as ethereal as a Buddhist chant. World leaders routinely chastise Beijing for its actions on Tibet, and Beijing routinely ignores the charges as politically motivated. In the meantime, the conquest of Tibet moves forward at a speed never before seen in the Himalayas.

Beijing's successful efforts to bring a mass migration of ethnic Han Chinese to the Tibetan Plateau, along with the plan to construct a railroad from Beijing to Lhasa, look like the pincers of a brilliant, if tragic, strategy to bring cultural genocide to that ancient land.

As for the rest of the world, the chances that it will take significant action on the issue of Tibet are somewhere between remote and nonexistent. The value of Tibet to the West, or even the value of the principles at stake there, have been deemed insufficient to justify the risk of staring down the country that in the new millennium appears to be the most powerful rival to the U.S. and its allies in the Western hemisphere.

Spirit Soars, Heart Breaks in Today's Tibet
(July 2000)

(Lhasa, Tibet) Barkhor Square bustles with pilgrims on this cool summer morning. You can make out the hum of mantras recited by devout Tibetans as they make the route around their land's holiest shrine, the Jokhang Monastery at the center of this capital. People of all ages walk as if in a trance, spinning their prayer wheels, making the prescribed clockwise route and prostrating themselves in deep prayer. Inside the gates, pilgrims, monks, and tourists mix under the watchful eye of Chinese men in uniform.

This city on the world's highest plateau — some 12,000 feet above sea level — is breathtaking in every sense of the word. Is it the thin air, the majestic mountains, or Tibet's spiritual power that makes you gasp at every turn? Or perhaps it's the air of intimidation and the inescapable feeling that this is an invaded land that casts a pall on one of the world's most enigmatic places. Tibet can make your spirits soar and your heart break all in the same breath.

Since China invaded Tibet in 1950, Tibetans have experienced repression in many forms. Today, there's an element of subtlety in Beijing's tight control of what it calls the Tibet Autonomous Region. The Chinese have discovered that Tibet has the potential to become a tourist goldmine. Sleek brochures for foreigners advertise the great benefits of China's administration. A public relations effort is in full swing.

The original goal of retaining Tibet for its strategic value and its mineral reserves are paramount. But now Chinese brutality comes with a smile for the out-of-towner.

Reports of abuse and outright torture of Tibetans by the Chinese are frequent, and the degree of intimidation is plain to see. Tibetans are terrified to speak openly, constantly looking over their shoulders, not only for Chinese, but also for Tibetan spies in their midst.

"These are dangerous times. Very dangerous," whispers a Tibetan man. But before he can elaborate, a boyish looking Chinese soldier in a wrinkled, ill-fitting uniform materializes out of nowhere. We go back to discussing local cuisine.

Without a doubt, the most visible sign of Beijing's hand in today's Tibet is what is happening to the population mix. Tibetans may just be the gentlest people on earth, quick to offer the broadest of smiles, eager to befriend someone they just met. Their unique culture and profound Buddhist faith are at the center of their lives. But now they are drowning in a sea of Chinese immigration, as China works to build unbreakable demographic ties between Tibet and the Chinese "Motherland."

Already Tibetans have become a minority in their own land. Beijing claims 95 percent of the population of Tibet is made up of native ethnic Tibetans, but you don't need to take a census to see that that is plainly not true. Lhasa is awash in Han Chinese. The Dalai Lama, Tibet's leader-in-exile, says Tibetans now make up 44 percent of the population. In Lhasa, some Tibetans claim the ratio is now only one Tibetan for every seven Chinese. Tibet observers say this ancient culture, shielded from the world for generations, could disappear in a generation or two.

Still, China now exercises some restraint. Tourists will not cross the Himalayas to reach yet another modern Chinese city. The authorities are promoting Tibet's cultural heritage and allowing a degree of religious freedom. China may just allow enough of the real Tibet to survive to create a sort of Tibetan Buddhist Disneyland in the Himalayas. Religious freedom, though, is far from a reality. Pictures of the Dalai Lama are strictly forbidden. The 14th Dalai Lama, now leading a government in exile in Darhamsala, India, is a god to Tibetans. Their faces overflow with emotion when they see one of the outlawed photos of the man they believe to be the embodiment of compassion.

China accuses the Dalai Lama of working only to regain power and to line his own pockets. Monks in Tibet, who find it more and more difficult to continue their studies, are forced to repudiate the Dalai Lama. They tell of monastery searches of their meager personal belongings by Chinese officials who confiscate the banned pictures along with anything that might hint of Tibetan nationalism.

The Chinese maintain they are trying to bring progress to a backward land.

Today's Lhasa shows some jarring signs of development, along with some much-needed public works projects financed by China.

Traditional sun-baked brick and mud Tibetan homes display colorful prayer flags fluttering in the wind, carefully positioned to release prayers as the mountain wind blows through them. But Tibetan architecture is gradually being replaced, as many neighborhoods are destroyed to make way for modernization. Huge construction cranes, tipped with the red Chinese flag, stack tall buildings throughout Lhasa. Even neon signs are making an appearance.

Internet connections can be found all over town, although you could spend seven years in Tibet waiting for a usable line. The information super-highway has some unique traffic rules here. At the Internet room in a local hotel, a sign on the wall reads "Do not use Internet for political or any other unintelligent purposes."

Lhasa is being pushed into the 21st century, China-style. Beijing maintains it "liberated" Tibet, which it says is historically part of the Chinese mainland. But the Tibetans never asked to be liberated, and many scholars dispute Chinese assertions on Tibet's history.

A compromise between Tibet and Beijing, ironically, does not seem out of reach. The Dalai Lama says he is not asking for full independence, and he worries about the extinction of his people. As China curates Tibet into a museum piece, it too has little to gain by completely doing away with the people of the land it conquered. And yet, China has virtually nothing to gain by compromising with the powerless Tibetans.

In this age of global trade and economic integration, the world values trade with China above the matter of freedom for a few million people living where the air is thin. The world has made it easy for China to destroy Tibet.

In the meantime, the faith of the Tibetan people somehow endures in the face of cultural genocide. Perhaps it's something about living on the Roof of the World, several thousand feet closer to heaven than the rest of us. As they do most days, they make one more pilgrimage around the monastery, and say one more prayer for freedom, and for the successful return of their beloved Dalai Lama. So far, it hasn't worked.

The New Emperor of the World, Anointed

With the Soviet Threat out of the way, America declared itself the winner of the Cold War. It was a time of jubilation among conservatives, who promptly credited Ronald Reagan's policy with at long last defeating the "Evil Empire." The arms race, they said, had broken the Russians. Others maintained the Soviet system had collapsed as a result of its own ineptness. Communism, they declared, was simply not a viable structure for an economy. It just didn't work.

For critics of the right, the hundreds of billions of dollars spent on the arms race had proven a colossal waste. They pointed an accusing finger at the CIA for not realizing that the Soviet empire was crumbling from within. The USSR, they said, would have collapsed without the need for the U.S. to engage in an arms race that left the country with a national debt so large that most calculators didn't have enough digits to display it in all its grandeur.

Whatever the reason for the Soviets' calamitous exit from their superpower role on the world stage, the United States now had top billing, all by itself. It was a fact not lost on Washington, and not lost on the rest of the world. American politicians of all persuasions spoke proudly, with a tone that would quickly develop into arrogance.

Scholars called American power "hegemonic," meaning dominant and unrivaled. It was a term that would be used by adversaries as a corrosive solution, undermining American actions and bringing its intentions under suspicion.

Nobody, in the U.S. or anywhere else, was altogether sure what the new order meant. As the U.S. struggled with defining its own identity, perception of America beyond its borders took some unexpected turns. Europe, in particular, now feeling much less dependent on American protection against an outside threat, worked to reshape itself. It did it, to a large degree, in the image of America. As European states worked to integrate into a more cohesive European Union, the United States of America became a model for both what they wanted and what they did not want to become.

European views of what the U.S. was becoming in the new era were often sharply at odds with what the U.S. thought of itself.

The American economy entered an unprecedented period of prosperity, its economy became the one to emulate, but its values became a matter of debate.

In the early days of the post-Cold War era, the American economy was in a slump, and there was some doubt that the U.S. would continue its rise to preeminence. But the trend towards a global economy, coupled with unprecedented technological advances and the unexpected strength of the U.S. economy, demonstrated in short order that America's leadership position would remain unchallenged. It became apparent that many crises around the world went unresolved until the U.S. intervened. America unhumbly proclaimed itself the "Indispensable Nation."

On August 1996, Bill Clinton, speaking to relatives of the victims of the bombed Pan Am flight 103 at George Washington University, described America's role in the modern world, calling the U.S. the Indispensable Nation. Secretary of State Warren Christopher had used the same words only days earlier, in testimony before the U.S. Senate. By the time Secretary of State Madeleine Albright uttered the term in public, the emotional content of the label had been completely transformed, and the expression became inextricably linked to her.

What began as a statement of responsibility and commitment

somehow became a declaration of hubris that sent shivers of worry down the spines of world leaders. It worked its way around the globe to a public eager to find justification for a growing resentment of a disturbingly influential and successful America.

In his speech at George Washington, Bill Clinton was telling the victims (and perpetrators) of terrorism that the U.S. would take action to prevent and punish terrorist violence. "The fact is, America remains the indispensable nation," he said. "There are times when America, and only America, can make a difference between war and peace, between freedom and repression, between hope and fear. Of course, we can't take on all the world's burdens. We cannot become its policeman. But where our interests and values demand it and where we can make a difference, America must act and lead."

The policy had an altruistic bent. It was a new era filled with promise and the United States, standing at the crossroads of history, would make sure that the promise became a reality for all: "The worldwide changes in how people work, live, and relate to each other," Clinton explained, "are the fastest and perhaps the most profound in history. Most of these changes are good: the Cold War is over; our country is at peace. Our economy is strong. Democracy and free markets are taking root on every continent."

The U.S. would be a powerful force for good, the Superhero of the new world, upholding universal values for the sake of humanity. Washington thought everyone would welcome the new America in its altruistic role.

In December 1996, Bill Clinton nominated Madeleine Albright to become the first female Secretary of State, probably the most powerful woman in the world. He was choosing someone who had a passionate faith in the importance of the U.S., much as he did. In announcing his selection of Albright and of Bill Cohen for Secretary of Defense, Clinton declared the new team would "make sure that. . . America remains the indispensable nation — the world's greatest force for peace." But in her post at the State Department, Albright described the new American role in a way that raised hackles around the globe.

Albright had become something of a celebrity, as a combined result of the attention received for being the first female Secretary of

State, intensified by the startling discovery that, although she had been raised as a Catholic, she was born Jewish in a family where many perished in the holocaust. With media attention at its height and the world focusing on her profoundly interesting story, Albright described the role of the United States in the world in a way that sounded more menacing than altruistic. Explaining the U.S. threat to bomb Iraq, she said, "If we have to use force, it is because we are America. We are the indispensable nation. We stand tall. We see further into the future."

The same feather-ruffling mode was used by President Clinton when he engaged in a spree of self-congratulatory pontification at the 1997 G-7 Economic Summit in Denver, boastfully telling the major industrialized nations about the spectacular prowess of the American economy, a model for all to emulate. Clinton's triumphal description of America's role was not limited to economic issues. On one occasion he boasted of American leadership "from Prague to Port-au-Prince. . . from Kuwait to Sarajevo. . ."

America's two top foreign policy executives, the President and the Secretary of State, had become the country's P.R. agents. The world cringed as the American public puffed up its chest.

A *Chicago Tribune* series entitled "Alone at the Top: Foreign Policy in a New World" began: "The word is *hegemon. Get* used to it. It means Numero Uno, Mr. Big, the 800-pound gorilla. If you're an American, it means you." The gloating came from the left and from the right. It spread through the United States like an unstoppable virus. *The New Republic* had caught it, just as publications on the other end of the political spectrum had. The way they explained it, "Our labor markets, once considered chaotic, are now celebrated for their flexibility. Our capital markets, once denounced as citadels of greed, are now hailed for their transparency. Our culture, once derided as compassionless, is now recognized as a vital crucible of individual creativity."

The Emperor without Clothes

Around the world, reaction was less sanguine. An Australian publication, for example, talked about the American "ego trip," saying, "To anyone with a sense of history, this is all deeply worrying. If pride goeth

188

before a fall, the United States has one heck of a comeuppance in store."

Americans were convinced the 20th century had been theirs, and so would the 21st. And this, they believed, was good for the world. The world, on the other hand, wasn't sure it wanted to be saved by America. In fact, where Americans saw a model society, many outside the U.S. saw a deeply flawed one.

There was reason for Americans, especially the left-leaning ones, to feel optimistic about the country's new role on the international arena. For decades, during the Cold War, the U.S. had amassed a shameful record of supporting tyrants around the world, in the name of holding back the spread of communism. The United States had supported and armed dictators in Latin America and Africa. It had given aid to vicious regimes, and it had used the services of men it knew to be vicious criminals, all with an overarching foreign policy goal that in the end had succeeded. Communist revolution was dead.

For Americans on the political right, the triumph of the free market ideal around the world was vindication of their long-held beliefs. The political left also saw its credo affirmed in the nation's new role in world affairs. Now America could get on with using its extraordinary might in defense of human rights, democracy and the search for prosperity, values that, according to Washington, were now shared by everyone. A foreign policy for the Age of Aquarius was upon us. Deputy Secretary of State Strobe Talbott proclaimed, "American foreign policy is consciously intended to advance universal values."

Who could argue with America's reverence for life, liberty and the pursuit of happiness?

As it turns out, American values didn't always draw admiration.

It was true that in many Third World countries the U.S. was seen as a much more benevolent power. On university campuses, where during the Cold War walls used to be covered with graffiti demonizing "Yankee imperialists," the rhetoric became comparatively conciliatory. Bill Clinton enjoyed warm, even exuberant receptions during his trips to India, Africa and Latin America, in sharp contrast with previous U.S. presidents whose motorcades had been attacked by anti-American mobs.

Still, anti-American sentiment had not disappeared. The more the

U.S. exerted its influence and proclaimed its invincibility, the more the resentment grew. By the end of the 1990s, the European view of the United States was being cemented. The caricatured Ugly American was alive and well and living in France.

Parisian bookstores started serving a wide buffet of tomes dedicated to disparaging America and Americans. Opinion polls in Europe, but especially in France, showed growing disdain for the United States in its new role. For Americans, learning about the low esteem in which Europeans held them would have been shocking. They were spared the shock, however, because most Americans had little interest in what went outside their nations borders.

In France, a book like Noel Mamere's *No, Thanks, Uncle Sam* made the case for what the author and many of his compatriots saw as eminently justified disdain for post-Cold War America. Mamere described the United States as a callous nation where millions went homeless and without proper health care, a place where racism was rampant and citizens by the millions carried weapons. But nothing raised contempt for America more than the death penalty. In his view, the time was ripe to be "downright anti-American."

The French Foreign Minister, Hubert Vedrine, described the United States as a threatening force. He said the term "superpower" no longer applies. Rather, he said, the U.S. should be seen as a hyper-power, one whose dominance reaches to every sphere, and one that — in the absence of another major power — must urgently be counter-balanced.

Anti-Americanism was not just a French phenomenon. Throughout Europe, anti-American sentiment seemed to develop out of a deep skepticism about Washington's motives in its foreign and trade policies. The country's motives were viewed with suspicion, in large part because as the remaining super-power, the United States appeared ominously dominant on the world stage. America's vaunted efforts to help bring democracy and free markets to the rest of the world were seen by many as a cynical ploy to bring new markets and cheap labor for American companies.

When George W. Bush emerged as the new president after the surreal election debacle of the year 2000, many around the world who had complained about what they saw as America's heavy-handedness in world affairs suddenly felt nostalgic for the days of the Indispensable Nation. The new administration seemed much less interested in taking on the problems of the world as its own. In the Middle East, leaders clamored for American help in bringing back a peace process that once offered so much promise. Environmental activists, along with many European leaders, despaired of Washington's go-it-alone approach to global warming and a host of international issues. It was becoming clearer and clearer that, in a growing number of issues, America's absence made real progress impossible.

Even before the new administration came to office, while in the United States the people congratulated themselves for their exemplary democracy and enviable freedoms, much of the industrialized world already looked at America as a land whose economy might offer much to replicate, but whose treatment of the poor and the weak deserved contempt. More than the "Land of the Free and Home of the Brave," Europeans saw in American the land of the homeless and the home of the greedy.

The system that allowed tens of millions to go without health insurance, and often forced the elderly to choose between buying medication or food, was a wide-open target for criticism.

To be sure, the views reflected a great deal of bitterness at the loss of European influence in the world. Even as Europe unified and tried raising its profile on the global arena, it was clear that, in many areas, only the United States could make things happen. And that was a source of humiliation

The Field of Killings

While American diplomats spoke of democracy and human rights, international human rights groups deplored the widely supported use of the death penalty in the U.S. The practice, viewed as barbaric in much of the world, became a focus of anti-Americanism in Europe, where abolition of capital punishment became a requirement for admission into the European Union.

Europeans ardently criticized some of the most disturbing aspects of capital punishment, American style. Executions of minors, of the mentally retarded, along with statistics showing that blacks faced the death penalty much more frequently than whites and that almost nobody was ever sentenced to death for killing a black person, outraged millions, throwing fuel to their smoldering suspicions about the U.S.

While scores of countries abolished capital punishment, the United States held thousands on death row and showed no sign of shying away from executions despite a growing number of cases where people sentenced to death were exonerated by DNA evidence found through the efforts of non-profit organizations.

As the death penalty steadily lost support around the world, the United States executed more and more prisoners. At the same time, critics pointed out, many of the countries where executions still took place were the same ones regularly chastised by the U.S. as human rights violators, countries like China — executing more of its own people than all other countries — along with Iran, Iraq, the Democratic Republic of Congo, and Saudi Arabia.

Still, two in three Americans expressed support for capital punishment. As a result, virtually every candidate for president found it politically indispensable to say he too supported the death penalty.

When Michael Dukakis, the Democratic candidate in 1988 said he opposed it, he handed Republicans a major weapon. Dukakis was repeatedly portrayed as soft on crime by the Bush campaign, helping bring George Bush to the White House by a landslide.

The son of the man who beat Dukakis wore his support for capital punishment as a badge of honor. As governor of Texas, George W. Bush lead the state with the busiest death row in the country, executing more than 150 prisoners in the year 2000. Europeans were appalled. A former French minister of Justice, Robert Badinter, called him "a horrible symbol of [the U.S.] mania for the death penalty."

The European Convention on Human Rights, signed by 34 countries, banned capital punishment, classifying it on a par with torture and genocide. For many in Europe, George W. Bush represented one of the most reprehensible aspects of American civilization. The executions that became routine in Texas and garnered little media coverage in the U.S., drew enormous attention in Europe. As in America, politicians in Europe learned to exploit sentiments on capital punishment for political gain. In preparation for a run as a mayor of Paris, Jack Lang traveled to Texas to visit death row inmate Odell Barnes. A similar trip was carried out by a member of the German parliament, in advance of an execution of two men born in Germany who became causes célèbres in Europe.

In Italy, the Colosseum (where capital punishment took on the most gruesome traits during the Roman Empire), became a symbol of opposition to the death penalty. Every time a death sentence was commuted in the U.S., the ancient structure was bathed in bright lights. The city of Rome also became a focus of Europe's view of America's grotesque appetite for capital punishment when the clothing retailer chain Benetton started one of its trademark ad campaigns with a controversial display of photographs on the city's billboards.

Benetton showed enormous pictures of people on death row in the U.S., in an effort to humanize them. The campaign was pulled after angry complaints from the victims of the men on the billboards. At one point, before the ads were pulled, a human rights activist defended the campaign, explaining that no killer on death row had a hand in as many deaths as George W. Bush did as Governor of Texas.

Italy was the home of the first European government to abolish the death penalty: the Grand Duchy of Tuscany, which ended the practice in 1786. Capital punishment was outlawed in the entire country in 1899, and reinstated only for a few years under the Fascist dictatorship.

While Europeans writhed with revulsion, signing petitions and bringing up the subject in high level meetings (much as the U.S. does in meetings with Chinese officials), Americans seemed to pay little attention to the occasionally bizarre events in the world of capital punishment.

Of all the absurd moments in the annals of crime and punishment, few could surpass the case of Robert Brecheen, the man who would try anything to keep the state from taking his life. In 1995, Brecheen managed to set off a preposterous race of life and death — simultaneously — as the medical establishment and the criminal justice system contorted to comply with rules and principles to save his life, just so they could kill him.

To Save or to Kill:
The Twisted Tale of Life and Death for an Oklahoma Killer
(August 1995)

(Oklahoma City) The scene at Oklahoma's death row was one of mayhem on the night Robert Brecheen committed his last crime: he attempted to rob the State of his own execution. Brecheen's execution was scheduled for midnight, in accordance with the grizzly traditions of government-mandated death. But before the State could put the convicted killer to death, it had to save his life.

The death-row inmate almost threw the Oklahoma's neatly scheduled plans into total disarray by attempting suicide only hours before his execution. The State had to revive him before it could kill him, much like the nurse who wakes you up to give you a sleeping pill — a scene so tragically absurd, you couldn't hold back a remorseful laugh. Gary Larson's "The Far Side" couldn't have come up with a more baffling twist of logic.

The peculiar incident in Oklahoma points to another weak link in capital punishment, the weak link that gives us execution delays lasting decades, and rulings where confessed killers are not sentenced to die. The weakness is plain: we're simply not comfortable with killing people.

Near 8 P.M., Brecheen heard that one of his final appeals was denied. At 9 o'clock a prison officer came to wake him for his last shower — presumably one of the niceties of Hotel Death Row for victims in their last hours. But the guard could not wake up the prisoner. Brecheen had tried to kill himself. That would not do. The system kicked into high gear to save the man's life. Brecheen had an appointment for midnight, and he had to remain fully alert for the Big Moment. Unable to revive him in prison, officials rushed an ambulance to the scene. Paramedics there to save the inexorably-dying man were greeted with a cacophony of shouts from residents of death row at the Oklahoma State Penitentiary.

The incident came on the same day the government announced its indictments against the accused perpetrators of the Oklahoma City bombing, Timothy McVeigh and Terry Nichols.

Perhaps the day's elaborate recollection of the killing of 168 people on April 19 made it easier for those who work in Oklahoma's capital-punishment system to proceed with confidence, even in the face of unexpected developments in the execution of a man who had been called a model inmate. Brecheen, sentenced to death for the murder of 59-year-old Marie Stubbs, had helped nurse other ailing inmates and mediated in prison disputes, helping keep the peace in the explosive environment of condemned men. His appeals enjoyed the unprecedented support of prison staff who even testified in his behalf during clemency hearings.

Yet, with Brecheen's appeals exhausted, the machinery of death had to find a way to continue grinding. The system bans the execution of inmates who are mentally incompetent. The executed must understand what is happening to him. So Brecheen had to regain full use of his senses before he satisfied the requirements for execution.

At about 9:30, while traveling in the ambulance, the convicted killer regained consciousness. When he arrived at the hospital, doctors did what doctors do in normal cases. They worked to make their patient well. But this was not a normal case. Brecheen had to be made well so he could be killed. Doctors pumped his stomach, checked his vital signs, presumably asked him — with concern for his well-being — how he was feeling. Once he was out of danger, he could resume his busy schedule. By 1:55 am — just two hours later than planned — Robert Brecheen was declared dead of a lethal injection. The prison warden told reporters that the execution went "smoothly." Some witnesses, however, complained that Brecheen seemed disoriented. That he needed help to make it into the execution chamber. The law says that's no way to kill a man. Perhaps he wasn't quite well enough yet to die.

Officials say the prisoner had taken an overdose of tranquilizers. No one is really sure why. Doctors agreed that Brecheen was depressed. No kidding. So depressed he wanted to die a few hours early? Some say he wanted to postpone the execution. Others wonder if this was his way of thumbing his nose at the system. It's not clear what he achieved. The tortuous evening only made the hours more painful for Brecheen's family, and for the family of his victim. The Stubbs family wanted to see him die. They wanted this over.

Something about the events of the evening of August 10 is incongruous. But what exactly is it? Should Brecheen have been allowed to die at his own hand? Should guards have picked him up, taken him to the infirmary, and even given him another little push to the other side of life? Should doctors have taken him in and observed him, without trying to save him?

Every action taken by guards and paramedics and doctors, all of them taken individually, seem reasonable. Every action they took fits in with our principles and our values and our instincts. It is only the conclusion that doesn't belong. It is the killing that makes the evening surreal. Despite the nation's apparent fondness for killing our worst criminals, and regardless of the outrageous number of homicides regularly committed in this country, this is still a nation where killing is out of place. That's the reason for the disbelief; killing Brecheen after saving his life was absurd. Saving his life never was.

Love and Hate

Brecheen's case was not unique. Other death row inmates have attempted suicide, have been saved and later have been executed. In other cases, medical teams gave inmates treatment for heart conditions and other serious diseases, ensuring they'd be healthy enough to die. Every case was fodder for critics of capital punishment, particularly those in Europe.

For people in the U.S. who closely followed other people's views of America, European criticism didn't always seem imbued in principled morality. They pointed out that in some European countries, like Britain, for example, the death penalty enjoys widespread support. In Sweden many people also say they would support it. In America, meanwhile, a dozen states have already banned the practice and, in virtually all the others, the issue is at the center of a heated debate. Americans, they said, are not bloodthirsty brutes.

Whatever the criticism, there are aspects of American society that enthrall observes around the world. No country in the world, for instance, accords freedom of expression the same reverence the U.S. does. Against all human instincts, the American nation has learned to hold its nose and let all views be expressed, no matter how distasteful.

On the political and economic fronts, America truly is the land of opportunity. While it is clearly true that those born in positions of privilege are much more likely to succeed, the reality is also that in American more than anywhere in the world those who reach the pinnacles of power can come from the most unexpected places. The story of Bill Clinton, for instance, born after his father died, in a poor family in a poor state, is a telling one. The odds that the son of a Jamaican immigrant, like Colin Powell, would rise to the highest reaches of power, are greater in the United States than perhaps anywhere in the world.

And despite its profound difficulties with racial prejudice, the United States has become home to the most extraordinary population, with people born in every single nation of the world reaching its shores to make a new life. No matter how serious the criticism, a green card remains one of the most coveted pieces of paper in the world for millions who realize their best chance at a new life is in America. Perhaps nowhere in the world do immigrants have a better opportunity to start over and make a good life.

Homegrown Terrorism

After the end of the Cold War, Americans were aware of the great appeal their nation held for immigrants. They also knew that to radical groups in distant lands the U.S. remained the Great Satan. Terrorism had become one of the new troubles crossing the vanishing borders of the new world. That's why, when Americans faced the greatest single act of terrorism ever on U.S. soil, everyone immediately thought it was the work of Muslim fundamentalists.

The Oklahoma City bombing was a startling wake-up call for the United States. Not only was the target of the blast the American Government, but the perpetrators were Americans. The country discovered the so-called "Patriot Movement," a loose agglomeration of violent, extremist, anti-government activists. These fascist-leaning "patriots" believed the government had become too powerful. They tended to be white supremacists, and they were showing an increasing willingness to go to destructive extremes to sow mistrust in the government.

Timothy McVeigh, a disillusioned veteran of the Gulf War, with the assistance of his friend Terry Nichols, had built a massive bomb made up largely of fertilizer and diesel fuel. They had loaded the explosives into the back of a large moving truck. McVeigh had driven the bomb to Oklahoma City and parked it in front of the Alfred P. Murrah Federal Building. He wanted to avenge the actions of federal agents exactly two years earlier: on April 19, 1993, the Branch Davidian Complex in Waco, Texas had been stormed by federal agents, ending a standoff with David Koresh, the leader of a small religious cult, and killing 80 of Koresh's followers.

The bombing in Oklahoma City on April 19, 1995, showed a new face of evil to Americans. This time it wasn't the Evil Empire; it wasn't the Middle East. This time it was one of them. And this time, the threat had materialized into a heart-breaking reality.

Good and Evil in Oklahoma
(May 1995)

(Oklahoma City)   One of the most insidious occupational hazards faced by journalists is becoming jaded and cynical about human nature.

How can you look at cocky young men strutting their automatic weapons amid starving children in Somalia, without feeling a deep disappointment in humanity? How could you be untouched when you know they use their guns to steal relief supplies that would save lives? How can you witness cold-blooded killings over sometimes-petty political disagreements, without wondering whether the essence of people is good or evil? The capacity of human beings to bring sorrow to other human beings is plainly visible throughout the world in places like Bosnia, Rwanda or Haiti.

For many journalists rushing to Oklahoma City in the aftermath of the bombing, this seemed another bitter story of unnecessary suffering caused by the wretched, cruel side of human nature.

But something unexpected happened on the way to cynicism in Oklahoma City. Journalists could be seen crying. Maybe even more incredible, they did not quietly roll their eyes and scoff when they heard it said that some good would rise out of this terrible evil.

Somehow, the mightiest effort to harden, to keep one's composure, fails when you meet the families of the victims at any of the scores of funerals this city has seen in the last few days; the Coverdale boys, Aaron and Elijah, buried in the same casket, long, long before their time. At 5, and 2 years of age, Aaron and Elijah should be playing on an April afternoon, enjoying spring. Their grandmother should be smiling over them, feeling the special lightness of spirit that only children know how to bring. Instead, she watched their casket slowly lowered into the ground.

The haunting sounds of the grandmother calling over and over for "my babies. . ." was felt by all who were there. As the Coverdale boys were given a last good-bye, only a few dozen feet away another victim of the bombing was being laid to rest — Rona Chafey, 35.

And only a hundred feet away, flowers covered the grave of another couple of brothers buried the day before. The Smith boys, Colton and Chase, the two children of Edye Smith, also went to the daycare center at the Federal Building. Their mother had dropped off her boys for the day. Hugged them and walked away. Less than five minutes later ,she heard the explosion and knew her children were dead.

Of course, the journalists cried.

Despite the searing sadness of the Oklahoma tragedy, there is another equally powerful side to what happened here, a positive side. It is the response of the people of Oklahoma and of the United States that has helped to sand down the rough edges of mistrust and disenchantment with humanity so many feel today.

Perhaps for the first time in any major news stories, journalists joined the protagonists of this story — the people of Oklahoma — when, as survivors of tragedies often do in their search for comfort and meaning, they insisted that much good would come out of this tragedy.

It would take a lot of good to even up the score with the immense sorrow inflicted by the terrorists of Oklahoma. But the bomb set off a chain reaction, maudlin as this may sound, of sheer goodness. The Oklahoma bombers achieved to a large degree exactly the opposite of what they wished.

Far from destroying a part of an anonymous government, they gave the government an opportunity to shine. They made us discover that the government is made of people, and they gave the government at many levels an opportunity to make us glad we have them.

A while back the voters of Oklahoma approved a tax increase to improve their fire and police services. The services performed brilliantly. The Federal government was impressive as well. Only moments after the blast, they were on the trail of the perpetrators and on the scene helping to coordinate the rescue efforts. The words of comfort and support and shared grief coming from the President, and from the Governor of Oklahoma, helped articulate what America felt. They helped the country grieve, and made it clear that this great loss reached far beyond the bounds of this city and state.

Michael Lenz, whose wife Carrie, 26, pregnant with their first child, died in the blast, told me that the knowledge that all of America was grieving with him brought him a great deal of comfort.

The reality is that often wishful thinking makes us believe there will be a silver lining, glowing after we wipe our tears. But look at Oklahoma. Look at the country. And look. For once, look closely at the hate-mongers that appear to be implicated in the bombing, and see America's response to what they did. This is not wishful thinking.

We have ignored white supremacists in America, because we refused to believe they were worth taking seriously. That neglect is now over. Their effort to divide the country along racial and even religious lines is corrosive, and its explosive. But the blast made those divisions seem trivial. Who even thought about race when the shattered survivors were being pulled out of the rubble? The children were children. People — as they always are — were all people.

The Coverdale boys were black; the Smith boys were white. People of all races attended their funerals.

Prejudice, hatred, greed, selfishness, they all seemed to vanish in Oklahoma. People everywhere wanted to know how they could help. They took vacation time to volunteer, doing anything at all, giving support to the rescuers on a scale that firefighters could scarcely comprehend. Businesses contributed whatever they could conceive would be useful. And nobody took to the streets in hatred. Instead, they all came out to support the suffering, encourage the helpful, and — with the greatest dignity — to repudiate the evil-doers. How could journalists not be changed?

Hamburgers, Dollars and Rock'n'Roll

As the new post-Cold War order evolved, the new, powerful America, with its enormous prosperity, astonishing technology, frightening violence, and a myriad of other often-contradictory traits evoked a reaction from the rest of the world that sometimes appeared schizophrenic. While the criticism was unrelenting, the fascination with all things American also seemed unstoppable. Clearly, an element of bitterness was at play.

Benjamin Franklin once said that everyone had two cultures, their own and France's. At the turn of the millennium, there was no culture in the world, disparaged as it might be, that had a wider and deeper reach across national boundaries than American culture. The United States, with its military, economic, and cultural reach, left far behind countries like France, Britain, and Spain, all of which at one time had enjoyed enormous international supremacy.

The way novelist Tom Wolfe described it, "[America] now dominates the world to an extent that would have made Alexander the Great, who thought there were no more worlds to conquer, get down on all fours and beat his fists on the ground in despair that he was merely a warrior and never heard of international mergers and acquisitions, rock and rap, fireball movies, TV, the NBA, the World Wide Web, and the 'globalization' game."

The rise of American power didn't seem assured when the Cold War came to an end. The U.S. treasury was plagued with debt, the economy was stagnant and Japan seemed poised to buy up America at fire sale prices and move ahead of everyone else. In 1989, Toronto's *Globe and Mail* drew the gloomy picture this way, "The colossus of the free world is dogged at home by social and economic problems, and increasingly it faces constraints on its ability to influence the world single-handed. . . ." "With only 5 per cent of the world's population, it consumes 50 per cent of the world's cocaine. . . ." "Deficits, drugs, a falling dollar, rising foreign investment, stagnant living standards and a continually widening gap between the rich and poor are the staples of the domestic news that bombards the country daily. . ."

Ten years later, there was no question which country had pulled ahead — way ahead — of everyone else. Canadian economist James Laxer, hardly a devotee of the U.S., declared, "The USA is the most powerful human creation of all time."

No matter how strong the criticism, the world, to a large degree, accepted America's ideas about what economic system should prevail. The world accepted American music, American food, American movies, American television, and American fashion, as its own.

American athletes became worldwide celebrities, and Hollywood's superstars drew crowds in all continents. Coke, Pepsi, Kodak, CNN, Levy's blue jeans, Pizza Hut, Madonna, McDonald's, Michael Jordan, Tiger Woods, all became part of the global culture of consumption lead by the United States.

To the profound dismay of French authorities, English became the universal language, flowing like a spilled bottle of Coca Cola, as the spread of technology and the Internet became unstoppable. Ironically, much of the technological advances originating in the U.S. came from immigrants. Drawn from around the world, and attracted to the wealthy and dynamic business environment, many of the most talented people from Europe and the developing world brought their talents and skills and helped fuel the boom. In many cases, the wealthy elites sent their children to school in the United States, forging links that would provide important political and commercial contacts in the future. American education, ridiculed in some European capitals, attracted people from every country in the world, exporting U.S. values to every continent.

In Taiwan, for example, virtually every member of President Chen's cabinet was educated in the U.S. The President of the Dominican Republic studied in the United States, as did the President of the Philippines, who went to school with Bill Clinton. Alberto Fujimori, of Peru, attended the University of Wisconsin. His successor, Alejandro Toledo, went to Stanford University in California, as did Marta Suplicy (of Brazil's Workers Party), who was elected Mayor of that country's biggest city, Sao Paolo. The deposed President of Ecuador, Jamil Mahuad, who made the U.S. dollar the legal currency of his country, went to Harvard. Kofi Annan had part of his education in the U.S., and at least one of the sons of President Jiang Zemin of China studied in the U.S., along with thousands of other Chinese (much to the consternation of national security experts). The list is practically endless.

At the height of U.S.-Libyan animosity over the bombing of a Pan Am flight over Lockerbie, Scotland, I was at the Libyan embassy in Cairo, picking up a Libyan entry visa with CNN's Cairo bureau chief Gayle Young. The Libyan official handling the matter cheerfully told us, as we discussed whether American forces would again bomb his country, that his son was attending school in California. I was struck by how much more America's enemies knew about the U.S. than vice versa.

Some 450,000 foreigners attend American universities each year. In some fields, a U.S. education is the norm even for Europeans. According to the National Science Foundation, 81 percent of French citizens holding the highest degrees are either entirely educated in the United States or finished their degrees in the United States.

In many countries, the wealthy elites who can afford it routinely send their children to school in the United States, forging ties that provide important political and commercial contacts in the future.

People outside the U.S. understand America and have a profound interest in it. America's domestic problems often become topics of conversation around the world. Even trivial matters, magnified by the ever-present media, take on international dimensions as the entire world keeps a close eye on the U.S.

If it is true that Americans aren't all that interested in the world, the world, it seems at times, simply can't get enough of the U.S., and, like neighborhood gossip in a global village, nothing appeals more than America's dirty laundry. And few cases aired the country's dirty laundry like the now-legendary O.J. Simpson trial did.

The case of O.J. Simpson, the retired football player and actor accused in 1994 of killing his wife Nicole and her friend Ron Goldman, exposed some of the country's dirtiest truths to the entire world. The trial revealed to people inside and outside of the United States some of the deepest flaws of America's legal system. It brought into sharp focus the stark differences in how law enforcement is perceived by different ethnic groups. Most white people, absolutely convinced of Simpson's guilt, were shocked to discover how many blacks found completely credible the argument that Simpson had fallen victim to racism in the Los Angeles police department.

The case, in a hint of what would occur years later during the Clinton-Lewinsky melodrama, made celebrities of scores of journalists, lawyers and family members. The intensity of the coverage was without precedent. During the many months of the O.J. Simpson trial, little else mattered in the world. For those of us in the field covering other stories, the coverage was an outrage, a source of enormous frustration, as important stories, including those we were risking our lives to cover, were pushed aside. (Christiane Amanpour, on assignment in Haiti, told me once, while we sat watching CNN in Haiti, "This is an atrocity — a crime against journalism!") Americans watched the trial breathlessly, and the rest of the world watched the trial and watched America. It was another opportunity to get caught up in an American story, and for many, a way to do it under the guise of analyzing America's flawed obsession with celebrity and its willingness to be manipulated by the media.

O.J. Abroad: Americans Under the Microscope
(Feb. 1995)

Do you remember where you were on the night that made the white Bronco famous?

I was in Port-au-Prince, Haiti, glued to the television along with a group of American journalists. The scene was surreal. Not the chase: the journalists.

In Haiti to cover a tragedy that affected millions and could bring the U.S. to war, we all sat mesmerized watching American television show us a lone vehicle pursued by a posse of police cars and a gaggle of helicopters.

We formed a semi-circle around the television. In the second row, quietly behind the rest of us, sat a Haitian security guard, also hypnotized. The man spoke no English. He had no idea who was being chased or why.

When we tried to explain what was happening, we realized he had never heard of the sport that made the subject of the chase famous. He had never heard of America's brand of football, much less of O.J. Simpson. Why was he watching? What was he watching?

I think he was watching us. The screen showed almost exactly the same thing for what must have seemed an eternity. Yet we kept watching.

Like the Haitian security guard, the people of the world are watching. They're watching us looking at O.J., and they find us fascinating.

The *Weekend Australian*, for example, carried a full page story titled "In for a Killing." The subtitle charged, "The Hyenas of American journalism are alive and well and howling on the steps of an L.A. courthouse." Not all foreign publications singled out the media. Some think we're all hyenas of a sort. The newspaper *El Tiempo*, from Colombia, published a learned essay on the "obsessive" and "hysterical" attention Americans pay to these scandals. The article talks about our attention to the Simpson case and the Harding-Kerrigan melodrama and notes that the obsession is "almost sexual."

The show outside the courthouse, with the hundreds of journalists, the satellite transmitters, the round-the-clock vigils and the relentless pursuit of the scoop, has caught the attention of journalists from South Korea to South America. But the interest reaches beyond the mere peculiarity of a country entranced by a trial. It's all a part of the world's interest in things American.

The Australians may say the story is hyena feed, but that has not kept them from keeping a watchful eye on the case. A close read of their description of what's going on outside the court-room betrays the magnetic appeal of certain aspects of American culture.

Somehow the article manages to paint a picture that looks like a caricature of America, an Oliver Stone movie. There are Vietnam vets and bible-thumping preachers and, of course — in this land of racial strife — there's always the skin color, black or white or whatever, it must matter. It's America.

A long-time resident of Rio de Janeiro, in Brazil, says the case has all the elements of what people there see as America. Brazilians are tuning into *T.V. Globo*'s regular updates from their U.S. correspondents. What they see is a story of a poor man turned multi-millionaire, a dead wife, a black-against-white struggle. Wealth, violence, and race: that's America abroad.

The English have kept close tabs on developments, too. Sure they think we're a little weird paying this much attention to the trial of one man, compared to, say, the Bosnian war, but they too have made sure they stay on top of the story. That, even though this star of "American Football" was not a household name in Britain.

The Times of London has carried huge spreads on the O.J. case, complete with easy-to-read chronologies of the events and a companion Cliff Notes-style summary of the story, for those catching on a little late. After all, it doesn't matter who O.J. is, the Brits have always loved a good scandal. And the illustrious tabloid industry has taken it upon itself to keep British appetites whetted. Not that the distinguished *Times* could ever compare to a tabloid, but the "America" section of the paper has kept readers abreast of the case, with a correspondent in L.A. They even brought out a half-page review of the book where O. J. pleads his innocence.

The *Independent* would not be left behind. Readers have learned much about all the players in the case, including a long profile of one of the star prosecutors handsomely laid out in "The Super Marcia Show."

A young Philippine woman confesses she's been watching the developments as closely as possible. Like many in Manila, she remembers O.J. from his movie career. "People here care," she says. "We remember him well, from *Naked Gun*."

A Jordanian man, speaking heavily-accented English peppered with American slang, says — perhaps exaggerating a bit — "Everybody knows about O.J.; everybody's watching." But the truth is that to watch it closely you have to have a satellite dish, and everybody can't afford one. "O.K.," he admits, "all the rich people are watching." He believes the widespread interest is a natural outgrowth of a general interest in America. "A lot of Jordanians went to school in America," he explains, "and they like anything coming from the United States."

The trial is news around the world. In part, it's a function of the presence of American news agencies and popular culture in other countries. An agency photograph of O.J. Simpson, sitting in the courtroom, leaning over to confer with Johnnie Cochran, occasionally appears in a Third World newspaper with a simple caption explaining that the murder trial of the American sports superstar goes on in Los Angeles. Everyone knows Los Angeles. They saw pictures of the riots after the Rodney King verdict. They have heard about the gangs and, of course, *L.A. Law* is still a big hit in many countries. Televised proceedings of the courtroom drama can be seen around the world, and newscasts in places like South Africa, Hong Kong and Japan have covered the trial. Of course, the case has all the ingredients of a great story, with love and jealousy and sex and money, all running in great rivers of melodrama. But the world's attention has been captured by more than the dramatic tension. The trial is a glimpse into the United States and its people, objects of profound curiosity for people from Haiti to the Land Down Under.

Where Have All the Powers Gone?

The growing suspicion with which the United States came to be viewed, as it emerged to its lead role in the new world, developed in tandem with the world's affinity for American culture. In fact, the latter seemed to feed the former. As U.S. technology, culture and commerce broke through the filters of virtually every society, it came to be seen more and more as a threat.

That phenomenon was not just a European one. The explosive prosperity of the United States proved irresistible and invincible. Globalization became synonymous with Americanization, and as the global economy spawned vocal opponents, the rhetoric of anti-globalization became, to a large extent, the rhetoric of anti-Americanism.

America came to be viewed by many as a nation obsessed with material pursuits. Even as the country's leaders spoke of their reverence for democracy and freedom, many saw that as a thin cover for U.S. efforts to open markets and benefit from the poverty of others.

In 2001, with George W. Bush in office, concerns about the unrivaled power of the U.S. grew louder. When China, Russia and the Central Asian Republics joined in the so-called Shanghai Cooperation Organization, many in Asia thought it was high time for a counterbalance to the U.S.

Political historians pointed out that, throughout history, when one nation has emerged dominant, others have aligned against it to create a new balance of power. Some argued that over the course of the previous decade, the U.S. had been allowed to remain a single, dominant power because it was perceived by many to be pursuing the interests of the world, rather than its own interests at the expense of others. In the new millennium, with a White House that appeared much less interested in building international consensus, that view was clearly on the way out. When Bush announced that Washington was walking away from the Kyoto agreement on global warming, the sense of alarm was palpable around the world. This was a new United States. The new imagine gradually solidified as the U.S. rejected a draft of a protocol to enforce a ban on biological weapons, after every other country had accepted it. The pattern continued when the world tried a common approach to deal with sales of small arms. People around the world saw an America that would refuse to participate in solving global problems with global solutions, letting the planet pay the price of America's prosperity and its internal politics. To many in Europe, Russia, and the developing world, the time for a new balance of power seemed clear, and China looked like a promising anchor for a new center of power.

China Elbowing its Way Between U.S. and Asian Friends
(July 2001)

(Bangkok, Thailand) The editorial cartoon in the *Bangkok Post* shows a spoiled little boy — George Bush, the toddler — surrounded by his toys: refineries belching black smoke; oil rigs gushing petroleum, and nuclear plants spreading their pollutants into the air. Boy Bush, sitting in his playground, a map of the U.S., says, "I want more...more... more... and more."

The same issue of the *Post* describes preparations for yet another high-level meeting between China and Thailand. The two countries, it explains, will look for ways to strengthen their relationship and counter-balance U.S. power.

The United States and its new leadership are giving Southeast Asia a palpable sense of unease and the colossus of the east, China, is moving quickly and skillfully to capitalize on the growing mistrust of American intentions.

Just as the Bush administration unveiled its highly controversial new energy policy, the Chinese Prime Minister Zhu Rongji was carrying out a tour of Asia, spreading China's largesse, pointing to America's "excessive" power, and playing to Asian sensibilities in a way American officials could only hope to study in their diplomacy textbooks.

China also took the opportunity to promote its Olympic bid and undermine U.S. charges about the country's human rights records. Beijing's ascendancy, coupled with American's loss of prestige, makes it quite possible that U.S. rhetoric against China actually helped it win 2008 Olympics. The issue of human rights is increasingly being viewed as a tool of American foreign policy rather than a matter of universal human values. At the same time, the U.S. is more and more viewed as a selfish, hypocritical nation. One sports reporter, discussing whether China should host the Olympics, argued the U.S. is no better than China on human rights. "Do you remember," he asked his readers, "the Rodney King incident?" America too, he said, just as China, has a problem with human rights.

On the economic front, Asia has tied its fortunes to the West, developing export-based economies that target the U.S. and Europe as the markets that will buy their products and bring riches to their people. But the results have been mixed, at best.

While Asia worries about yet another major recession on the horizon, regional leaders wonder aloud whether their nations should rethink their economic strategy of competing with each other to see who can pay its people the lowest possible salary so they can sell their goods ever more cheaply to American and European consumers, as dictated by the global economic model promoted by the United States. They worry that the International Monetary Fund will again come in and force them to make painful and unpopular cuts to satisfy what they believe are the wishes of Washington, and an administration they believe has little interest in their countries.

Many Southeast Asian leaders stood by, carefully watching the new policy proclamations coming from the White House. The new American president spoke about an energy crisis, about economic problems in the U.S. American allies in Europe were accusing the U.S. of worrying about its own wishes at the expense of the world's environment. Asian leaders intently followed the debate. Now America, the nation whose economy they had tried to emulate, was also on the brink of a recession, and the motives for its new policies were under fire from its allies.

Enter China, with its deep pockets; China, with its enormous cash reserves; China, with an economy that has managed to grow strongly even as the rest of the world seems to be slipping away from the coveted mountaintop of prosperity.

China's Zhu came to Thailand bearing neatly wrapped gifts and brightly polished promises. His briefcase contained more than $4 billion worth of economic and military assistance. China offered an alternative to the West's callous economic prescriptions, proposing a multi-billion dollar fund to help prop the currency. He offered hundreds of millions of dollars in military aid, much of it to be spent buying Chinese-made weapons.

A few weeks after Zhu's visit, Thailand's Defense Minister, Gen. Chavalit Yongchaiyudh, paid a visit to Beijing. The event was carefully choreographed to boost Thai spirits.

General Chavalit, who doubles as Deputy Prime Minister, received red carpet treatment, meeting not only with his counter-part at China's defense ministry, but also with the country's President and Prime Minister. Chinese officials were quick to point out it is "quite rare for a foreign official to see all the top leaders."

During one of his meetings, General Chavalit heard high praise for a member of the Thai royal family. It is impossible to overstate the degree to which the Thai people revere their king and his family. When China's president Jiang Zemin spoke of Princess Sirindhorn, you could almost feel the collective pride of Thailand. Apparently, the princess had dazzled the Chinese leaders, and they were quick to tell the Thai Defense Minister. General Chavalit wasted no time in telling Thai reporters what Jiang Zemin had told him. "The President said he never before witnessed any dignitary who could write complex Chinese poetry so beautifully." Score one huge point for China.

Many experts believe the U.S. is losing ground in Southeast Asia. Beijing is using its $120 billion in foreign reserves and its profound understanding of the neighborhood as powerful strategic tools in the region, and every step forward it takes, gives a push backwards to the U.S.

After years of close relations with the U.S., Thailand, for one, seems to be inching closer to Beijing. Thailand holds regular military exercises alongside the U.S. The country was home to American military bases during the Vietnam War. Now, after his meetings with China's top brass, General Chavalit spoke of his wish to see an expansion of the new Shanghai Cooperation Organization, recently established by Moscow, Beijing and four Central Asian nations. The Thai Defense Minister said he would like to see it become something like the Warsaw Pact, the old Soviet-Eastern European alliance that functioned as a counter-part to NATO.

China and Thailand agreed to hold annual meetings of their defense leaders as a way to "provide balance" in the region. Translation: the U.S. is no longer the only game in town.

To ensure the new love affair in Asia doesn't die with the current generation, the two countries agreed to start a youth exchange program. And, yes, China will loan some pandas to Bangkok. According to Chavalit, that means, "Thailand is regarded by China as one of its most trusted allies."

As far as Thailand, and much of Southeast Asia is concerned, the U.S. is taking its toys and going to play somewhere else. But they won't be left to play alone. They've already found a new friend in China.

Even before the younger Bush came to Washington, the world's new power structure inevitably led to criticism. Not only did the U.S., as the only superpower, one with worldwide interests, feel it had to influence events around the world, but regional powers also vied for American support when they felt threatened by their rivals. At times, the United States was simultaneously asked to use its influence and criticized for meddling.

Harvard's Samuel Huntington described the layers of the new world structure. The second level of power, below the United States, was made up of major regional powers like Russia, China, Brazil, Franco-German Europe, India, etc. The third level of power included "secondary" regional powers, with rivalries in relation to regional members of the second tier. Huntington counted in that group Pakistan, relative to India, Britain, in relation to the Franco-German force, Ukraine to Russia, Japan to China, etc.

As nations developed institutions to help manage relations with one another, American preeminence resulted in suspicions of the institutions as well. Entities designed to play a role in managing free trade and economic growth around the world, institutions like the International Monetary Fund, the World Bank, and the World Trade Organization, were perceived, in varying degrees, as instruments of U.S. policy. When the IMF required governments of poor countries to cut expenditures and work towards fiscal responsibility as a condition for obtaining loans, the resulting cuts in basic subsidies for food and transportation (which helped the poorest of the poor scrape by) created waves of anti-Americanism.

In a world where decision-makers worked to move their countries towards the American free market economic model, governments everywhere endeavored to create a better environment for business investment, often at the expense of social services and labor entitlements. For nervous populations and for political activists, the prospect of prosperity was appealing, but there was cause for concern. Governments, they feared, were emulating a system of callousness, where the individual would lose at the hands of the corporation. Small businesses would lose to multi-nationals, the weak would be left behind, and society would become less caring. As the world became more like America, and the U.S. preached to the world the benefits of its ways, many resisted. Resistance focused on American business institutions.

McProfits and Cappuccino

U.S. corporations became symbols of what was seen as the new imperialism. The ever-present McDonalds and Starbucks became a target of anti-globalization activists, their windows smashed at demonstrations from Seattle to Davos.

To Starbucks executives, the vilification was totally unexpected. Their chain of coffee houses had always embraced New Age causes, giving every appearance of being a responsible corporate citizen of the world. What shareholders and employees viewed as a profitable but benevolent expansion, bringing the joys of cappuccino to every corner of the world, to others looked more like the frightening tentacles of capitalism reaching for the pockets of unsuspecting consumers, and pushing small café owners out of business.

McDonald's, on the other hand, had a long history of enduring international criticism from political activists. After decades of pioneering multi-national expansion, the hamburger chain had suffered the slings and arrows of anti-U.S. activism throughout the Cold War. Animal rights activists, environmentalists and others had focused their anger on the golden arches. But perhaps no attack brought more embarrassment than the case of the two young British vegetarians, Helen Steel and Dave Morris.

The so-called McLibel trial emerged when, to the astonishment of observers, the giant corporation initiated legal action against the two unemployed anarchists in an effort to stop them from sullying its name. The two were accused of defaming the company with their participation in the distribution of a leaflet that read "McDollars, McCancer, McMurder, McDisease, McProfits, McHunger, McRipoff, McTorture,

McWasteful, McGarbage." Among other charges, they accused the corporation of destroying the environment and fostering the spread of disease by encouraging people to eat their unhealthy products.

McDonald's gray-suited lawyers faced off against the sandal-wearing rebels, making heroes of them as their accusations against the corporate giant were debated in court. The activists considered the entire process a victory, as public relations specialists scratched their heads in disbelief at the predicament McDonald's had brought upon itself.

McDonald's won the initial verdict, but its corporate reputation was left splattered on the appeals court floor. Although the court agreed that the corporation was defamed by charges that its hamburgers were cancer-causing poison, and that its practices contributed to deforestation and starvation, it reduced the fine imposed on the two anarchists, saying they were justified in their claims that McDonald's customers increased their risk of heart attack by eating the company's products and that McDonald's paid its employers poorly.

As if to add credibility to the paranoid conspiracy theorists in the ranks of the anti-globalization movement, in July 2000, Scotland Yard agreed to pay the couple $15,000 after it was revealed the agency helped McDonald's in the libel case by providing confidential information during the trial.

The case received widespread coverage in Europe. In the United States, most people never heard of it.

As the seemingly perennial struggle between the forces of Capitalism and Communism came to an end, the battle over trade mobilized the new foreign policy armies. Again, the Unites States headed the "free world," pushing with all its might to open markets. And much like in the old ideological battle, many of the world's poor (whose freedom American claimed to protect) were suspicious of, if not openly hostile to, Washington's efforts. The United States became the indispensable nation for anti-globalization activists, the home of the corporations they despised and the advocate of the policies they saw as criminal.

Under the New World Order, the subject of food took center stage repeatedly and raised tensions between the U.S. and Europe, becoming one of the catalysts of the anti-globalization movement. The

European left, which successfully identified American corporate interests as the enemy, gained passionate followers in the developing world.

European food-safety activists and farmers determined to hold onto protectionist measures joined in their struggle against unfettered free trade. Issues like the safety of genetically modified crops or irradiated foods made the headlines in Europe, while the same products took their places in American supermarkets with consumers paying little notice. Public health advocates in the U.S. directed their efforts against cigarette companies and smoking, while European activists held rallies where they passionately decried the evils of modified and irradiated food — pausing only to take a deep puff on their cigarettes.

Not surprisingly, one of the icons of the European movement made a name for himself by attacking and destroying a McDonald's restaurant. The emerging Che Guevara of the healthy-food movement was a French sheep farmer, Jose Bove, who spoke perfect English after — not surprisingly — having lived for several years in the United States while his father conducted research at the University of California at Berkeley.

Bove's meteoric rise came in August 1999, after he and his followers demolished a McDonald's, still under construction, in the town of Millau, in the south of France. Bove, head of France's Peasant Confederation, became an instant celebrity in his country and abroad. With his trademark pipe and enormous handlebar moustache, he was instantly recognizable. When he appeared in court the next year, an estimated 40,000 sympathizers jammed the town square. By then, he had already become an international star and the darling of the movement, after playing a prominent role in the victorious anti-globalization protests that brought a halt to the WTO meeting in Seattle.

Bove had a gift for theatrics and a knack for finding the right issues and making them resonate among his audiences. In Seattle, he held a chunk of Roquefort cheese in hand as he stood in front of a McDonald's restaurant. The crowds ate it up, so to speak. Plainly, it was evil versus good, or so the message read at the hands of the folk hero.

When the World Economic Forum met at Davos, Switzerland in 2001, the anti-globalization forces decided to hold their own anti-Davos meeting. The World Social Forum — starring Jose Bove — met in Porto Alegre, Brazil, the same day the Davos gathering began. This presented a wrenching dilemma to globetrotting activists. Brazil or Switzerland? Some 4000 people from more than 120 countries met in Brazil, foregoing the Swiss protests, for a meeting that — despite the heated rhetoric — turned out to produce an acknowledgement that globalization would not be derailed. Activists in Porto Alegre declared they wanted a more benign version of globalization.

Rather than breaking windows and chanting slogans, many at the meeting acknowledged that the globalization trend has, in fact, brought jobs to millions in poor countries. Still, they pointed to rising inequalities, with the richest people in the world holding an ever increasing share of the wealth and more than a billion people still living in absolute poverty. They noted World Bank figures showing that the average Swiss makes in one day what the average Ethiopian makes in a year.

Gradually, institutions like the World Bank, and proponents of Globalization, recognized the shortcomings of the system, while anti-globalization activists wearing Levy's blue jeans, chewing Wrigley's gum and smoking Marlboro cigarettes recognized the potential benefits of a system they now said needed to be tamed and humanized rather than eliminated.

Despite what organizers described as a more mature movement, Bove's stay in Brazil would not have been complete without an attack on U.S. corporate interests, ending with a visit to a Brazilian jail. In another strange-bedfellows instance of the movement, Bove joined forces with Brazil's vocal Landless Peasants organization. By some accounts, Brazilian and European peasants are at war over unfair subsidies to farmers in countries that compete against each other in world markets. But they united against the big corporations. Nothing, it was clear, had become more globalized than the anti-globalization movements. Bove declared, "Today the battle is not in one country, but in every country." The adoring crowds chanted "Somos todos Jose Bove," "We are all Jose Bove."

The new allies took on the American agricultural corporations, which they said threaten farmers by patenting crops and consolidating agriculture in a few hands, and threaten consumers with their bioengineered products. Activists marched on land owned by the giant American corporation Monsanto and did their best to destroy the plantation of genetically modified soya. Bove was arrested, and his comrades honored him by attacking a McDonald's.

The Porto Alegre meeting, ironically, had been the brainchild of American activists. Americans counted prominently in the anti-Americanization movement, and many attended faithfully the protests around the world. But as the world moved towards the American model, the U.S. suddenly acquired a new and disturbing preoccupation.

The President's Zipper

In the midst of the greatest wave of prosperity in their history, and without a Soviet enemy to worry about, Americans, in the eyes of the world (and of many in the U.S.) developed a bizarre puritanical obsession with the sex lives of public figures.

Long before Bill Clinton took office, the private lives of politicians had become fodder for public debate. The political career of Gary Hart came to an early demise in 1987, when the presidential candidate was caught spending the night on the aptly named boat "Monkey Business" with his extra-marital girlfriend Donna Rice. The career-ending disease came to be known as the Gary Hart Syndrome. It was considered politically fatal, until Bill Clinton, through his personal clinical trials, appeared to have found the cure.

In earlier times, the private lives of politicians had been an intimate matter for politicians, their spouses, and their loyal press corps. The escapades of the likes Franklin D. Roosevelt, his wife Eleanor, John F. Kennedy, and other prominent figures were kept out of bounds and out of print. But the celebrity culture put an end to that. The American press and the American public found what seemed a good rationale for prying and judging: if he lies to his wife and betrays her trust, people argued, how can we trust him to be president? If he doesn't stand by the commitments he made when he wed, how can he be trusted to stand by commitments he makes as president? If his character is flawed, how can we trust him with the most important job in the world?

In many countries, the logic led to almost the opposite conclusion. In Latin America, many (men) maintained that a man without a girl-friend could not be considered a real man. And who would want anything less than a real man holding the world's most important job?

Opinions outside the U.S. were irrelevant. In the U.S., before Bill Clinton, an extra-marital affair disqualified a candidate for president. Candidate Clinton, by that logic, didn't stand a chance. But he didn't give up. He and his wife Hillary took the bull by the horns, so to speak, and addressed the subject head on.

In the earliest days of the 1992 campaign, the tabloid *The Star* reported that Clinton had engaged in a multitude of encounters with one Geniffer Flowers. Clinton's run for the White House seemed to be over before it started. Then, Clinton and his wife appeared on the program *60 Minutes* for a public confession. Displaying what would become a trademark ability to manage public opinion, he partially revealed his sins while denying accusations and ultimately winning the hearts of America with his heartfelt sincerity,

With wife Hillary faithfully by his side, he movingly confessed to "causing pain in my marriage." While denying the Flowers allegations, Clinton attacked what years later would come to be known as "the politics of personal destruction." The show was a hit and so was the candidate. Clinton finished second in the 1992 New Hampshire primary. He promptly baptized himself the "comeback kid," a label he hoped would send into oblivion the disparaging old nickname, "Slick Willie," coined by Paul Greenberg, an Arkansan editorial writer repulsed by the governor's antics.

Throughout the 1992 campaign, Clinton's former Chief of staff Betsy Wright took on the job of dousing so-called Bimbo Eruptions. She won many battles, but in the end it would prove impossible to win the war.

Clinton's ability to evoke the most passionate of emotions was visible from the earliest moments of his presidency. In Little Rock, working on CNN's election night coverage in 1992, I was struck by the nervousness of a middle-aged African American woman working at the convention center where we had our workspace. She repeatedly found excuses to walk into our area, looking for the latest information on the election. When we at last had the final tally, the news that Clinton had won, she broke into tears. She was so overjoyed, it was hard to believe she was simply another voter whose candidate had won. "He's such a wonderful man," she said, apologizing for her outburst.

Moments later, another worker from the Little Rock convention center walked in, looking sullen and angry. "Just wait," he warned me, "Just wait." America, he said, had made a huge mistake in electing Bill Clinton. One it would come to regret. "He's no good," he said shaking his head in disgust. "That man is no good."

Because Clinton evoked such powerful emotions, and because people who despised him were already working hard to publicize his flaws, it was simply astonishing that he handed his enemies all the ammunition they needed by becoming involved with Monica Lewinsky. Clinton was not the first president to have extra-marital sex while in office. He was not even the first to have it in the White House. But he was the only one to do it while under federal investigation, where a special prosecutor leading an office with a huge staff was devoted full-time to sorting through the president's dirty laundry.

Engaging in the affair was so unbelievably stupid, the only apparent explanation was that Clinton, at the time, was incapable of clear thought. The pop-psychologists and the PhDs all agreed the president suffered from a grave case of sexual addiction.

The Lewinsky scandal broke during what was supposed to be a major international news event: Pope's John Paul II's trip to Cuba. All the major news organizations were set up to cover the Pope's trip extensively. The principal anchors for the networks traveled to Havana, and large budgets were apportioned for coverage. I was traveling to each one of the Pope's scheduled masses in the Cuban provinces, sharing transmission facilities with other networks, as we all filed live reports from each location. As is customary, we had set up a rotation, where each networked was allotted approximately two minutes on the live platform, using the same camera and satellite facilities to file our reports. It was a hectic pace with tight rotations.

Our daily routine was to cover a mass with live reports, put together a quick taped story for play throughout the rest of the day, and then get on our little bus and drive to the next location. After arriving at night, we would get details of the next day's mass and try to get some rest before an early start the following morning. But in the middle of our Cuban tour, we discovered we no longer had to share the facilities. Everyone else, it seemed, had stopped covering the Pope's trip. Something to do with another sex scandal in Washington, we were told. The rest of the trip was much easier. We could go live any time we wanted. Everyone else had lost interest in the Pope's historic visit to Cuba.

Everywhere around the globe, the soap opera of Bill Clinton's life became front-page news, complete with in-depth analysis of why this was happening in America. In some countries, there was a degree of admiration. Even the most powerful man in America had to account for his actions. But the more common reaction was one of astonishment. Fidel Castro was said to be astounded at how the press was allowed to treat the President, while his people in the streets displayed their frank admiration for the American President's prowess with women. In France, where monogamy is not exactly revered, there was one more reason to despair over the questionable values of the remaining superpower. One newspaper called it "The Tyranny of the Puritans," boasting, "there are some days when it's good to be French."

Saddam Hussein, meanwhile, worried that Clinton would go to war to distract attention from the scandal, predicting the scenario from the unbelievably prescient film *Wag the Dog*. (Just weeks later, when we, in fact, found ourselves in Baghdad after flying almost directly from Havana, foreign journalists were all over the Iraqi Ministry of Information building waving Cuban cigars while they discussed the latest from Washington.)

In Cuba, when we returned to our headquarters in Havana, the CNN staff had also been thinned out considerably. About half the people had returned to the U.S. Around the table in our makeshift newsroom, a debate was raging over whether or not the term oral sex could be discussed on television. Having been somewhat disconnected from events, I thought the discussion was, shall we say, tongue-in-cheek; the giggles were certainly there. But the subject was hardly academic. Journalists would end up talking about details of the President's sex life in a way nobody could believe even then.

Months later, I would find myself giving live reports to Latin America on CNN's Spanish language network, describing a report from Special Prosecutor Ken Starr where Clinton's erotic use of a cigar was explained along with information about semen stains on a dress, and oral sex in the Oval office.

The topic proved challenging in more ways than one. It was perilously easy to say precisely the wrong thing. An anchor in the studio asked a colleague in the field about Americans' reaction to the lurid report. Innocently, the reporter replied, "It has left a bad taste in their mouths."

Publications like the conservative British magazine *The Economist* called for Clinton to resign, even as the President was impeached and tried, and his popular support remained strong. But around the world, public reaction was more one of disbelief, not so much with the President's actions but with America's puritanical obsession.

For the next year, the United States would have little time for anything beyond the Clinton sex scandal, which would ironically end up ruining the political careers of Clinton's harshest critics like Newt Gingrich.

Politicians, editorial writers and common people worried about the world's most powerful government devoting all its energy to investigating the sexual escapades of one man. A French minister expressed outrage that the President had to spend all his time defending himself, rather than governing. Still, the scandal had all the elements of great gossip. In China the Starr report was banned as pornography, but still became widely available. People were either disgusted with the President for what he had done, or with the press for publicizing it, or with Americans for caring enough to let the crisis derail the government. Regardless of the focus of their disapproval, everyone wanted to know the latest gossip on the President.

The Pope and Fidel versus Bill and Monica: A Lopsided Battle for TV Ratings

(January 1999)

(Havana) One of the most unlikely victims of the recent Clinton fiasco became the people of America, who lost a once-in-alifetime opportunity to have a front-row seat to view history when Pope John Paul II made his unprecedented visit to Cuba.

The world press was poised for the Pope's arrival. Friends and enemies of Fidel Castro could almost be seen rubbing their hands together in anticipation of the potential for major changes they believed the pontiff could trigger in the island. But it was not to be. At least not immediately, and not with the undivided attention they had expected.

Just as the Pope arrived, the world heard of Monica Lewinsky.

In the view of some in the world of journalism, the American public is capable of consuming only one major story at a time. So the choice was made: it would be White House sex on the first page. The Pope would have to yield the lead as Americans devoured information that coated moralistic introspection with a heavy layer of voyeuristic tale telling.

All the while, the Pope — struggling mightily against his considerable physical weakness — presented the Cuban people with some of the most serious and important moral questions that face human beings.

What is the meaning of true freedom? As the Pope arrived in Cuba, Fidel welcomed him with a speech listing some of the achievements of his revolution. He talked of the lofty literacy rate of Cubans. He spoke of access to health care. His welcoming speech proclaimed, as do the officially graffitied walls of Havana, that of the millions of children who live in the streets around the world, none is Cuban.

But the Pope challenged the Cuban people. He told them they should be free to worship as they wished. He hinted of the shortcomings of their system and urged them to reconsider the morality of their own lives. Cuba has staggering rates of both divorce and abortion. The island's people live without political freedoms that have become commonplace in most of the world, certainly in Latin America. Cuba is the only nation in the hemisphere whose leader is not democratically elected.

The Pope's visit held out the promise of change for all sides of the Cuban system. Opponents of Fidel Castro's defiant Marxist regime believed the Pope would inspire the people of this island less than 100 miles away from the U.S. to push for an end to their political system, just as the Pope's landmark visit to his native Poland is believed to have been a catalyst for the beginning of the end of Communism in the Eastern Bloc. On the other side, Castro expected the Pope to help him point to the effects of the United States' embargo that continues to strangle the Cuban economy. The Pope did just that, speaking of the harshness of the economic measures imposed by the giant to the North in a struggle that Castro called David versus Goliath.

But who was paying attention? In the United States everyone was in the thrall of the latest chapter of Washington melodrama. This was a unique opportunity to learn about the real moral questions of our time.

It was an opportunity to understand a very close neighbor that one day will again be treated as a friend. It was an opportunity to better understand Cuba, and examine the controversial American policy of total isolation against the island, a policy that has been criticized by many countries around the world, but continues to be fiercely backed by Cuban exiles in the U.S. and their supporters in Congress. It was one of the last opportunities to listen to and watch Pope John Paul II in the twilight of his remarkable life.

Instead, Americans watched the media scramble to discover the details of Bill Clinton's sex life and strain to decipher its legitimate significance.

Me, My Friends and I

The new world leader, even if occasionally playing out unseemly private dramas on the public stage, continued to play a critical role in world events before, during and after the scandals that captured the public's attention. The United States spent the better part of the 1990s riding the fences around Iraq, regularly firing on the country's anti-aircraft installations, and occasionally launching a bombing raid when Washington thought Saddam Hussein had strayed too far.

When Europe couldn't devise a strategy to end conflict in the Balkans, the U.S. spearheaded international action, leading its NATO allies.

Now that the world was not neatly divided in two camps, the U.S. struggled to decide just how much it would rely on international institutions to legitimize its own actions. Many argued that America's real power derived from its values, and that in order to exercise its power, the country should work as a part of the international community rather than as a lone enforcer of its own will.

Others maintained that it had reached the status of Lone Super-power by not being afraid to influence events around the world and if America now stopped utilizing its influence, another country would move in and work to shape the world to suit its own needs.

The debate was not new. Woodrow Wilson, the quintessential idealist, had passionately believed in the need for international institutions. When the Soviet Union and the U.S. vied for international influence, many American leaders worked to develop international institutions from which the country could work to radiate its ideology to the rest of the world.

The first president George Bush, in the White House during the fall of communism, spoke of a New World Order, and built the wide-ranging coalition that followed U.S. forces into the Gulf War. International institutions like the U.N., previously paralyzed by the enmity between the U.S. and the USSR, suddenly appeared to be bursting with world-improving potential. Bill Clinton, particularly in his days as a candidate, emphasized the need for America to work within the United Nations in its efforts to bring democracy and prosperity to the world.

The problem was that international organizations didn't always go along with America's wishes. The U.N. Security Council would not have supported an attack on Serbia in defense of Kosovar Albanians. China and the USSR would have stopped it. Without U.N. support, the U.S. moved within NATO in its Kosovo campaign. And because no European country, indeed, not all European countries combined, had the capacity to carry out the sustained bombing needed for a successful campaign, it was again the U.S. that conducted the war, albeit under a NATO banner.

When the world moved towards agreements on an International Criminal Court, a ban on land mines or a far-reaching environmental treaty, the United States balked, fearing its own range of action would be limited by international restrictions. Working under the umbrella of the international community was desirable, but only if the U.S. felt it could control the rules.

By the time George W. Bush came to office, the emphasis on "multilateralism" appeared to be a thing of the past. The administration of George Bush the son, in sharp contrast with that of the father, focused on American action outside the constraint of the international community.

Beginning with the 2000 campaign, Bush promoted the plan for building a missile shield to protect the U.S. from incoming missile attacks from so-called rogue nations. The idea was strongly opposed by foes and friends alike, but that had little influence on the candidate's, and later the president's, views. The U.S. would do what it deemed necessary to fight what it saw as a growing threat of terrorism, with or without the world's help.

The new administration would continue the country's search for identity in a changing world. Humanitarian intervention, it seemed, would no longer be a major activity of the armed forces. With a touch of sarcasm, Bush's National Security Adviser, Condolleezza Rice, explained that American soldiers would not be escorting Kosovar children to kindergarten.

As a candidate, Bush had said he wanted to have fewer American troops in the Balkans, leaving the bulk of the peacekeeping duties to the Europeans. During the debates, Bush said he wanted to "work with our European allies to convince them to put troops on the ground." In fact, U.S. troops already constituted only about 13 percent of the total number of peacekeepers in Kosovo, and Europe was already paying about 80 percent of the cost of the operation.

America's allies viewed talk of a reduced role in the Balkans with concern, and extremists in the region saw it as an opportunity to gain ground.

Europe intensified its efforts to build its own military force, partly out of a desire to grow less dependent on Washington.

In Latin America, U.S. strength continued to produce irritation even after decades of American support for anti-Communist dictators had ended. Washington's obsession with the drug war became a source of friction.

The annual ritual of "certification" was despised by the people and the governments of Latin America, who found it humiliating and hypocritical. The practice required the U.S. State Department to determine whether a country was doing all it could to stop drug trafficking.

Whether the criticism was legitimate or not, many in the developing world grew tired of Washington's lecturing and moralizing. The United States had become, if not the world's police, perhaps the world's nagging mother, constantly complaining and judging the behavior of others. The criticism from the U.S. was often well founded and well intentioned, but it wasn't always well received.

With the benefit of many decades of international diplomacy, the venerable George Kennan, once a U.S. ambassador to the Soviet Union and to Yugoslavia, warned, "This whole tendency to see ourselves as the center of political enlightenment and as teachers to a great part of the rest of the world strikes me as unthought-through, vainglorious and undesirable. . ." Observing the U.S. at the height of its political and economic hubris, Kennan observed, "We are not, really, all that great."

Kennan advised more work on the country's own serious social problems. It was a prescription that the rest of the world would have heartily endorsed, especially if the treatment came at the expense of the lecturing of others.

Against that background, the extraordinary U.S. election of the year 2000 brought enormous glee to America's foes and its resentful friends.

When the contest between George Bush and Al Gore proved to be a tie, the rest of the world (much like the U.S.) could hardly believe its eyes. Internet jokesters called for former President Jimmy Carter and his election monitors to go to Florida. The U.S. looked like a Third World country just learning the ropes of free elections, the kind of country where a few shortcuts are excused in the name of advancing the general principles of democracy. When the election's outcome was finally decided by a vote of the Supreme Court, the former president, whose Carter Center witnessed more than 30 elections in some 20 countries, was unequivocal in his judgment. "If the basic rules in those countries for holding elections were the same as those that prevailed in the United States — in particular, Florida — we would not even go into those countries to try to ascertain if the election was fair or not."

Just like the United States, the world was astonished at the failure of democracy in America. Outside U.S. borders, however, the astonishment was bathed in sudsy joy.

American Election is Gored, Voters Totally Bushed
(November 2000)

Could there be anything more delicious for the rest of the world than watching the self-appointed judge of everyone else's democracy squirming in electoral limbo? Hardly. After years of hearing the U.S. tell them what they're doing wrong, other countries are savoring with delight the drama of America's 2000 election.

Already Russian President Vladimir Putin has offered to send advisers to help with the crisis. Putin says his government is greatly experienced in crisis management. (Massive electoral irregularities when Putin was elected were not a great cause for concern, since the election was such a landslide.)

But joy is greatest among those whose democracy has been the target of criticism from Washington. In Zimbabwe, where the same man has been president for 20 years, the state-controlled newspaper editorialized on the front page with a proud headline, "Election Intrigue Not Monopoly of the Third World."

Another man who never loses an election could hardly contain his glee. Cuban President Fidel Castro, the man who has led his country for four decades, mocked the American electoral process even before the election took place. He made fun of the candidates — for much the same reason Americans did — and his officials found the perfect explanation for the electoral standoff: clearly, corruption in the state of Florida is at the heart of this case. When it comes to Florida, Cuba has a lot to say. Cuban authorities explained that the state with the largest Cuban population outside of Cuba is "anti-democratic."

Among the major democracies of the West, the situation was cause for both sarcasm and erudition. Experts pondered the American system and the consequences of the confusing results. In Germany, one scholar declared the Electoral College system

227

"an idiotic system of government." In Italy, the country most used to being the butt of political jokes, now enjoying its 58th government since the end of World War II, the word was, "It sounds like Italy."

Long before the election, many Europeans have ridiculed American voters as self-absorbed and ill informed. In many countries, but especially in Europe, the campaign leading up to these elections was astounding for what it did not address.

Social problems in the U.S., which preoccupy the European public, were far from the political spotlight during the interminable campaign season.

It is France where America's high opinion of itself grates the most. And it is France where sarcasm drips the thickest. In France, the sound of an American calling his president the Leader of the Free World is as distasteful as cheap wine poured out of a box. The French, like many others, have despaired at the show-biz aspects of American politics and the lack of interest in foreign affairs by voters here. A reporter for the daily *Le Monde* highlighted the "Third World" traits of the 2000 contest: a dead man wins in one state, the President's wife wins in another, and a recall is called in the state where a leading candidate is the governor's brother. How can the Americans complain about other people's elections, the article asked.

But in the Third World it wasn't all criticism. There was more head shaking than anything. In Colombia, the daily *El Tiempo* marveled, "The most advanced country in the world can't figure out who won the election." *The Times* of India, in keeping with the worldwide outbreak of headline cuteness, explained "U.S. Caught in Florida Twister," while another headline writer declared "U.S. Bushed, Presidency Gored."

And yet, there were words of praise for the American system. An editorial in Kenya's *Daily Nation* said that young democracies have much to learn from the maturity of the American system. Recognizing how severely democracy has been tested in the United States — first an impeachment of the president, then a seemingly tied election — the editors were impressed with how a recount was undertaken without objection, and the complaints of voters were not automatically dismissed.

In other young democracies like Indonesia, where the right to choose a leader was only recently won after decades of dictatorship, many expressed amazement at the American system holding together under such extraordinary circumstances.

The incredible election of the year 2000 has given voters in the United States, and U.S.-watchers around the world, a crash course in democracy, American-style. But anyone hoping that America's opinion of itself will change after this election doesn't need to wait for the final chapter of this saga.

The United States will sort out the results of the election and will, undoubtedly, go on telling other countries what is wrong with their democracies

The Perils of Predictions

In the early days of April 1917, President Woodrow Wilson stood before the U.S. Congress to announce that the U.S. would march into war, joining the effort to "make the world safe for democracy." In the ominous scenario that called for U.S. intervention in the European war, the President noted, there was at least one cause for rejoicing. Wilson spoke of the "wonderful and heartening things that have been happening within the last few weeks in Russia." Now that they had shaken off the shackles of the old autocratic rule by the Czars, Wilson proclaimed, "the great, generous Russian people have been added in all their native majesty and might to the forces that are fighting for freedom in the world, for justice, and for peace."

In short order, the events in Russia took a sharp turn away from Wilson's dreamy words. Western pressure to keep that troubled nation in World War I proved too heavy a burden for the democrats. Before the year was over, Russia was in the grip of the Bolsheviks, sowing the fast-growing seeds of the rivalry that would dominate world politics for most of the 20th century.

Studying history in retrospect is a much safer endeavor than gazing into the future in search of understanding. Predicting the course of history is a perilous art. Just as Wilson's premature and ultimately mistaken assessment of the direction of Russia's history proved so utterly incorrect, our interpretation of the world's unfolding history at times seems designed only to prove how easy it is to be wrong.

With the Cold War over, the direction of the world is open to infinite possibilities. The rosiest projections for immediate worldwide peace and prosperity after the fall of the Berlin Wall proved incorrect, just as the doomsday forecasts of open warfare between rival republics of the old Soviet Union did.

But history takes time, much more time than journalists, particularly today's television journalists on permanent deadline, are prepared to allow.

While it is true that world revolution, Bolshevik style, is all but dead, there is little doubt that many of the reasons why, for decades, so many people throughout the planet believed such a drastic solution was necessary still remain in place today. The ideologies that have taken hold around the world in this new era have yet to prove they have the power to bring a minimum of well being to the 6 billion people who crowd the globe. The majority of the planet's inhabitants still live in poverty; fully half of all people barely survive on less than $2 per day, while those lucky enough to live in the affluence of the West have little understanding of what real poverty is.

Paradise Postponed

In the final years of the prosperous 1990s, with globalization engulfing the entire world and soaring stock markets creating explosive wealth, a U.N. report showed that the combined income of the three richest *people* in the world was greater than the income of the 48 poorest *countries* — hardly a vision of global utopia.

As the new millennium started, 34,000 children were dying every single day from hunger and hunger-related diseases. Over the last 40 years, the gap between rich and poor steadily expanded, offering little proof that the new world will be one of universal prosperity. By all appearances, globalization has brought enormous prosperity to many at the expense of many more. And yet, it is quite possible that globalized trade will prove the only viable method of raising incomes at the very bottom, even if it is by an amount so minuscule that standards of living remain sub-human. Other systems, however good their intentions, have shown little promise. It seems plain that there are no easy answers.

As Octavio Paz, the Mexican Nobel-winning writer noted, the fact that Communism turned out to be the wrong answer doesn't mean the questions were wrong. At the end of the millennium, Paz despaired over the important question looming over the lives of millions, noting that, "the triumph of the free market over planned economies has not brought abundance to the poor. . ." The late Paz spoke gloomily about the plight of the poor in their seemingly unsolvable predicament. "Is there no remedy for this situation? And if there is, what is it? I would be lying if I said that I knew the answer. No one knows it. Our century will end with an immense interrogation: what can we do?"

In the new century, the belief that free markets will magically bring an end to poverty while making the rich even richer still permeates the corridors of power. For now, opening new markets is the economic strategy of virtually every country in this era without a name. Some leaders of the developing world are quietly questioning the era's mantra, wondering whether the price of being part of the global economy isn't too high, when it means that those at the bottom of the heap must vie with each other to keep workers' wages down in order to attract investors.

The invincible economies of the West will inevitably show they too can suffer from the unavoidable cyclical ravages of the global economy. The side effects of unrestrained laissez-faire will, in the end, force the hands of free traders, bringing some restrictions to the market. When troubled times bring truly painful times to wealthy nations, they too will feel pressure to take some action, however subtle, rather than allow the market to take its course without interference. Just as the Capitalism of the West is now hued with welfare benefits, retirement protections and other programs, the age of free trade will in time take on a new character.

Despite its many shortcomings, globalization does offer a great deal of promise. The pressures of the world economy have made "transparency" one of the hallmarks of progress, forcing corrupt governments to clean up or face the wrath of investors and their regimes' potential downfall. Fleeing foreign investors can mean economic trouble for the masses and trouble for the people in power. The new economy has brought a measure of fiscal discipline, which, however painful, has virtually eliminated the devastating effects of hyperinflation, the scourge that destroyed economies in the old days. Some poor countries are seeing the emergence of a middle class, with some of the most desperately poor managing to climb slowly out of the abyss.

As the world marches rather optimistically into this new era, the question is, will we rely completely on market forces to solve our problems, allowing the new era to forge a planet resembling a typical Third World country, where a few are opulently rich and the majority live in abject misery, or will we take the reins of the world economy and claim responsibility for the well being of millions who are still starving in the new millennium?

No Island is an Island

In the few places that still cling to Communist theory, the reality of the market and of technology has become inescapable even to the most recalcitrant leaders. Even Fidel Castro — who points to the disastrous Russian experience after the collapse of the Soviet Union as proof that he was right in not giving up on Communism — cannot escape the power of today's world communications.

In 1999, as he prepared to host an Ibero-American summit in Havana, Castro was forced to stage a charade for the benefit of the world media, after local dissidents were prevented by authorities, in full view of the press, from expressing their views.

We had been invited to cover a small demonstration by Cuban dissidents in advance of the summit. The event had been openly announced, and the authorities went into action. When we arrived at the local park where the demonstration was supposed to begin, it was clear that nobody would be allowed to say a word against the system. Enormous loudspeakers were blaring deafening salsa rhythms. The square was filled with high school students in uniform, joyfully swaying to the music. They had been brought in purportedly to celebrate a historic date in Cuban history. Also on the square, pacing nervously, were the members of a "construction brigade" with a reputation for brutality in putting a stop to dissidents' attempt to speak out in public.

Suddenly, in the noisy plaza, a man quietly approached one of the cameras. He pulled his identity card from his pocket, and said, "I am Cuban, and I have a right to speak." Before he finished the sentence, the construction workers jumped into action, attacking him viciously with punches and kicks. The scene was repeated three times. Each time, a man would try to speak, only to be attacked by the people who were brought in specifically for the purpose of keeping the protesters quiet. The streets around the park quickly filled with people shouting down the dissidents and shouting at us, the media, for offering our microphones to "enemies of the revolution."

When I asked a woman there why she wouldn't let someone with a different view speak, she shouted back, to cheers from the crowd behind her, that everyone had a right to speak out in Cuba, as long as they don't say anything anti-revolutionary. A novel take on freedom of speech. I spoke to some of the teenagers in school uniform, who told me plainly they had been brought in because "anti-revolutionary activities" were about to take place.

In the melees of the morning, our camera was hit with a hammer, which narrowly missed the cameraman himself. The pictures were damning, and they were quickly spreading beyond Castro's area of control.

A couple of hours later, as I was putting the finishing touches on my report for transmission to the U.S., the phone rang. I was being invited to a meeting with Fidel Castro. Along with a small group of journalists, I met with the Cuban leader for an astonishing display.

Castro, visibly aging but no less authoritative and defiant in his trademark military fatigues, told us he was disturbed by what he had heard about the morning's events, saying he wanted to get to the bottom of what happened just as much as we did. He joked that he would have to talk to his friend Ted Turner, because he just couldn't afford to pay for CNN's broken camera. Then the show began. He brought in a group of school children, and regular "compañeros," who, as he explained, had just happened to be at the scene of the disturbance. One after the other they explained how their hearts had been deeply wounded by hearing these unpatriotic men say such awful things about their beloved revolution, and they had shouted them down from spontaneous patriotic rage.

One of the teenagers who had told me earlier that morning that she was brought in because dissidents were planning an event averted her eyes from mine and told her Comandante that she had come to celebrate a holiday, with no knowledge that anything else was about to happen, and had acted spontaneously in defense of her revolution. I had her on videotape saying quite the opposite.

Castro also read to us what he said were the criminal records of the men who had been detained. They all, he said, were common criminals, with a past of stealing bicycles, taking drugs and worse.

After the invited patriots left, Castro took questions from journalists, displaying a dazzling knowledge of world events and of the economic and political theory that was taking over the world. He reminisced about history, giving us his version of some of the major events of the past several decades. He told us how he had convinced Omar Torrijos of Panama not to announce unilaterally that he was taking over the canal, lest he should give the U.S. an excuse to attack.

We listened to Castro for more than seven hours. When it looked like we might finally get home after an exhausting day, a Chilean journalist threw in one more question. "Comandante," he said, "how do you see Latin America in the year 2000?" We tried to keep our groans low, as the Comandante expounded for at least one more hour.

The meeting was recorded in its entirety and later played and re-played, over and over, on national television. Before long, the new Truth, with the government's seal of approval, had become reality among all the Cubans with whom we spoke. Castro had found it necessary to respond to the images and words the media had broadcast, and to do it not only to his people, but also to the rest of the world. Although the reality we had seen had made its way beyond Cuban shores, Castro had found it necessary to at least try to get his version of events to the rest of the world. Cuba could not afford to live in a cocoon without regard for local and international opinion. The survival of the regime, even one that was living on the margin of the globalization revolution, also depended on maintaining a modicum of international legitimacy. And what better way to do it than by using modern communications technology? The effort, however, was not altogether successful on the international front.

By the time hemispheric leaders met for the 2001 Summit of the Americas in Quebec, every head of government in the Americas had been invited, except Fidel Castro, the leader of the only country in the hemisphere without a democracy.

236

The Summit again saw loud demonstrators, tear gas, and a commitment to expanded free trade. The leaders seemed unanimous in their desire to expand free trade and the demonstrators, most of them not really opposing globalization, were determined to continue demanding restraints on unfettered capitalism.

Action and Reaction

As the world has grown smaller under the spell of global markets and dazzling communications technology, the interests of nations have converged. And yet, nationalist impulses have not subsided. In some cases, they have exploded with volcanic force.

Nationalism and similar movements like religious fanaticism have, in some cases, been revived by the removal of the powers that used to suppress them during the Cold War. In others cases, the fervent desire to reach for a group's roots and for the aspects of ancestry, culture or religion that distinguish it from all others, comes as a reaction to the powerful forces of globalization. We seem to be marching inexorably towards a homogenized world, where everyone's culture and values blend into one — one that closely resembles the nation whose economy is predominant. To some who find themselves swimming against the current to preserve national identity, the answer is in poisoning the waters with nationalist intolerance.

The waves of intolerance washing over parts of the world will undoubtedly carry more persuasive power in the anxious atmosphere of difficult economic times.

Scapegoating has a long tradition during economic recessions and no country, however diverse, is immune. In the United States, the economic squeeze of the early 1990s allowed candidate Bill Clinton to use his "laser beam" focus on the economy to propel him into the White House. But economic distress also opened the door to the neo-fascist rhetoric of Pat Buchanan.

Some three million Americans voted for the man who labeled his political movement "America First," displaying from the day of the announcement that he was a candidate what would become a campaign based on prejudice against foreigners, Jews and gays. "When we say we will put America first," Buchanan explained, "we mean also that our

Judeo-Christian values are going to be preserved and our Western heritage is going to be handed down to future generations, not dumped onto some landfill called multiculturalism." Buchanan, who worried aloud that immigration from various ethnic groups was "a threat to the Euro-Americans who founded the U.S.A." and suggested building a fence along the enormous border between Mexico and the U.S. in order to stop illegal immigration from the south, had also praised Hitler as "an individual of great courage" and "extraordinary gifts," and described AIDS as "nature's retribution on gays." He came nowhere near winning the election, but he became influential enough to help pull his party to the right, setting the tone for a Republican Convention in 1992 that is still remembered by many as a beehive of bigotry — this, in a country where prejudice is, for the most part, not socially acceptable.

In countries where there is no taboo against such hatred, the distance between the fuse and the explosives is much shorter. Prejudice, however muted, is a fact of life everywhere, but it some parts of the world it is viewed without any suspicion. In the West, social restrictions often bring an awareness of one's prejudice, coupled with an effort to diffuse it. In regions like the Balkans, one can witness prejudice in the most unexpected ways. Far from ethnic cleansing and war, regular people pepper their conversations with proof of their prejudice.

In Bosnia, for example, I was driven to total frustration when a young Croatian employed by CNN insisted on calling an Israeli producer on our staff "the Jew." All my efforts to explain why that was inappropriate fell on deaf ears. "He's Jewish, isn't he?" was as far as our discussions ever got. My trip to Bosnia had come unexpectedly, while I was working temporarily at CNN's Jerusalem bureau. I flew to Zagreb, Croatia, and had to rush to buy a winter coat. The charming Croatian driver who took me shopping offered his opinion on my purchase. He steered me away from an Italian-made coat, saying, "I'm sure it's made by Turks." He preferred the coat from Slovenia, assuredly made by Slavs like himself, a simple logic that sent shivers down my spine no matter what the quality of the coat may have been.

The new era will continue to see outbreaks of violent nationalism and militant fundamentalism, as well as assaults on the dignity of minority group members even in the most progressive countries.

Fading Borders?

The shrinking world, where people move from country to country more easily than ever in history, provides a ready target for those who feel threatened. Immigrants and minorities will remain in the crosshairs of hatred of those who feel they are losing influence in a world moving out of their control.

The debate over whether countries are made stronger or weaker by having a diverse population will continue. A Japanese observer once predicted that America's diversity would sow the seeds for a destructive race war. Racial conflict has been violent and remains a fundamental problem in American society. But few can argue that the U.S. has benefited greatly from attracting talented, motivated people from around the world. In the end, exposure to different cultures has the potential to create understanding and avert conflict at home and abroad.

Whatever one's position, it is clear that nations and societies benefit from explicitly expressing their disapproval of prejudice. Prejudice is contagious, and its worst epidemics bring catastrophe. Just ask the survivors in Bosnia or Rwanda.

In the Middle East, the end of the Cold War, the advent of globalization, the advances of technology, and the efforts of an American president were unsuccessful in bringing peace. Some conflicts seem to mock the naïve optimism of the early 1990s.

For the more dominant players on the world scene, for the nations enjoying the prosperity of the new era, a crucial decision remains in its formative stages. What role will they play in the affairs of other nations — particularly when humanitarian crises develop? Will the West and its allies intervene in the wars of the future? Will they fight to stop carnage, even if there is no economic gain in the process? For those who would like to see humanitarian values play an important role in foreign policy, there is some reason for hope: There is usually something to be gained by bringing peace, even to the most remote corners.

The first U.S. administration of the new millennium announced even before moving from Austin to Washington that it intended to become much less involved in solving other nations' problems. George W. Bush proclaimed America would not use its energy to fix broken countries. But this new age makes it increasingly difficult to draw the line between one country's problems and their impact on the rest of the world.

Just as American pollution contributes to global warming for the entire planet, chaos in one place has a way of spilling across national borders. Just as poverty in Africa contributes to diseases that can now more easily travel from one country and one continent to another, and just as decay in one region contributes to bitterness, violence and terrorism across the world, practically every action in a remote jungle eventually has a reaction in a big Western city. Every instance of degradation in one nation can add to a reservoir of instability, with a potential to eventually overflow into terrorism, refugee migrations, and political upheaval. It may take years to realize when London or New York will feel the breeze from the fluttering of a butterfly's wings in a South American jungle, but it will be felt.

The United States, for example, has made the war on drugs a major foreign policy priority. Massive aid to Colombia is designed to help solve America's drug problem. But every day it becomes more obvious that poverty in Colombia has opened the door to the narcotics industry, and as long as poverty is rampant, the lure of drug money will draw violent and unscrupulous people to the business, and to what is now a war. Colombia's war presents a threat to the entire neighborhood, a neighborhood that includes Venezuela, one of the U.S.'s principal petroleum providers, and Panama, home of the strategic canal Washington once controlled.

The Not-So-Lone Rangers

The U.S. may not be interested in "fixing" broken countries in South America, but even in the unlikely case that Washington's war on Colombia's drugs were to succeed, poverty in the neighboring countries would roll out a welcome mat to the narcotics industry.

Ignoring early signs of a looming crisis can prove costly in the long run. Still, there is little evidence that the West wants to become very deeply involved in combating the gargantuan difficulties that are destroying the lives of millions of African citizens and the future of the African continent. For now, a decision seems to have been made to write off the continent. Sooner or later — probably later — that decision will change, when the West realizes that the entire world is everyone's problem. For now, deciding what character the new era will have, what values will guide it, is a slowly evolving process, a work in progress.

Also a work in progress is the effort to define what kind of nation the United States will be as a global leader in the new era.

America's unchallenged preeminence in the world seems just as secure today as Soviet dominance of Eastern Europe seemed in the 1970s and early 1980s. In the early 1990s, Japan's economy seemed poised to grow powerfully into the future; but as the millennium came to a close, the U.S. seemed unstoppable.

European nations coordinating their policies and solidifying their union may pose a threat to America's ability to act unilaterally in the world, but they will largely continue to work in concert with Washington. (Their own unity will undoubtedly be tested one day, when one European country finds itself unable to adjust policy to its own interests, because that policy has to be coordinated for the whole of Europe.) The West remains, for the most part, unified in its basic principles and objectives, although disagreements over tactics may cause friction. Differences in priorities on issues such as the environment will also contribute to that friction, as Europe generally is more willing to sacrifice short-term prosperity for the sake of environmental concerns, whereas the U.S. under George W. Bush clearly values prosperity above just about everything else.

In the end, issues like the environment, terrorism, and refugees are a source of enormous frustration as it becomes increasingly obvious that they have an impact that transcends national borders, so that the decisions of one government affect the populations of many others.

The future of China is particularly difficult to predict. The massive nation is joining the world economy but remains dismissive of many of the basic principles of an era that many people thought would bring a new freedom to all humanity. Beijing remains undaunted in affirming its territorial sovereignty over Tibet, with little regard for human rights concerns expressed by the West. The country is spending more money revamping its military forces. Whatever China does, however offensive to human sensibilities, the appeal of its enormous market

241

overwhelms everything in the eyes of hungry investors and the governments that protect their interests.

And a new dangerous trend has developed in the country since the crushing of the Tiananmen Square uprising. The authorities there deliberately engaged in a program of stoking the embers of nationalism. The program has proved enormously successful. What was expected to become a controllable fire may burn out of Beijing's control. Chinese nationalist passions could burn their way onto the international scene, complicating matters for the Communist Party and for the rest of the world. The West could find itself ambivalent about people-power on the mainland.

China's position in the world will be determined in part by the world's response to the actions of the country's leadership and its efforts to retain control of a fast-changing nation.

The country whose transformation made the new era possible, Russia, remains another puzzle. The days of Yeltsin, "friend of the West," are over. Vladimir Putin is determined to regain some of his nation's former pride. Putin is open to money and technology from the West, but he has his own views about Russia's role in the world. Putin is asserting Russia's claim to a sphere of influence in what used to be the Soviet Union. The "near abroad," as it is known in Moscow, will become a boundary to NATO's threatening expansion — unless the latest hints are serious, and Russia itself comes into the club. Moscow's transformation from a feared adversary whose expansionist policies spurred the creation of NATO, to a fledgling democracy wanting to join the alliance, has gone full circle.

In the eyes of a humiliated nation with not-so-distant memories of its status as a superpower, America's uncontested power on the international arena is hardly cause for rejoicing, especially after the U.S. and its NATO partners undertook the bombing of Serbs over events in Kosovo, ignoring Moscow's objections. The new chapter in Russia's history is, to a large degree, about gaining respect — self-respect, and the respect of the world. However disastrous the country's condition, the fact remains that no nation outside the U.S. has a more lethal arsenal of weapons. The United States and rest of the world ignore Moscow at everyone's peril.

The Character of the Future

If Moscow is suffering from a case of low self-esteem at the start of the new millennium, the United States is experiencing just as critical a case of the opposite malady. The United States deludes itself in thinking its economy will remain forever dominant. The delusion that every nation in the world today envies and admires practically every aspect of the U.S. may not change among much of America's population as long as the country remains more inward looking than almost any industrialized country in the world.

America's democracy, business climate and lively popular culture are, without a doubt, a powerful magnet. But the United States could benefit from looking outside itself with a degree of humility. There is much to be imitated in other places, and there is much that could stand improvement in today's United States.

Every time the media saturate the nation's households with news of another school shooting, or drug use statistics; whenever the harshness of the country's health care system becomes a reality to yet another family; when parents realize in horror that their children place more value on making money than on just about anything else — every time these realities crash America's blissful ignorance — little is done to look for answers away from U.S. shores, where some answers might be found, or where they may have at least been discussed more productively than in the short-attention-span world of modern day America. A country with a strong social fiber is a country that can speak with much greater authority on the world stage.

The United States, today's indispensable nation, must decide what kind of a nation it wants to be: what kind of a nation for its own citizens and what kind of a nation to the rest of the world.

On the global arena, America finds itself powerful, if somewhat confused. Perhaps the best description came from Jeffrey W. Legro at the University of Virginia. He likened the U.S. since the end of World War II to Hollywood's *Gladiator*. "We entered the arena reluctantly but once inside we vanquished all challengers. Now we stand alone inside the Coliseum, victorious and sword in hand, but with little idea now what to do with Rome."

For a time, the United States wanted to use its newfound power to create a world of democracy, global trade and the rule of law. The plan, for a time, was to do so under the aegis of the United Nations and other respected international institutions. But when other powerful nations disagreed with Washington, the U.N. proved to be less willing to cooperate than planned. Then the U.S. started to act with less concern for international consensus, securing approval from its friends in Europe. Now, it appears, the country is prepared to make its own decisions and move with or without their agreement. Whether or not the U.S. decides to proceed with its missile shield, for instance, over the objections of much of the world, remains to be seen.

The way in which the U.S. will use its influence around the world, and the goals of the country, also seem to be changing. The Bush administration shows little inclination to expand the definition of national interest beyond the direct interest of American taxpayers, mostly in terms of their personal prosperity. The administration will probably find it difficult to stay out of the problems of other nations. But at least its intention appears to exclude becoming involved far from the country's shores to stop the slaughter of ethnic minorities, to help end wars, or to otherwise fight the suffering of human beings.

The decisions the U.S. is making about what kind of nation it wants to be are, in the end, not very different from the choices facing today's world as a whole. The planet is undergoing a prodigious transformation — an adolescence of sorts. We are deciding what character the future will have, what kind of a world this will be. There can hardly be a more important question.

Printed in the United States
4667